Hotel Accommodation
Operation and Management

HOTEL ACCOMMODATION

Operation & Management

V.K. SRIVASTAVA
Principal
Govt. Institute of Hotel Management
& Catering Technology
Almora (Uttrakhand)

AMAN PUBLICATIONS
NEW DELHI (INDIA)

Published by
Rajiv Jain for Aman Publications
LG-4A, Ganpati Bhawan,
4675-B/21, Ansari Road,
Darya Ganj, Delhi - 110002
PH: 23255012, 23282127
E-mail: sshjbs@yahoo.com

First Edition 2008
ISBN-81-8204-045-0
ISBN-978-81-8204-045-8

SOLE DISTRIBUTOR
JINDAL BOOK SERVICES
LG-4A, Ganpati Bhawan,
4675-B/21, Ansari Road,
Darya Ganj, Delhi - 110002

Laser Typesetting by:
S.M. Graphics, Delhi,

Printed by:
Indus Press , Delhi, India

Preface

A hotel is an establishment where primary business is to provide to the general public lodging facilities and which may also furnish one or more of the various services such as food: beverage, laundry, uniformed services etc. Hence, hotel can also be called as home multiplied by commercial activities. Managing a hotel means working in a bustling centre of business and leisure activity, making sure that everyone who visits enjoys the experience. Hotel managers are one part accountant, one part salesperson, one part entertainer, one part diplomat, and a little bit of a magician.

Describing in great depth and detail all areas of hotel management and operation, this book provides an up-to-date and comprehensive examination of the responsibilities of a hotel general manager. Covering of topics such as human resource management, front office operation, customer relationship, hotel security and modern trends in the industry, this book provides a practical approach to how professionals in all areas of the industry manage the many different aspects of their operation.

This book helps readers develop the wide-ranging knowledge and analytical skills they need to succeed in today's burgeoning and dynamic hotel industry. It encourages critical thinking by providing different points of view through contributions from sixty leading industry professionals and academics. It will be suitable for university hospitality programs and management training programs within the hotel industry.

Contents

Preface v

1. Overview of Hotel Industry 1
2. Organisational Structure 50
3. Developing a Hotel 81
4. Operating a Hotel 110
5. Human Resource Administration 133
6. Front Office Operations 160
7. Customer Relationship Management 204
8. Operation and Management of Spas 230
9. Managing Hotel Security 255

Bibliography 297

Index 299

1

Overview of Hotel Industry

A hotel is a place where all who conduct themselves properly, and who being able to pay and ready to pay for their entertainment, are received, if there be accommodation for them, and who without any stipulated engagement as to the duration of their, stay or as to the rate of compensation, are while there, supplied at a reasonable cost with their meals, lodging and other services and attention as are necessarily incident to the use as a temporary home. A hotel may be called as an establishment where primary business is to provide to the general public lodging facilities and which may also furnish one or more of the various services such as food: beverage, laundry, uniformed services etc. Hence, hotel can also be called as home multiplied by commercial activities. The term 'Hotel' refers to 'a house of entertainment of travelers'.

The word 'Hotel' is of ancient origin, but its use in English for a house offering lodging and food for travelers is recent. The Hostlers of London took the name of Inn keeping in 1473. The world Hostler' or 'Ostler' having come to mean an inn servant. The term 'Hotel' was used in England in about 1760. British law as a "place where a bonafide traveler can receive food and shelter, provided he is in a position to pay for and is in a fit condition to be received" defines hotel or inn. In legal terminology a: hotel is an inn and is required under common law to offer to its visitors lodging, food and protection, 10 their baggage. Hotel service is generally based on these three fundamental necessities of life. In addition to these a modem hotel provides its visitors many luxuries of modem urban city living, all under one roof.

Early history of accommodation for travelers can be traced back to the Greek word 'Xenia', which not only meant hospitality but also the protection given to a traveler from discomforts. The city was bound to offer hospitality. In Sparta city, although due to rigorous customs visitors were not encouraged, yet goddess Athena was considered as protector of strangers and hence her name was 'Xenia Athena'. In this period travelers were mainly diplomats, philosophers; intellectuals arid researchers. Guests were invited to stay with noblemen. In ancient Olympia, buildings constructed with the aim to accommodate strangers can be seen. They were called 'Leonidio' and were, built in 4th century B.C. The concept of hospitality can also be drawn back to ancient times. Homer finds mention of it in 'Iliad' and 'The Odyssey'. Hotel keeping can also be traced back to many centuries and its evolution through the, ages has been brought about by Britain's economical and industrial changes and developments.

During the seventh and eighth centuries, it was thee monasteries that applied hospitality to strangers and, as no charge was made for the accommodation, a travelers were expected to contribute according to their means to the Abeey funds. As more people began to travel they grouped themselves together not only for company but for mutual protection from highway and robbers. Consequently travelers arrived in groups at a monastery and it was often difficult to accommodate them all. To overcome this, separate lodging houses, called 'Inns' were built. The word 'inn' came to mean a 'Lodging House' and until the passing of the Hotel proprietors Act in 1956, it was the legal term for 'Hotel' and hotel proprietors were legally referred to as 'Common innkeepers'. 'Common' in this sense referred to Common Law. In the thirteenth and fourteenth centuries, manor houses, being hospitable places; willingly gave accommodation to travelers. As no payment was expected, travelers tipped the servants as a 'thank you' for the generous hospitality received—thus the practice of tipping was born.When high taxes crippled the generosity and hospitality of the owners of the manor houses, many became commercial inns. During Elizabeth the First's reign, posting houses were established and travelers, in addition to getting refreshment were able to change horses before continuing their journey.

The turn of the century saw an era that was called the 'Belle Epoch' when the grand and luxurious hotels flourished. A few hotels are still operating today. In London and some other cites attempts have been made to recapture some of the grandeur of the past era in the making of modem hotels, and bring back the memories the grand hotels of olden days. The next stage in the cycle of evolution of the hotel industry was the coming of the motorcar. It enabled people to visit those parts of the country not reached by railways. This gave birth to inland resorts and the hotel Industry began to flourish. International air, travel has helped create the modem 'stop-over' hotel. With the increase in this form of travel, the number of hotels built close to airports has multiplied.

Geographical Dispersion of Lodging Facilities

Lodging is an important component of the tourism industry, providing accommodation to travelers while away from home. Lodging operations are diverse, ranging from small bed-andbreakfast properties in rural locations to large hotels with several thousand rooms in major cities.

Table 1 provides an overview of geographical dispersion, showing that the majority of the world's hotel properties are concentrated in Europe (55 percent) and North America (22 percent).

Table 1. Geographical dispersion of hotels

	Total Revenue (109) US$	Number of Hotels	Percentage of total Hotels	Total Number of Rooms	Average Size of Hotel (Rooms)
Africa	6.3	10,769	3.5*	343,347	32
Caribbean	7.9	5,290	1.7*	155,253	29
Central America	1.2	1,160	0.3*	41,221	35
North America	62.1	66,943	21.7*	3,738,977	56
South America	9.8	14,576	4.7*	487,787	33
Northeast Asia	23.7	10,192	3.3*	719,480	71
Southeast Asia	12.8	13,211	4.3*	453,657	34
South Asia	3.1	3,663	1.1*	159,417	44
Australia & Pacific	6.6	10,082	3.2*	229,319	23
Middle East	9.2	4,735	1.5*	162,178	34
Europe	87.5	151.945	49.4*	4,242,193	28
Other areas of Europe	22.5	19,178	6.2*	676,631	35
Total	247.8	307,683	100*	11,333,199	37

*Source:World Travel and Tourism Council 1995. *Total does not add up to 100 due to rounding.*

The Table also demonstrates that the average property size in North America is larger than that in Europe (56 versus 28 rooms), with chain-affiliated properties being more common in North America. Despite controlling only a minority of room stock (approximately 30 percent of total room supply) hotel chains dominate the lodging sector and tend to exert a disproportionate influence on industry operations and performance.

In addition to generally having higher occupancy and average daily rate, chain properties tend to be more profitable, delivering trading profit per room seven times more than their independent counterparts. As a result, the industry is expected to continue to consolidate, with an increasing number of mergers and acquisitions resulting in a small number of large companies dominating the marketplace. A differentiation must be made between hotel ownership, hotel branding, and hotel operations. Historical developments with Real Estate Investment Trusts (REITs) in the United States gave rise to a situation where many owners could not operate their own hotels.

Instead they must use a separate management company to oversee day-to-day operations, resulting in a split between hotel ownership and hotel operations.The situation is further complicated by the widespread use of both franchises and marketing agreements that provide a consumer brand and require compliance with brand standards.

At any one time there may be up to three parties holding a stake in the operations of a particular property:

(1) the owner, who holds title to the assets, is responsible for mortgage payments and provides the capital for the operation;

(2) the brand, which brands the property and provides standards, distribution services, marketing, technology, and other services; and

(3) the management company, which provides management talent and operates the property on a day-to-day basis.

Within each management company the brand portfolio is quite mixed, with each company operating under a variety of competing flags in different geographical markets. In the US lodging industry there are multiple stakeholders with, at times competing, interest in the operations of the property.

A working knowledge of the classifications used in the hotel industry is important to understanding its organization. The various types of properties, their market orientation and location, sales indicators, occupancy, and revenues as they relate to levels of service and various types of business affiliations are all means of classifying hotel properties. Table 2 serves as a reference point throughout this discussion.

Table 2. Overview of hotel industry

I. Types of hotel properties
   a. Hotels
   b. Motels
   c. All-suites
   d. Limited-service hotels
   e. Extended-stay hotels

II. Market orientation/location
   a. Residential
      i. Center-city
         1. Hotels
         2. All-suites
         3. Limited-service
         4. Extended-stay
      ii. Suburban
         1. All-suites
         2. Limited-service
         3. Extended-stay
   b. Commercial
      i. Center-city
         1. Hotels
         2. All-suites
         3. Limited-service
         4. Extended-stay
      ii. Suburban
         1. Hotels
         2. Motels
         3. All-suites
         4. Limited-service
         5. Extended-stay

- iii. Airport
  1. Hotels
  2. Motels
  3. All-suites
  4. Limited-service
- iv. Highway
  1. Motels
  2. All-suites
  3. Limited-service
  4. Extended-stay

III. Sales indicators
- a. Occupancy
- b. Average daily rate (ADR)
- c. Yield percentage
- d. Revenue per available room (RevPAR)

IV. Levels of service
- a. Full-service
- b. All-suites
- c. Limited-service
- d. Extended-stay

V. Affiliation
- a. Chain
  - i. Franchise
  - ii. Company-owned
  - iii. Referral
  - iv. Management contract
- b. Independent

Types of Lodging Facilities

Classification of hotel facilities is not based on rigid criteria. The definitions can change depending on market forces, legal criteria, location, function, and, in some cases, personal preference, but the definitions that follow are generally accepted.

Hotels

A hotel usually offers guests a full range of accommodations and services, which may include reservations, suites, public dining and banquet facilities, lounge and entertainment areas, room service, cable television, personal computers, business services, meeting rooms, specialty shops, personal services, valet, laundry, hair care, swimming pool and other recreational activities, gaming/casino operations, ground transportation to and from an airport, and concierge services. The size of the property can range from 20 to more than 2,000 rooms. Hotels are found in center-city, suburban, and airport locations. Guest stays can be overnight or long-term, as much as several weeks in length. Properties sometimes specialize in catering to particular markets, such as conventions or gambling. Casino hotels usually take a secondary role to the casino operation, where the emphasis is on profitable gaming operations. Marriott's hotels operated as JW Marriott Hotels & Resorts and Renaissance Hotels, as well as Hyatt Hotels & Resorts brands operated as Hyatt Regency, Grand Hyatt, and Park Hyatt Hotels, are examples in this category.

Motels

Motels offer guests a limited range of services, which may include reservations, vending machines, swimming pools, and cable television. The size of these properties averages from 10 to 50 units. Motels are usually in suburban highway and airport locations. Guests typically stay overnight or for a few days. Motels may be located near a freestanding restaurant.

All-Suites

The all-suites concept was developed in the 1980s as a separate marketing concept. These hotels offer guests a wide range of services that may include reservations, living room and separate bedroom, kitchenette, optional public dining room and room service, cable television, videocassette players and recorders, specialty shops, personal services, valet and laundry, swimming pool, and ground transportation to and from an airport. The size of the operation can range from 50 to more than 100 units. This type of property is usually found in center-city, suburban, and airport locations. The length of guest stay can be overnight, several days, or long term. Although this type of hotel may seem new, many downtown, center-city hotels have offered accommodations with in-room kitchenette and sitting room since the early 1900s. Now with mass marketing—advertising products and services through mass communications such as television, radio, and the Internet—this type of hotel is considered "new." Examples of the all-suite concept include Hilton's Embassy Suites and InterContinental's Candlewood Suites.

Limited-Service Hotels

Limited-service hotels appeared in the mid-1980s. Hampton Inn and Marriott were among the first organizations to offer limited-service properties. The concept of limited service was developed for a specific segment of the market: business and cost-conscious travelers. The range of accommodations and services may include reservations, minimal public dining and meeting facilities, cable television, personal computers, personal services (valet and laundry), and ground transportation to and from an airport. The size of the property can range from 100 to more than 200 rooms. Limited-service hotels are found in center-city, suburban, and airport locations. They are usually located near restaurants for guest convenience. Guest stays can be overnight or long term. These properties sometimes specialize in catering to the business traveler and offer special business technology centers. Limited-service hotel properties include Holiday InnExpress, operated by InterContinetal Hotels Group; Comfort Inn, by Choice Hotels International; and Marriott's Fairfield Inn.

Extended-Stay Hotels

Extended-stay properties were designed to offer guests a home-away-from-home atmosphere over long stays precipitated by business, leisure, or personal necessity. For example, a person may have to attend to a business project for several days or weeks; another may want to visit with relatives whose home does not have adequate accommodations for visitors; a third may be accompanying a relative or friend receiving an extended health treatment at a medical center and require overnight accommodations. The patient himself may appreciate the homelike atmosphere of the extended-stay hotel in which to recover between treatments.

Classification of Hotels

Hotel is an establishment selling service-food, drink and shelter. The value and the potentiality of a hotel is assessed by the size, location, the number of rooms and other revenues earning points it possesses. The classification of hotels with in the industry is a complicated task. Hotel can be classified on different basis. Followings are some of the basis of classification:

Classification based on Tariff Pattern

Most of the hotels generally run on plan system. There are various types of plan, which are internationally recognised. Hoteliers according to their convenience or the policy of the management can adopt these. The list in which the prices of hotel services are incorporated is known as hotel tariff. On the basis of tariff pattern hotel are divided as follows:

— *European Plan*: In this case only the lodging i.e. bed is offered. Thus the charges are made for lodging only. The client is free to take or not to take teas, breakfast, and meals in the hotel. He has a choice of eating at any other good restaurant. The guest is booked to pay for lodging only and is charged separately for all other things or services he enjoys or consumes. This system is generally followed by youth hostels or hotels which are situated in metropolitan cities. European plan hotels fix the prices of rooms separately so that guest may either have their meals in the hotel dinning at its regular prices or go to the other restaurant. In India most of the hotels are being run on European Plan. Almost all the public sector hotels are run on this basis.

— *Continental Plan:* In the case of continental plan bed and breakfast are included in the charges. Thus bed is offered along with breakfast and the client is, however, free to take his meal and tea as he likes. Thus the guest tariff includes lodging and breakfast and for other he is separately billed.

— *American Plan*: Hotel where American plan is prevalent, board lodging is provided in the charge. The tariff fixed includes board and lodging. It is an all inclusive full board tariff. Accommodation and three meals daily are included in the price of the room. It includes bed, breakfast and two principal meals and evening tea. It does not include EMT nor coffee after lunch, or dinner. The needs are usually 'table d' hote'. It is also known as 'full pension'.This means that guests day ends about 24 hours after his arrival that is, the guest arriving between lunch and dinner is entitled to retain his room until the next afternoon and to have dinner the first night and breakfast and lunch the following day for the fixed rate. This analysis is mostly used at those tourist resorts, which are not situated in big cities. Most of the tourists who do not want to carry too much, has go for all inclusive accommodation so that the entire amount is paid at the starting point. These terms are supposed to be sold to the guest, though for internal record, a clear apportionment of charges between accommodation and meal is made. This is particularly important where some guests stay on inclusive terms and others not.

— *Modified American Plan (MAP):* The tourists mostly prefer this plan, as it is comparatively flexible. It is offered in most of the good hotels and is normally by arrangement. It includes hotel accommodation, breakfast and either lunch or dinner in the price of the room. Thus, in this type of accommodation bed and breakfast and along with it one principal meal, lunch or dinner, at the discretion of the client is also included. It generally includes continental breakfast and either 'table d' hotel' lunch or dinner in the room rates. It is also known as demi-pension. It has been observed that the Indian style hote Is in India follow the European plan, and the western style hotels which cater the foreign tourists, operate the American plan. In the past foreign tourists used to visit India for pleasure and leisure trips. They had plenty of time to travel and stay. Nowadays, we have typical tourists, businessmen or travelers, who would like to visit the country for a week and the city for a day. They do not have time and desire to return back to their hotels again and again.

International Hotels

There are modem western style hotels in all large cities as well as important tourist centers. These have been classified on the internationally accepted star ranging from

5 star to 1 star hotels. These are the hotels of international repute having more than 200 rooms with their counter parts in all the large cities. These establishments provide accommodations, restaurant facilities, grillrooms, banqueting suites and bars as an integral part of their businesses. There normal activities are often 'supplemented by shops' of diverse kinds, garages, laundry and similar services. Also, in many instances, residential, furnished and unfurnished flats equally belong to the over all operating company.

Hotels in the international grouping are mostly owned by public companies and controlled by a Board of Directors. The President/Chairman of the Board is usually a prominent figure of the industry, the secretary, a chartered accountant, and the managing director, a leading personality in the hotel industry. The overall operational responsibility of the company's affairs falls to the managing director. These hotels are generally divided into various departments under a resident/general manager who is, directly responsible to the managing director. The relationship and responsibilities of the departmental heads, general manager and. Managing director should be clearly defined and understood. The general manager manages the hotel through his departmental heads and all immediate operational data are his responsibility. The managing director takes charge of the broad operational and financial policies of the company.

Apart from the profitable lettable accommodation—the suites, flat lets, and studio rooms:-a considerable revenue is extracted from catering. There is a restaurant, which opens for luncheons and where also there are tea dances, and evening dinner dances. Good band and international fame cabarret artists are employed. The cliental dances to famous bands and are entertained by well-known cabaret artists. True to tradition the restaurant specialises in entertainment, the grillroom caters for the epicures and the banqueting suites, large and small, handle all the special and functional catering. The new thought in maximum revenue promotion from catering advocates three main regular activities over and above the banqueting business and the room service on the floors a large restaurant for entertainment operating a moderate "allin" tariff, a popular priced cafe complete with snack-bar and a small, select grillroom, a rendezvous of the gourmet working on a high price allocate service in return for the finest fare that money can purchase.

Residential Hotels

A purely residential hotel is not a hotel in the legal sense of the word since its tenants are not transients. Its methods of operation are quite similar to those of residential hotels. They serve a few rooms for visiting friends of their tenants, and most of them are glad to accommodate other transients in order to fill rooms that may be vacant. Example of such hotels is Oberoi Apartments, Qutab Hotel, and Oberoi Maiden etc. These are the largest group of all. They meet great need that of the resident. An endless mixture of varied sizes of residential establishments exists ranging from a few exclusive hotels to boarding houses of all kinds. Many of the quieter residential towns, large cities abound with these establishments. This group can be classified by the wealth of their patrons. The guests are drawn from different walk of life, people of independent means, from retired folk living on investments or pensions and from-men women wage earners. The residential hotel is the development of USA, evolving after people discovered that permanent living in hotels offer many advantages. A residential hotel usually apartment building with the service of a hotel, maid and linen services, dinning room and room services with board and possibly a cocktail lounge. Some are luxurious, and offer full suites, whereas others are moderate and feature single rooms. Although they are few in numbers, they usually let a room for a long period of time. In some of the cases their terms are weekly. They have fixed hours for breakfast lunch tea, dinner etc. These hotels are generally in the hands of private operators. Services and amenities provided are comparable to that of average well regulated home. The food is more or like a home style. As the residents are having fixed income, therefore it arises a number of economic problem for the owner.

The revenue of residential are more or less fixed where as the operating cost is increasing day by day. There are some advantages. The rent from room is fixed although most of the times these people are away from their rooms and secondly they are much less trouble some than any other residential. These types of hotels are the product individualistic family system. These hotels are found in USA. Terms are weekly. The turnover of residential is very slow, especially in good houses, although the more enterprising of residential housekeepers frequently set rooms aside for regular short stay visitors. The general standard of comforts of establishment can be described as adequate and resembles that of the average well regulated home. There are set hours to rise, to breakfast, lunch, and dinner. Though public rooms are provided the guest spends much of their time in their bed sitting studio type rooms. These hotels are usually privately owned owner operated. The staff consists of one or more waitresses or waiters, cook, kitchen and floor maid etc. The food is more home style. The economic of residential establishment has its problems.

The future of the residential establishments relies upon the service flat Service flats range from great block to smaller houses letting out one room letting out one room flat lets. The block of flats has its own restaurant, catering for residents and chance customers alike, and operates a room catering service. Experience has shown, that with this type of restaurant unless there is a possibility of strong and regular chance trade, both luncheon dinner and functional, the venture can prove very precious. Small one room flat both furnished and unfurnished are always good propositions. The latest thought advocates the equipping of small kitchen units comprising cooker, freezer and wash-up for those who find for themselves. Sometimes a room service is available in the form of room trays. The flats are centrally heated and serviced. Apartment houses of this nature are more reasonable to live in than guest houses, offering a fuller and more personal service. Residential premises equipped to be operated in the self-help idiom with a much labour—saving equipment as possible and the entire outfit designed to warrant the minimum of maintenance is the answer to high costs will become the guest house of the future for people of limited means.

Commercial Hotels

Commercial hotels depend mainly on executives and on the individual traveling for pleasure. Thus these hotels mainly cater for the commercial traveler and they are not found in all the larger provincial towns. As the hotel caters primarily to business people, it is generally convenient to establish these hotels near to office buildings, restaurant and entertainment outlets. All firms with connexions upon a nation wide scale send out their representatives on the road. Some 'reps', hilly an area to cover, others range the whole country, some travel with a display of goods, other travel light all have travel and lodging allowances.

Commercial travelers, with their set and often-limited expenses require in expensive accommodation. But being for the most men from good homes, they require a certain standard of comfort. These businessmen like company and enjoy getting together with their fellow travelers. For these reasons there are commercial hotels catering for their needs. The commercial requires good, plain, home-style food, a comfortable bed, clean surroundings and a place where they may read or write in peace. Stock rooms, let at a rental for displays, are usually available at these hotels. Facilities typically include small meeting and conference room, a medium sized restaurant and lounge and a swimming pool. Since occupancy at there hotels usually declines on weekends, many hotels have installed elaborate recreational amenities, health club, tennis court, all-year-round swimming pools.

Commercial hotels are normally owner run and a successful business depends upon their operating on a friendly and comfortable use. A good name is a sound asset with the 'knights of the road', who, amongst their community will recommend the good and warn against the not so good house. Success again depends upon the building of a consistent and regular business. The commercial is certainly a regular caller and will always patronise and remain faithful to a house where he is known and where a warm and comfortable welcome is guaranteed. The number of rooms in these hotels varies around the fifteen mark. The average guest stay is of short duration, though some have a wide area to cover and make the hotel their headquarters.

In some of the big industrial towns largely fully licensed commercial hotels exist complete with grill room, functional accommodation and garage, It must be emphasised that the commercial hotel is not and should never be taken for a poor type of lodging house. Neither should a bad concept be formed of the traveler. The modern commercial is an important businessman, a representative carefully selected by his firm. Marked attention is paid by the sales director to engage the right type—a man of education and integrity, because its representative knows a firm and obviously he must be carefully selected. Hoteliers who make a specialisation of catering for the commercial traveler not only find a regular and remunerative business, but a pleasant task as well.

Star Hotels

The hotel on completion is inspected as a functioning establishment or approval and placement in the appropriate star category. There are five such categories ranging from 5 star for hotels which offer luxury features, to one star for hotels which offer adequate standard of comfort and cleanliness. There are no uniform criteria at international level for grading and classification of hotels. When inquired the reaction of the tourists, it was pointed out that it is more important to list facilities alone with the rates fixed, thereby giving them the choice to select. Quality is more important to them than the physical aspects of a hotel.

The star system creates an impression of luxury and waste—an artificial label with unwanted connotations. Material criteria's are unsatisfactory. These criteria's 30 not contain any built in guarantees. Facility wise, a luxury hotel will not merit any consideration of, for instance, it does not employ sufficient personnel. Quality of service is very important consideration. After all, hotels constitute a service industry. The standard for gradation of hotels in India are laid down by the government of India from the points of view of the suitability of the hotel for foreign tourists. All hotels which are approved get worldwide publicity through tourist literature published by the government and distributed in India as well as abroad/ overseas and are eligible for foreign exchange for their essential imports of equipment and provision and for their advertising, publicity and promotion abroad, from the government's special quota of foreign exchange for tourist promotion.

There are certain general features, facilities and services expected of establishments in each category. For example, hotels in the category of four, five star, and five star deluxe should be completely air-conditioned, three star hotels need have airconditioning in only 50% of rooms; two star hotels need not serve continental cuisine and one star hotels need have only 25 attached baths.According to the regulatory conditions for approved hotels, the officials of the government or any other officer deputed by it to inspect hotel premises from time to time will be allowed free access with or without prior notice. In the event of breach of any of the conditions by the hotels, the government shall have the right to withdraw the approval. The characteristics of star hotels of different categories are described below.

— *One star hotels*. The general construction of the building of one star category hotels should be good and the locality and environs including immediate approach should be suitable. The hotel should have at least 10 lettable bedrooms of which at least 25% should have attached bathroom with a bathroom for every 4 of the remaining rooms. All bathrooms should have modern sanitation and running cold water with adequate supply of hot water, soap and toilet paper. The rooms should be properly ventilated and should have clean and comfortable beds and furniture. There should be a reception counter with a telephone and a telephone for the use of guests and visitors. There should be a clean and moderately well equipped dining room/restaurant serving clean wholesome food, and there should be a clean, wellequipped kitchen and pantry.

— *Two star hotels*. The building of two star category hotel should be well constructed and the locality and environs including the approach should be suitable for a good hotel. The hotel should have at least 10 lettable bed room of which at least 75% should have attached bath rooms with showers and a bath room for every four of the remaining rooms and should be with modern sanitation and running cold water with an adequate supply of hot water, soap and toilet paper. 25% of the rooms should be air-conditioned,and all rooms must be properly ventilated, clean and comfortable, with all the necessary items of furniture. There should be a well-furnished lounge.There should be a reception counter with a telephone. There should be a telephone or call ball in each room and there should be a telephone on each floor unless each room has a separate telephone.

— *Three star hotels.* The architectural features and general construction of the building of three star category hotels should be of a very good standard and the locality including the immediate approach and environs should be suitable for a very good hotel and there should be adequate parking facilities for cars. The hotel should have at least 20 lettable bed rooms, all with attached bath room with bath tubs and/or showers and should be modem in design and equipped with fittings of a good standard, with hot and cold running water. At least 50 per cent of the rooms should be airconditioned and the furniture and furnishings such as carpets, curtains etc., should be of a very good standard and design. There should be adequate number of lifts in buildings with more than two stories including the ground floor. There should be a well appointed lounge and separate ladies' and gentlemen's cloak rooms equipped with fittings of a good standard.

— *Four star hotels.* The facade, architectural feature and general construction of the building of four-star category hotel should be distinctive and the locality including the immediate approach and the environs should be suitable for a hotel of this category. There should be adequate parking facilities for cars. The hotel should have at least 25 lettable bedrooms, all with attached bathrooms. At least 50% of the bathrooms must have long baths or the most modern shower chambers, with 24 hours service of hot and cold running water. All public rooms and private rooms should be fully airconditioned and should be well furnished with carpets, curtains, furniture, fittings, etc. in good taste. It would be advisable to employ the services of professionally qualified and experienced interior designers of repute for this purpose. There should be an adequate number of efficient lifts in buildings of more than 2 storeys including the ground floor. There should be a well-appointed lobby and ladies' and gentleman's cloaks room equipped with fittings of a standard befitting a hotel of this category.

— *Five star hotels.* The facade, architectural features and general construction of the building of five star and five star deluxe hotels should have the distinctive qualities of a luxury hotel of this category. Five star deluxe category hotels are a qualitative extension of the five star categories, while quantitatively, the basic features are as of a five star category. In a five star deluxe hotel, the comparative all around standard of service and amenities are of very superior quality and high standard. The locality including the immediate approach and environs should be suitable for a luxury hotel this category, and there should be adequate parking space for cars. The hotel should have at least 25 lettable bedrooms, all with well appointed, attached bathrooms with long baths or the most modern shower chambers, with 24 hours service of hot and cold running water. All public rooms and private rooms should be fully air-conditioned and should be well appointed with superior quality carpets, curtains, furniture, fittings, etc. in good taste.

Concepts of Hotel Management

The history of the hotel industry is filled with concepts

that shaped the products and services offered. The atrium concept design, limited-service hotels, and technology were notable innovations. Management concepts such as marketing and total quality management (TQM) offered managers a new way to do business in hotels. The major U.S. economic reorganization in the late 1980s shaped the way hotels could be profitable. Also, in the 1990s, a new financial approach—real estate investment trusts (REITs)—changed the financial structuring and operation of hotels. The terrorist events of September 11, 2001, continue to affect how hotels market their products and services and deliver hospitality.

The hotel industry has seen many notable developments over the past years. The atrium concept, an architectural design in which guest rooms overlook the lobby from the first floor to the roof, was first used in the 1960s by Hyatt Hotels. The dramatic approach to hotel style [was] exemplified by the Hyatt Regency in Atlanta. Designed by architect John Portman, with a striking and impressive atrium soaring up its 21 stories, the hotel literally changed the course of upscale hotel design. As a result hotels became more than a place to rest one's head. They became hubs for excitement, fun, relaxation and entertainment. This 1,260-room hotel "is now one of the nation's premier convention and trade show facilities with 180,000 square feet of ballroom, exhibit, meeting and hospitality space."

Total quality management (TQM), a technique that helps managers look at processes used to create products and services with a critical eye on improving those processes, is practiced in hotels today. This emphasis on analyzing the delivery of services and products, with decision making at the front lines, in the 1990s and continues today under terms such as quality assurance and service quality.

The movement of hotel construction from the downtown, center-city area to the suburbs in the 1950s coincided with the development of the highway system. The limitedservice concept—hotels built with guest room accommodations and limited food service and meeting space—became prominent in the early 1980s, when many of the major chains adopted this way to serve business travelers and travelers on a limited budget. Hampton Inn revolutionized the hotel industry with the creation of the first national brand targeted to the new limited-service hotel segment. The hotels featured spacious, comfortable rooms but eliminated or reduced other elements common to hotels at that time, such as restaurants, lounges, and meeting and lobby space, passing the resulting cost savings on to guests in the form of lower rates. The company pioneered a number of ideas, including the mounting of the first site by a hotel brand on the Internet. In 1989, Hampton Inn became the first national brand to offer guests an unconditional 100 percent satisfaction guarantee, which today is the cornerstone of all Promus brands and a testament to the company's commitment to quality.

Technological Developments

Technology has played a major role in developing the products and services offered to guests. Reservations systems, property management systems, and in-room guest checkout are only the most obvious advances in technology. Impressive firsts in the adaptation of technology to the hotel industry are shown in Table 2. Note how many of the developments we call technology are recent adaptations.

Recent additions to the list include applications of wireless technology that allow front office staff to alert others on VIP check-ins, housekeeping staff to report guest room cleaning and release, marketing staff to maintain guest profiles, and bell staff to process baggage handling. Guests have also found technology in the 2000s to increase their ability to work and play at the same time; they can check email and print documents as needed from so-called hot spots, or designated wireless transmission and reception areas in the hotel.

Table 2. Introduction of technological advances to the hotel industry

1846	Central heating
1859	Elevator
1881	Electric lights
1907	In-room telephone
1927	In-room radio
1940	Air-conditioning
1950	Electric elevator
1958	Free television
1964	Holiday Inn reservation system with centralized computer
1965	Message lights on telephone
	Initial front office computer systems introduced followed by room status capability
1970s	Electric cash register
	POS (point of sale) systems and keyless locks
	Color television standard
1973	Free in-room movies (Sheraton)
1980s	Property management systems
	In-room guest checkout
1983	In-room personal computers
	Call accounting
1990s	On Command Video (on-demand movies)
	LodgeNet Entertainment (interactive video games)
	Interactive guest room shopping, interactive visitor's guide, fax delivery on TV, interactive guide to hotel's facilities and activities, reservations from the guest room for other hotels within the same organization, and interactive weather reports
	Internet reservations
	Introduction of legislation that monitored hotel ownership through real estate investment trusts (REITs)

2000s	Wireless Technology—Wireless Technology VIP Check-In, Housekeeping Guestroom Glean and Release Status, Marketing Guest Profile, Bell Staff Baggage Handling; Guest "hot spot" centers in hotels for wireless transmission and reception of emails and documents.

Modern Trends

An emphasis on niche marketing to guests was the theme in the 1970s. This technique surveyed potential guest markets and built systems around the needs of identified segments. The larger hotel-management and franchise companies also were discovering the advantages of forging strong reservations and marketing systems. For a guest, this meant that by calling a single phone number, he or she could be assured of a reservation and feel confident of the quality of accommodations expected. The marketing emphasis continues in the 2000s through the routine use of the Internet to place guest reservations.

The economic period of 1987–1988 saw a major reorganization of the hotel industry. 1986 Congress unraveled what it had stitched together in 1981. The revised Tax Act made it clear that passive losses on real estate were no longer deductible. Hotels that were previously economically viable suddenly were not. At this time, there were plenty of Japanese who seemed intent on buying up, at astronomical prices, any piece of U.S. property with a hotel or golf course on it. As a result, the value of American hotel properties continued to increase. Between 1990 and 1995, the recession began and ended, and the full impact of the 1986 law and overbuilding were experienced. Some investors who had built properties in the early 1980s found their properties sales or replacement value had fallen to 50 percent or less of original cost. Some owners simply abandoned their properties to their mortgage holders—which in many cases turned out to be Uncle Sam, because of the simultaneous S&L debacle.

Hotel Investment

Real estate investment trusts (REITs) provide an investment opportunity for hoteliers. In the Spring 2000 Virginia Hospitality and Leisure Executive Report, P. Anthony Brown of Arthur Andersen wrote the following about the U.S. Tax Relief Extension Act of 1999. This information will be useful as you plan your career. The most significant provision, however, is creation of a new type of corporation—a "Taxable REIT Subsidiary" (effective January 1, 2001)—which will allow REITs to create new incremental income streams. With new growth opportunities, shareholders should be rewarded with higher stock prices since companies with increased growth rates typically trade in the market at higher earnings multiples. Under the terms of the 1999 legislation, Taxable REIT Subsidiaries can provide non-customary services to tenants through their subsidiaries. This legislation should enable REITs to provide better customer service, create stronger customer loyalty and sell new, non-customary services to tenants. In addition these new subsidiaries can lease lodging facilities from REITs. However, the lodging facilities must be managed by an independent contractor that is actively engaged in the trade or business of operating lodging facilities for any person other than the REIT.

With these changes, hotel REITs will be able to reorganize their structure in order to retain more of the income generated by their hotels. For example, FelCor Lodging Trust Inc., a hotel REIT based in Irving, Texas, currently leases its hotels to two tenants:

1) a company owned by its executives and directors; and
2) Bristol Hotels and Resorts, a publicly traded company.

With the new legislation, FelCor will be able to form a new Taxable REIT Subsidiary and transfer the leases of its hotels to this new subsidiary. Accordingly, the net income of the existing lessee would be transferred to the new Taxable REIT Subsidiary. However, a management company must manage the hotels and must be actively engaged in the trade or business of operating lodging facilities for any person other than the REIT.

The terrorist events of September 11, 2001, will have a lasting effect on how a hotel markets its products and services and delivers hospitality. The immediate impact of the terrorist attacks was a decrease in the number of people willing to fly and, thus, a decrease in demand for hotel rooms. Hotels and the federal, regional, and state tourism associations continue to cooperate to address the issue of fear as it relates to travel and tourism. Hoteliers reviewed their marketing plans and determined how to attract the post-9/11 corporate traveler. The huge corporate guest market can no longer be taken for granted. Corporate executives, travel planners, and traffic managers now must be greeted personally by hotel staff and asked when business might be expected. New methods of attracting markets such as local and regional residents are being developed. These efforts include special packages emphasizing local history and culture, businesses, sporting events, and natural attractions and are combined with the products and services of an individual hotel. Is this an easy challenge? Indeed no, yet it is one that hoteliers had to grasp with eagerness and enthusiasm in order to succeed.

R. Mark Woodworth reports that this effort is indeed a formidable task in light of the data revealed in Trends in the Hotel Industry—USA, published by PKF Consulting and the Hospitality Research Group (HRG). The 2003 edition reported that "the operating profit for the average U.S. hotel dropped 9.6 percent in 2002, this after a 19.4 percent decline in profits in 2001." Rick Swig of RSBA & Associates notes that although hotel revenues increased by 2 percent from 2003 to 2004, "other issues such as supply of hotel rooms of 4.4% since June 2001 versus average number of rooms sold increasing only by 3.3%." He urges, "Hotel operators should focus on pricing power for the next 24 months until occupancy returns to pre-2001 levels and compression begins to build. . . . National consortium and high volume travel contracts are being finalized for 2005. Hotels will have to be successful in achieving significant rate hikes through these conduits, since the past two years of negotiations have yielded little or no rate increase as operating expense inflated." Further insight into the challenge facing hoteliers is expressed by Tom Belden of The Philadelphia Inquirer, who relates that 94 percent of the 112 corporations surveyed by the Business Travel Coalition of Radnor, Pennsylvania, cut their travel spending over a three-year period. He reports that one participant increased its use of web-based meeting software by 50 percent in one particular year. The delivery of hospitality in hotels has also come under review. For example, hoteliers are reviewing security plans to include the front-line employee who must take immediate action based on observations at the front desk, in the dining room and recreational areas, and on guest and public floors. The front-line employee who sees uncommon activities has to know the importance of reporting concerns to supervisors. Special training in what to look for in guest interactions in public areas and on guest floors assists the front-line person in becoming proactive.

Hoteliers must also be concerned with how to support hospitality as part of responsible community citizenship. Hotel general managers should develop emergency plans that allow immediately offering public space to medical personnel and disaster victims. Shortterm concerns such as feeding disaster victims and emergency personnel and long-term commitments such as housing displaced members of the community are among the many issues faced by the hotel industry. Liability implications for the owner, management contractor, or lessee with respect to repair of facilities have arisen in addition to concerns for the safety of guests resulting from terrorism. Andrew MacGeoch, reporting in Hotel, notes:

The obligation of an owner to repair the hotel under a management agreement usually depends on the extent of the damage. In general, if the costs of repair do not exceed a certain threshold specified in the management agreement [which is usually a certain percentage of the replacement costs of the hotel], the owner will be obliged to repair the hotel to its condition prior to the destruction. However, if the costs of repair exceed the specified threshold, the owner will have the right to choose not to undertake the repair and to terminate the management agreement.

MacGeoch continues with a note on liability toward guests by acts of terrorism. Generally, neither the operator nor the owner would be held liable for any injury or death caused by terrorist activities, unless the owner or operator has failed to exercise reasonable care for the safety and security of their guests. Therefore, to make sure that the reasonable-care standard is met, it is necessary and advisable for owners and operators to take reasonable and necessary steps to protect the safety of guests, including implementing appropriate security policies and measures and providing crisismanagement training to all employees. These issues of marketing, delivering hospitality, and the ramifications of possible terrorism are ongoing concerns that hoteliers must continue to discuss. They must focus on goals and subsequent planning for implementation of a safe environment for guests and employees.

Market Orientation

Market orientation in the hotel industry is categorized into two segments:

(1) residential hotels, which provide guest accommodations for the long term; and

(2) commercial hotels, which provide short-term accommodations for traveling guests.

Residential properties include hotels, all-suites, limited-service, and extended-stay properties. Services may include public dining, recreational facilities, social activities, and personal services. These hotels are usually located in center-city and suburban areas where other activities are available to round out the living experience.

Commercial properties service the short-term transient guest. Services include computerized reservation systems, public dining, banquet service, lounge and entertainment areas, personal services, and shuttle transportation to airports. These hotels may be located almost anywhere.

It is essential to note the gray areas where these two categories overlap. A commercial lodging establishment may have a certain percentage of permanent residents. Likewise, a residential hotel may have nightly rentals available. Owners and general managers must exhibit a great deal of flexibility in meeting the needs of the available markets.

Sales Indicators

Sales indicators, including hotel occupancy and average daily rate, are another way of describing hotels. This information is necessary for business investors to estimate the profitability of a hotel.

Four factors measure a hotel's degree of financial success:

— occupancy percentage,

— average daily rate,

— yield percentage, and

— revenue per available room (RevPAR).

Occupancy percentage is the number of rooms sold divided by the number of rooms available. Average daily rate (ADR) is the total room revenue divided by the number of rooms sold. Yield percentage, the effectiveness of a hotel at selling its rooms at the highest rate available to the most profitable guest, reveals a facility's success in selling its room inventory on a daily basis. RevPAR is used to indicate the ability of each guest room to produce a profit. Once the daily sales opportunity has presented itself, it cannot be repeated.

Occupancy

Occupancy percentages measure the effectiveness of the marketing and sales department as well as the external and internal marketing efforts of the front office. Occupancy percentage is also used by investors to determine the potential gross income, or the amount of sales a hotel might obtain at a given level of occupancy, average daily rate, and anticipated yield. However, it is important not to assume that occupancy is standard each night. Variations occur daily and seasonally.

Average daily rate

The average daily rate is also used in projecting room revenues—the amount of room sales received—for a hotel. However, this figure also affects guests' expectations of their hotel experience. Guests expect higher room rates to correlate with higher levels of service; the hotel with a rate of $175 per night is expected to offer more services than a hotel in the same geographic area with a rate of $85 per night. These expectations have been extensively capitalized on by major hotel chains, which develop different properties to meet the expectations of various segments of the hotel market.

Yield percentage

Yield percentage measures a hotel manager's efforts in achieving maximum occupancy at the highest room rate possible. It is sufficient to note here that this concept is relatively new in the hotel industry.

Prior to the 1990s, hotel managers relied on occupancy and average daily rate as indicators of meeting financial goals. Yield percentage forces managers to think in more active terms.

RevPAR (Revenue per Available Room)

RevPAR is determined by dividing room revenue received for a specific day by the number of rooms available in the hotel for that day. The formulas for determining RevPAR are as follows:

$$\frac{\text{Room Revenue}}{\text{Number of Available Items}}$$

or

$$\text{Hotel Occupancy} \times \text{Average Daily Rate}$$

For example, RevPAR for a hotel that has $10,000 in room revenue for the night of September 15 with 200 rooms available equals $50 ($10,000 ÷ 200 = $50). This same hotel on September 15 with 200 rooms, room revenue of $10,000, 125 rooms sold at an average daily rate of $80 ($10,000 ÷ 125 = $80), and with hotel occupancy of 62.5 percent (125 rooms sold ÷ 200 rooms available × 100 =

62.5 percent), produces the same RevPAR (0.625 × $80 = $50).

RevPAR is used in hotels to determine the amount of dollars each hotel room produces for the overall financial success of the hotel. The profit from the sale of a hotel room is much greater than that from a similar food and beverage sale. However, the food and beverage aspect of the hotel industry is essential in attracting some categories of guests who want conference services.

Levels of Service

The four commonly used market segments—identifiable groups of customers with similar needs for products and services—are full service, all-suites, limited service, and extended stay. There is a great deal of overlap among these divisions, and much confusion, some of which occurs because leaders in the hotel industry do not agree on terminology.

Some industry leaders avoid the "budget" tag because of its connotations of cheapness and poor quality. Others welcome the label because it appeals to travelers looking for basic accommodations at inexpensive rates. Nevertheless, the following definitions provide some idea of what is offered at each level of service. Full service is a level that provides a wide range of conveniences for the guest. These services include, but are not limited to, reservations, on-premises dining, banquet and meeting facilities, and recreational facilities. Examples of full-service hotels include Marriott Hotels and Resorts, Renaissance Hotels, and Holiday Inns.

The all-suites category indicates a level of service appropriate for a guest who desires an at-home atmosphere. Services include separate sleeping and living areas or working areas, kitchenette facilities, wet bars, and other amenities at the midprice level. This concept appeals to the business traveler as well as to families. Marriott's SpringHill Suites and Embassy Suites Hotels are examples of all-suite hotels. It is interesting to note that this concept is also employed in older center-city commercial hotels, in which rooms adjoining the bedroom and bath have been remodeled as living rooms and kitchenettes to create suites.

Limited service emphasizes basic room accommodations, guest amenities, and minimal public areas. A continental breakfast and/or an evening cocktail is often included in the price of the room. The guest has the opportunity to trade the public meeting room for free in-room movies, the dining room for free local phone calls. Hampton Inns and Holiday Inn Express Limited are examples of limited-service hotels. Extended stay is a level of service that offers a home-away-from-home atmosphere for business executives, visitors, and families who are planning to visit an area for an extended period. A fully equipped kitchenette allows international guests to prepare comforting foods in a new environment. The spacious bedrooms and living areas provide work and recreational areas. Light breakfast and evening meals included. Examples of this level of service include Hilton's Homewood Suites hotels, InterContinental's Staybridge Suites, and Choice Hotels International's MainStay Suites.

Business Affiliations

Business affiliations, which indicate either chain or independent ownership of hotels, also categorize the hotel industry. These classifications are the most easily recognizable by consumers with regard to such features as brand name, structural appearance, and ambience. Long-lasting marketing effects develop a brand loyalty and acceptance that are most important to the long-term profitability for a hotel.

Chain Affiliation

When asked to name several chain operations (a group of hotels that follow standard operating procedures such as marketing, reservations, quality of service, food and beverage operations, housekeeping, and accounting), most people would probably mention Holiday Inn, Marriott, Sheraton, Days Inn, Hyatt, Hilton, or Econo Lodge. Students should stay up to date regarding developments in the industry, such as acquisitions, restructuring, and other changes in these organizations. This information, important to know when making career decisions, can be obtained from trade journals such as Hotels, whose annual July issue includes a listing of hotel chains, addresses, and number of rooms; the Wall Street Journal; and other newspapers, magazines, and websites.

Chain affiliations, which include hotels that purchase operational and marketing services from a corporation, are further divided into franchisee, referral, company-owned properties, and management contract companies. Franchise corporations offer support to the franchisee, who is the owner of the land and building, in the form of reservation systems, advertising, operations management, and management development. In return for these services, the franchisee pays fees for items such as initial startup, rental of signs and other equipment, use of the corporation's reservation referral system, and national advertising. Anyone wishing to enter the hotel business by investing personal funds wants to be sure of realizing a profit. Perhaps due to lack of experience in operating a hotel or motel, a lack of business acumen, a poor credit rating, or limited knowledge of real estate development, this type of entrepreneur may need to seek the guidance of others. He or she can receive direction from a corporation, such as Days Inn, Sheraton, or Hilton, concerning land, building, and management development.

Referral Property

Sometimes a hotel organization chooses to become a referral property—that is, to operate as an independent in association with a certain chain. Because the property is already physically developed, the entrepreneur may want assistance only with management, marketing and advertising, or reservation referral. Likewise, the fees are based on services required. The chain's quality assurance standards must, however, be met by the referral property.

Company-Owned Property

A company-owned property, a hotel that is owned and operated by a chain organization, allows the hotel company developer to act as an independent entrepreneur. The hotel company developer operates the hotel property in competition with all other properties in the area. It uses its own expertise in site selection, property development, marketing and advertising, and operations management. The hotel company developer recruits talented professions into the organization to manage such properties. It uses the chain's reservation system. The hotel company developer may set a limit on the number of franchises so that a majority of the properties remain company-owned.

Management Contract Property

A management contract property, a hotel operated by a consulting company that provides operational and marketing expertise and a professional staff, is similar to a referral property. Several management contract organizations develop business relationships with existing hotels and operate the hotels as their own. Their business relationship requires financial accountability and profitability. Management contract companies may choose to operate each hotel as a member of a franchise or as an independent.

Brands

Hotel brands are an important part of the lodging industry, especially in consumer marketing.

Branding allows a hotel company to create a concept in the mind of a consumer. This mind-concept helps the consumer classify a hotel's offerings. For example, a fictitious brand such as the Hotel Flower Chain may have three distinct offerings in its portfolio of lodgings: the Tulip Extended Stay, the Rose Limited Inn, and the Violet All-Suites. Another fictitious brand such as the Timber Chain may have seven more brands in their chain with similar facilities, such as the Pine All-Suites, the Maple All-Suites, the Sunset Extended-Stay Suites, the Timber Express, the Timber Grand Hotels, the Timber Falls, and the Pine Limited Service. Each of these brands has distinct product and service offerings such as communication via website, reservation service, reservation reward point program, room accommodations, food service, personal fitness and business equipment, and meeting and convention facilities. Therefore, when guests have certain needs for business or pleasure traveling, they can match them up to a certain brand.

Independent Properties

An independent hotel is one that is not associated with a franchise. It provides a greater sense of warmth and individuality than does a property associated with a chain. Independent hotel characteristics include an owner who functions as a manager, room rates similar to chain properties, rooms decorated in different styles, and inviting dining rooms. These hotels may be residential or commercial, with locations in the center city, suburbia, along the highway, or near an airport. The number of rooms can range from 50 to 1,000. They may offer full services to the guest, including suites, dining room, room service, banquets, gift shop, beauty shop, athletic facilities, swimming pool, theaters, valet services, concierge, and airport shuttle service. Some older independent hotels have refurbished their suites to capture a share of the all-suites market.

With all of these advantages, why aren't all lodging properties independent? The answer lies with the U.S. economy. The development of large chains and of smaller properties often brings tax advantages and improved profits to investors. Millions of dollars in capital are required to develop a 2,000-room full-service property. Business, financial, and managerial expertise is more readily available in a company in which there is a pool of skilled experts. Large corporations can also offset financial losses in certain fiscal years or from certain properties against financial gains of other companies or properties in their diversified portfolios.

The independent entrepreneur operates his or her business without the advantages of consultation and assistance. This person may have worked for a large chain or gained a great deal of operations and development experience in the industry. He or she may also purchase a hotel property to balance an investment portfolio. As for any financial investment, the entrepreneur seeks a professional to manage and operate the establishment. The person chosen for this job must manage all aspects of the business: room, food and beverage, housekeeping, security, maintenance, parking, controller's office, and marketing and sales. All business decisions on expenditures must be coordinated with a profit-andloss statement and a balance sheet. Every sale of a guest room, every guest purchase of food and beverage, occurs because the management of that property has been able to market and manage the property effectively. The challenge of managing an independent property can be overwhelming. It can, however, also offer enormous satisfaction and financial independence.

Trends that Foster Growth

Future professionals in the hotel industry must be able to analyze who their customers will be and why they will have customers. Marketing classes teach how to determine the buyers of a particular product—who the potential guests of a particular hotel property are. Such courses show how to evaluate demographic data (the size, density, distribution, and vital statistics of a population broken down into, for example, age, sex, martial status, and occupation categories) and psychographic data (emotional and motivational forces that affect a service or product) for potential markets. The second question—why there will be customers—is an important one. Students will explore this question many times during their career in the lodging industry. A manager must plan for profitable results. This plan must take into account the reasons customers purchase a product—what trends will increase or decrease the need for hotel facilities? Factors include the growth of leisure time, the development of the me/pleasure concept, increases in discretionary income, the trend toward smaller families, changes in business travel, and expansion of the travel experience. Other economics and political trends—such as public liability, insurance costs, overbuilding, the value of the U.S. dollar overseas, gasoline prices, safety from random danger while traveling, and legislation—affect commerce; labor and the airline industry also have an impact on current sales as well as growth in the lodging industry.

Leisure Time

The trend toward increased leisure time—in the form of three-day weekends, paid vacations and personal days, a workweek of 40 hours or less, and early retirement—sets the stage for the growth of the lodging industry. As more people have available leisure time to explore new geographical areas, try new hobbies, sample culinary trends, participate in sporting events, and just relax, the customer base of the hotel industry expands. Workers are spending fewer years in the labor force as the concept of early retirement becomes more popular. As the population segment known as the baby boom ages, the number of retirees is projected to soar. Many of them will take on a second career, but part-time jobs will likely be more common. With the two prime ingredients for using hotel facilities—time and money—readily at hand, these people will be a primary market for the hotel industry.

Me/Pleasure Concept

The idea of deserving recreation away from the job to restore mental acuity and improve attitude has evolved over the years. The work ethic of the eighteenth and nineteenth centuries strongly influenced the way Americans played, as recreation and leisure were considered privileges reserved for the wealthy. Today, most workers enjoy vacations and the feeling of getting away from it all. This trend toward fulfilling personal needs continues in the twenty-first century. The isolated nature of many jobs increases the need for respite. As more and more people find themselves spending more time communicating via computer and other machinery rather than face to face, social needs continue to grow. Workers need the away-from-job experience to balance their social and mental needs with their daily-life demands.

Discretionary Income

Discretionary income, the money remaining from wages after paying for necessities such as food, clothing, and shelter, is the most important of all the trends that support the growth of the hospitality industry. One of the main reasons for the increase in discretionary income of American families is the emergence of the two-income family. An almost double-income family unit has emerged over the years as more married women join or stay in the labor force. The strong growth in this labor segment will undoubtedly continue. As more income becomes available to pay for the necessities of life, discretionary income for leisure time and corresponding goods and services also becomes available. Discretionary income is not a constant. It is strongly affected by economic factors; an economic downturn with increased unemployment reduces discretionary income, for example. Different economic conditions tend to favor different ways of spending discretionary income; for example, low interest rates, which make the purchase of high-ticket items more desirable, make less discretionary income available for short vacations or quick day trips. Students of the U.S. economy need only review the effects of recessions, the energy crisis of the 1970s, and September 11, 2001, to see how quickly discretionary income formerly directed to the hospitality industry can evaporate.

Family Size

The current trend toward smaller families also indicates growth for the hospitality industry. The discretionary income available for a family with two children is greater than that for a family with five children when total incomes are equal. Household size—the number of persons in a home—has decreased over the years. Like the trend toward smaller families, the increased number of small households indicates that more discretionary income is available. The costs associated with a one- or two-person household are less than those for a household of four or more people. Moreover, people who live in smaller households are more likely to dine out, travel, and participate in leisure-time activities.

Business Travel

Corporate business travel should not be taken for granted by hotel managers in today's world of high energy prices and speedy communication. Oil prices significantly affect business travel; as the cost of fuel oil rises, higher prices for air travel and other means of transportation result. A business is not always willing or able to increase its travel budget. When travel costs increase, less travel is undertaken and the necessity for any business travel is reviewed. Executives no longer hop the next plane to clinch a deal if the same task can be accomplished via a phone call, (conference call) in which three or more persons are linked by telephone (or PictureTel, which is the use of telephone lines to send and receive video and audio impressions). Shorter trips (day trips or one-night stays) are another response to the increased cost of travel.

Business travel often represents the largest portion of the regular income of a hotel property. This prime market must be constantly reviewed for economic details that affect its viability. Female business travelers represent an increasing segment of the corporate travel market. Their travel is affected by energy prices and speedy communication. This particular market segment requires close attention to fulfilling special needs. Female travelers request particular amenities and demand close attention to safety. Mar-keting and sales managers must develop products and services to capture this growing market segment.

Travel as Experience

At one time, people traveled primarily out of necessity; business and family visits were the usual reasons for traveling. Today, people travel for many reasons, including education, culture, and personal development. Many people want to learn more about the society in which they live. They have studied American or world history and want to see the places they have read about. Cultural pursuits—art, theater, music, opera, ballet, and museums —can attract a constant flow of people. Sports and nature attract travelers who want to enjoy the great outdoors as well as those who prefer to watch their favorite teams. The push for lifelong learning has provided an incentive for many to take personal development/ enrichment courses, whether to update professional skills or to increase knowledge of a particular hobby. Ecotourists, people who plan vacations to study the culture and environment of a particular area, want to enjoy nature in its unblemished and unsullied form.

Career Development in Hotel Management

People planning a career in the hotel industry need to review the fundamentals of career development, which revolve around five important concepts: educational preparation, practical experience, membership in professional organizations, ports of entry, and growth areas for the industry.

Educational Preparation

The educational base you build now will serve you well over time. The classes you are taking in your major course of study—including management and supervision, cost control, human resources management, quantity food production, hotel management, purchasing, sanitation, layout and design, accounting, and marketing—constitute a strong foundation for your continued development of technical skills. Courses outside your major—such as

English, speech communication, computer training, arts, economics, psychology, sociology, nutrition, science, and math—will help develop the skills you need to cope in the professional world. The formal education you receive in your classroom study will be enhanced by extracurricular activities such as clubs, student government, sports, and other areas of special interest. These activities are a microcosm of the environment in which you will apply your technical, liberal arts, and science courses. Clubs associated with your major, in particular, allow you to apply theoretical concepts learned in class to a real-life business environment.

Your educational experience will open the door to your career. You must apply your skills and knowledge after graduation to be an effective, successful employee in the hotel industry. Use your degree as a starting point for an exciting career in hospitality. The educational experience you are now obtaining must be nurtured beyond graduation day. There are many opportunities for in-service education, which are courses that update a professional's educational background for use in current practice; these are offered by professional organizations, sponsors of trade shows, community colleges and universities, technical schools, correspondence schools, trade journals, and other industry groups, providing the professional an opportunity to stay current in industry practices. Just as professionals in other industries take classes to refresh their skills and learn new concepts and procedures, so must professionals in the hotel industry maintain awareness of industry advances.

One particularly relevant area is computer training. Professionals who attended school before the early 1980s had little exposure to computers and their ever-changing technology; even recent graduates are not always aware of the most current trends and advances. The professional has the choice of overlooking this need or enrolling in computer applications courses. The next choice is to determine whether these new procedures and equipment are applicable to a particular establishment. Professional organizations—such as the American Hotel & Lodging Association, the Hotel Sales and Marketing Association International, and the National Restaurant Association — offer professionals continuing education opportunities through correspondence courses and seminars.

The American Hotel & Lodging Association offers opportunities for hotel employees to become a Certified Hotel Administrator (CHA) and Certified Rooms Division Executive (CRDE), among other certifications. Trade shows sponsored by these organizations promote the latest concepts in technology, products, and supplies as well as providing miniseminars on how to use current technology in human resources management, food production, marketing, and general management. Community colleges and technical schools offer special-interest courses in management and skills application to keep you and your staff abreast of new areas and to review basic concepts. Attending these courses can provide new insight into operational problems. Each of these professional organizations sponsors a website and provides opportunities to access the abovementioned career information.

Correspondence courses are another way to learn new skills and understand new areas. New technology in distance learning—classes offered via satellite broadcasts, cable, PictureTel, or online computer interaction—is offered by colleges, universities, and professional groups.

Trade journals are also extremely helpful in keeping professionals up to date with new management concepts, technical applications, marketing principles, equipment innovations, and the like. The isolation experienced by managers in out-of-the-way hotel establishments can be alleviated by reading trade journals. Such journals help all managers feel connected to the community of hotel industry professionals, perhaps providing insight into solving technical problems as well as boosting morale. Some trade journals are offered free on the Internet. Education is a lifelong venture; it does not stop with the attainment of a degree from a university or community college. The degree is only the beginning of a commitment to nurturing your career.

Work Experience

The practical experience you obtain from entry-level hotel jobs—whether you are a desk clerk, waiter/waitress, host/hostess, maid/houseman/room attendant, bellhop, or groundskeeper—will be invaluable as you plan and develop your career in the hotel industry. It will give you an opportunity to learn what hotel employees do and how departments interact, and it will expose you to the momentum of a hotel—the time frame of service available for the guest, management applications, and service concept applications, to name just a few.

Your work experience will enable you to evaluate theoretical concepts offered in the classroom. You will have a basis for comparing your work experiences with those of other students. You will also develop your own beliefs and behaviors, which can be applied to other hotel properties throughout your career. At times, you will have to think on your feet in order to resolve a guest complaint, evaluate equipment proposals, reorganize work areas for efficiency, or achieve cost-effective spending. Your work experience provides you with the proper foundation on which to base a successful career.

Professional Memberships

A professional trade organization is a group of people who voluntarily pool their efforts to achieve a set of goals.

These goals may have a political nature, such as lobbying legislators or providing certification of achievement.

Professional trade organizations in the hospitality industry serve members in many ways. First and foremost, they are a political voice in government. Through use of membership fees, trade organizations are able to lobby local, state, and federal legislators to be sure the entrepreneur's views are recognized. Members can opt not to have their membership fee used to support legislators who they don't politically support on personal issues. These organizations also offer significant opportunities for continuing education by sponsoring seminars and trade shows. They offer group plans for insurance and other programs that can be cost-efficient to the entrepreneur. Professional trade associations also allow you to interact with others in the industry on both a professional and a social level. Valuable advice and rewarding friendships often result.

Ports of Entry

A review of the organizational structure of a hotel shows many departmental managers in a large organization. Which area is the best for you to enter to develop your career goals? Four of the ports of entry are marketing and sales, front office, food and beverage, and controller. It is impossible to say which the best port of entry is; all are avenues for career development.

The hotel industry demands a great deal of its professionals. All employees must have extensive knowledge of all areas of the facility, and they must understand the overall function of all departments. This understanding must be reflected in professional business plans. Employees must also have good communication skills and good interpersonal skills. The industry requires great flexibility in scheduling work responsibilities and personal life. It demands that the professional understand the entrepreneurial role of corporate owners while operating within budgeted resources.

Students who enter the lodging industry will find that each area in which they work contributes to a good background for the ultimate position of general manager. When trying to decide where to begin, consider reviewing the job responsibilities of department managers to learn what tasks are required to complete each job and who is involved in doing so.

Try to work in as many areas as you can before taking the leap into a general manager position. The job will be a lot easier, and you will go a long way toward meeting the establishment's goals if you are well prepared. You will make mistakes, no matter how much experience you have had; however, your success rate will be much higher if you have a varied background in many departments.

Researching Growth Areas in the Hospitality Industry

Areas that offer the most potential for growth should be explored. Because such areas change frequently, it is not possible to list them in a textbook. However, factors that support continued growth and strong business activity are regularly reported in such publications as Trends in the Lodging Industry, by Pannell, Kerr, and Forster. Hospitality industry futures projections publications usually cover such issues as new hotel developments; hotels under consideration; activities of convention and visitors' bureaus; strength of local economies; development of business, recreation, and arts activities; the need for office space; and area hotel occupancy percentages and average room rates. This information is listed for selected cities both within the United States and at international sites. The Internet is increasingly used as a method for researching career opportunities in hospitality management. Search engines will produce multiple listings of hospitality recruiters with key words such as "hotel manager," "front office manager," and "hotel careers." Also, professional hospitality organizations usually offer a job-posting service on their websites.

The Internet provides many opportunities for a new graduate to examine trends that are driving the industry and new technologies that will shape a career in hotel management. This information can assist job applicants in exploring the employment possibilities and prospects in different geographic areas.

Your survey of career possibilities should include a review of a potential employer's economic performance on a balance sheet and other features of its profit-and-loss state-ment. This information is available on computerized business databases. Take the time to research the economic potential of the company you are considering. Your interview preparations should include reviewing the regional economic prospects and the company's economic performance. This preparation could set the stage for an investment that lasts many years, perhaps a lifetime.

2

Organisational Structure

A hotel is an establishment that provides lodging, usually on a short-term basis. Hotels often provide a number of additional guest services such as a restaurant, a swimming pool or childcare. Some hotels have conference services and encourage groups to hold conventions and meetings at their location. Hotels differ from motels in that most motels have drive-up, exterior entrances to the rooms, while hotels tend to have interior entrances to the rooms The cost and quality of hotels are usually indicative of the range and type of services available. Due to the enormous increase in tourism worldwide during the last decades of the 20th century, standards, especially those of smaller establishments, have improved considerably.

All hotels are organised around the following functions:

1. Front desk operation
2. Housekeeping
3. Building maintenance/engineering, and
4. Security.

Beyond these common services, hotels and their departments can vary tremendously. For example, most luxury hotels include a restaurant and beverage department, while most budget facilities do not. The performance of these functions can also vary widely among different types of hotels. Business guests of a convention centre may expect hi-tech front desk operations, and guests at a resort may prefer a more personal approach. At any rate, all hotels carry out these functions both behind the scenes and at the front of the house.

Hotel Departments

There are two approaches to classify departments in typical hotels:

— *Revenue generating versus cost centers*: The first approach is trying to differentiate between departments revenue-wise. In fact, this approach entitles that if a department generates revenue to the hotel (eg., rooms division department, food and beverage department), it is called a revenue generator. On the other hands, if a department incurs costs without directly contributing to hotel profitability, it is called a cost or support centre (eg., accounting department, maintenance and engineering department).

— *Front of the house versus back of house*: This approach classifies departments according to department staff's frequency of communication with guests. If communication between staff and guest is frequent, then the department is said to be a front of the house department. On the other hand, if the communication between department staff and guests in nonexistent or on occasions, then the department is said to be back of the house department.

Following are some important departments of a hotel:

Rooms Division Department

The majority of hotels revenues (60.2 %) is generated from

Rooms Division Department under the form of room sales. This very department provides the services guests expect during their stay in the Hotel. It is typically composed of five different departments:

a) Front office:

- — Sell guestrooms; register guests and design guestrooms
- — Coordinate guest services
- — Provide information
- — Maintain accurate room statistics, and room key inventories
- — Maintain guest account statements and complete proper financial settlements

b) Reservation:

- — Receive and process reservation requests for future overnight accommodations.
- — With technology development, the Reservation Department can, on real time, access the number and types of rooms available, various room rates, and furnishings, along with the various facilities existing in the hotel
- — There should be close relationships with Sales and Marketing Division concerning Large Group Reservations

c) Housekeeping:

- — Inspects rooms before they are available for sale
- — Cleans occupied and vacant rooms
- — Communicates the status of guestrooms to the Front Office Department
- — Cleans and presses the property's linens, towels, and guest clothing (if equipped to do so, free of charge or for a pre-determined fee)

— Maintains recycled and non-recycled inventory items

d) Uniformed services:

— *Bell attendants:* Ensure baggage service between the lobby area and guestrooms

— *Door attendants*: Ensure baggage service and traffic control at hotel entrance(s)

— *Valet parking attendants*: Ensure parking services for guest's automobiles

— *Transportation personnel:* Ensure transportation services for guests from and to the hotel

— *Concierge:* Assists guests by making restaurant reservations, arranging for transportation, and getting tickets for theater, sporting, or any other special events

Responsibilities of the rooms department include reservations, guest reception, room assignment, tracking the status of rooms, prompt forwarding of mail and phone messages, security, housekeeping of guest rooms and public spaces such as lobbies, and answering guests' questions. To perform these many duties effectively, the rooms department may be divided into a number of specialized subunits. To complicate matters, in many instances these subunits are also referred to as departments. The laundry department is responsible for cleaning and pressing all the hotel's linens and employee uniforms as well as guest laundry. Because of its specialized function, little of the knowledge and skills required to manage a laundry operation is transferable to other areas of hotel operations. The front office is one of the most important departments in a hotel, as it often offers the only contact between guests and staff. A hotel's front office is where guests are greeted when they arrive, where they are registered and assigned to a room, and where they check out.

The reservations department takes and tracks the hotel's future bookings. The housekeeping department is responsible for cleaning guest rooms and public spaces. Because of their specialized nature, the security and engineering departments are discussed in separate sections. A great deal of interdependence exists among the subunits of the rooms department. The front office must let reservations know whenever walk-in guests register. A similar level of cooperation is required between the front office and housekeeping. When a guest checks out, the front office must inform housekeeping so that the room may be cleaned. Once a room is cleaned, housekeeping must inform the front office so that the room may be sold. Certain tasks within the rooms department must occur in a specific order.

Housekeeping cannot properly provision a guest room if the laundry does not supply enough clean towels or bed sheets. Engineering cannot replace a defective light switch in a guest room if housekeeping does not report the problem. Effective management of this busy department calls for standardized plans, procedures, schedules, and deadlines, as well as frequent direct communication between the executives who manage the key operating units of the rooms department.

The hotel and lodging business is vulnerable to security and safety problems. Problems can be created by guests, employees, or intruders. Security breaches can result in embezzlement, theft, arson, robbery, and even terrorism. Depending on the size of a hotel or a lodging establishment, the security function may be handled by a fully staffed department on site, contracted to an outside security company, or assigned to designated staff members sonnel in the rooms department. In a larger, full-service hotel, the director of security may report directly to the general manager. In smaller hotels, the security function might become a task of the rooms department. Engineering department's responsibilities include preventive maintenance; repair; replacement; improvement and modification to furniture, fixtures, and equipment (FFE); and ensuring uninterrupted provision of utilities (gas, electricity, water).Preventive maintenance involves routine checks and inspection of the key components of all equipment.

Maintenance of recreational facilities may be part of the engineering department's responsibilities. In particular, swimming pools require extensive maintenance to ensure proper filtration and to prevent the accumulation of algae and other conditions unsuitable for swimming. Prompt repair minimizes loss of productivity in other hotel operating departments and inconvenience to hotel guests. When a particular FFE has reached the end of its useful life and repair is no longer cost-effective, replacement is indicated. Improvement projects enhance the existing operation or reduce operating costs of the facility.

Modification projects alter the existing operation to accommodate one or more new functions. One hotel might have a large engineering staff that includes plumbers, carpenters, painters, electricians, and other technicians. Another might have maintenance personnel who have general knowledge and understanding of the hotel's operations but rely on outside contractors for specialized jobs. In larger, full-service hotels, engineering may be a separate department, with a director who reports directly to the resident manager.

Food and Beverage Department

Food and beverage department constitutes the second largest revenue generator of a typical hotel with an average of 23.1 for Food sales, and 8.6 % for Beverage sales. In a five-star hotel, Food and Beverage outlets might have the following forms:

— Quick service
— Table service
— Specialty restaurants
— Coffee shops
— Bars
— Lounges
— Clubs
— Banquets
— Catering functions
— Wedding, birthdays, etc.

The primary function of the food and beverage department is to provide food and drink to a hotel's guests. In earlier times, when an inn had a single dining room that could hold a limited number of guests, this was a fairly simple task. Today, however, providing food and drink is much more complicated. A large hotel might well have a coffee shop, a gourmet restaurant, a poolside snack bar, room service, two banquet halls, and ten function rooms where food and beverages are served. It might also have a lounge, a nightclub, and a lobby bar. On a busy day, it's quite likely that functions will be booked in many outlets at the same time. In addition, some outlets may have multiple events scheduled for a single day. As you can see, there is great diversity in the types of activities performed by a food and beverage department, requiring a significant variety of skills on the part of its workers. Because of the diversity of services provided, the food and beverage department is typically split into subunits. The executive chef, a person of considerable importance and authority in any full-service hotel, runs the food production, or kitchen, department.

A variety of culinary specialists who are responsible for different aspects of food preparation report to the executive chef. The actual serving of food in a large hotel's restaurants is usually the responsibility of a separate department, headed by the assistant food and beverage director. The food service department is composed of the individual restaurant and outlet managers, maitre d's, waiters, waitresses, and bus help. Because of their special duties and concerns, many large hotels have a separate subunit that is responsible only for room service. Because of the high value and profit margins associated with the sale of alcoholic beverages, some hotels have a separate department that assumes responsibility for all outlets where alcoholic beverages are sold.

The person responsible for this department is the beverage manager. Most full-service hotels also do a considerable convention and catering business. The typical convention uses small function rooms for meetings and larger rooms for general sessions, trade shows, exhibits, and banquets. As a hotel or lodging business increases the use of its facilities for conventions and meetings, it may form a separate convention services department. The convention services department and its personnel are introduced to the client, a meeting planner, or an association executive by the marketing and sales department. The convention services department then handles all of the client's meeting and catering requirements. Individually catered events include parties, wedding receptions, business meetings, and other functions held by groups. To provide for the unique needs of these types of customers, hotels often organise separate catering and convention departments. Depending on the size of the hotel, the job of cleaning the food and beverage outlets themselves as well as of washing pots and pans, dishes, glasses, and utensils is often delegated to a subunit known as the stewarding department. It is only through continuous cooperation and coordination that a hotel's food service function can be carried out effectively.

Sales and Marketing Department

A hotel, usually have sales and marketing division. However, if the staff size, volume business, hotel size, expected group arrivals is low enough, the hotel might have marketing staff placed under the reservation department. A typical sales and marketing division is composed of four different departments:

a) Sales

b) Convention services

c) Advertising

d) Public relations

The marketing and sales department is removed from most of the day-to-day operational problems faced by other departments. The division of work among the sales managers is based on the type of customers a hotel is attempting to attract. Individual sales managers often specialize in corporate accounts, conventions, or tour and travel markets. Sales managers' accounts are sometimes subdivided along geographical lines into regional or national accounts.

Accounting division

The accounting department is responsible for recording financial transactions, preparing and interpreting financial statements, and providing the managers of other departments with timely reports of operating results. Some of the activities that are undertaken in the accounting division are listed below:

a) Pays outstanding invoices

b) Distributes unpaid statements

c) Collects amounts owed

d) Processes payroll

e) Accumulates operating data

f) Compiles financial reports

g) Makes bank deposits

h) Secures cash loans

i) Performs other control and processing functions

The accounting department combines staff functions and line functions, or those functions directly responsible for servicing guests. Other responsibilities, carried out by the assistant controller for finance, include payroll preparation, accounts receivable, and accounts payable. Another dimension of the accounting department's responsibilities deals with various aspects of hotel operations, cost accounting, and cost control throughout the hotel. The two areas of central concern to the accounting department are rooms and food and beverage.

The accounting department's front office cashier is responsible for tracking all charges to guest accounts. At the close of each business day, which varies by hotel but typically occurs at midnight or after the bulk of guests' transactions have been completed, the night auditor is responsible for reconciling all guest bills with the charges from the various hotel departments. Although the front office cashier and the night auditor physically work at the front desk and, in the case of the cashier, have direct contact with guests, they are members of the accounting department and report to the assistant controller of operations.

The accounting department is anything but a passive staff unit contending with routine recordkeeping. The accounting department is also responsible for collecting and reporting most of a hotel's operational and financial statistics, which provide important data for decision making and budget preparation purposes. The head of the accounting department may report not only to the hotel's general manager but also to the hotel chain's financial vice president or to the hotel's owner. The reason for this dual responsibility and reporting relationship is to afford the hotel corporation an independent verification of the financial and operating results of the hotel.

Human Resources Division

The three functions of the human resources department are employee recruitment, benefits administration, and training. The director of human resources is also expected to be an expert on federal and state labor laws and to advise managers in other departments on these topics. The human resources department's major challenge is in its interactions with other hotel departments.

Although the human resources department recruits, interviews, and screens prospective employees, the final hiring decision rests within the department in which the potential employee will be working. The same is true of promotion and disciplinary decisions; the human resources department's input is, in most cases, limited to advice and interpretation of legal questions. The human resources department's effectiveness depends on its manager's ability to form effective working relationships with managers of other departments.

Security Department

Security department personnel are usually screened from inhouse personnel, security officers or retired police officers, across certain physical skills, and prior experience. The functions of the security division mainly include:

a) Patrols the property

b) Monitors supervision equipment

c) Ensures safety and security of guests, visitors, and employees.

Maintenance Division

This very department maintains the property's structure and grounds as well as electrical and mechanical equipment. Some hotels might have this very division under different names, such as maintenance division, property operation and maintenance department.

ORGANISATIONALCONTROL

Organizational control is a multilevel control approach in which explicit organizational goals, roles, and responsibilities are dynamically developed, distributed, and maintained to serve as guidelines for making detailed operational control decisions by the individual agents. By restricting the scope of local control decisions and communication actions, these organizational guidelines lower the cost of distributed resource allocation and agent coordination, help limit inappropriate agent behavior, and reduce communication requirements.

The factors determine the most appropriate span of organizational are:

1. task similarity,
2. training and professionalism,
3. task certainty,
4. frequency of interaction,
5. task integration, and
6. physical dispersion.

When a large number of employees perform similar tasks, the span of control can be increased. When the employees perform very different tasks, the supervisor must give each subordinate more individual attention in order to keep in touch with the different types of tasks; this requires a narrower span of control. For example, the rooms department manager might easily manage the front desk agents and housekeepers until the brand standards for check-in or checkout of a guest increase in complexity and the standards for the various types of rooms and their cleaning procedure increase in detail. At this time, the rooms department manager's span of control must be narrowed.

The better trained and more skilled a subordinate is, the less supervision is required. For example, a front desk agent might require a higher level of training and skill than a room service waiter. Thus, a front desk supervisor can supervise more employees than the room service supervisor. Task certainty refers to the predictability of a task. Routine tasks allow management to devise standard procedures for subordinates to follow, minimizing questions about the job and widening the span of control. On the other hand, close supervision is called for when tasks are ambiguous and uncertainty is great.

For example, the task of checking a guest in or out of the hotel can be documented and standard procedures can be created, so the front desk manager can have a relatively wide span of control over the front desk agents. However, because of the diversity of customers the sales manager encounters, the tasks of a hotel sales manager are less certain. The director of sales is responsible for coaching the sales managers, observing sales calls, and ensuring deal closings; these tasks require a hands-on approach that limits the number of employees the director of sales can handle, narrowing the span of control.

If the supervisor-subordinate relationship requires frequent interaction, the span of control must be narrow. If interaction is infrequent, the span of control can be wide. For example, the hotel controller must review regularly the status of collections and payments with staff. In contrast, the frequency of interaction between the chief engineer and his or her subordinates is directed by written work orders in most circumstances and thus requires less direct communication, enabling a wider span of control. If the supervisor must integrate and coordinate the tasks of subordinates, the span of control narrows. For example, in the production of a meal for one table of four guests with different appetizers, salads, and entrées, the chef must have a narrow span of control to ensure that each component of the meal is assembled correctly and delivered to service personnel on a timely basis. The span of control of the executive housekeeper can be much wider because the procedure for cleaning and preparing each guest room is similar, if not exactly the same, for every room.

One of the most important strength of a functional organisational design is efficiency. The performance of common tasks allows for work specialization, which increases overall productivity. Workers develop specialized skills and knowledge more rapidly. Training is easier because of the similarity of tasks and the resulting opportunities for inexperienced workers to learn from experienced workers. This helps new employees quickly learn the kinds of behavior that lead to success and promotion. Coordination of activities within functional departments is easier than in more broadly based organisations. A functional organisation fosters efficiency, teamwork, and coordination of activities within individual units. However, the functional organisation's most important strength is also the source of its great-est shortcoming. The success of a hotel as a business is measured by its overall performance and not by the performance of any one department.

A hotel with spotless guest rooms will not be successful if guests' front desk experiences are not up to par. Even if guests' dining experiences are superb, the hotel will fall flat on its face if its rooms are dismal. It is sometimes difficult for each department to fully appreciate its role in the overall success of the organisation. It is vital that each department keep in mind the hotel-wide goals of customer service and profitability rather than focus narrowly on its own concerns. Some means must be found to coordinate the activities of functional departments and to set hotel-wide strategies and goals. A hotel's functional organisation demands strong leadership. New initiatives in hotels often require cooperation and coordination between functional departments. New ideas tend to be stillborn if department heads lack a hotel-wide perspective or have difficulty coordinating their activities. The tendency to concentrate on doing things right often overshadows the organisation's ability to do the right thing.

The GM, as the chief executive of the hotel, emerges as the single person capable of providing the overall organisational direction, decision making, coordination, and arbitration needed to make a hotel's functional departments work together effectively. A hotel simply cannot run itself from the departmental level. Thus, the GM must be a strong leader to be effective.

The executive operating committee (EOC) of a hotel, made up of the general manager and senior executives from each department, is designed to increase the level of coordination between departments. There is no standard membership for this committee, but it usually comprises those executives who report directly to the general manager. The EOC is also responsible for a hotel's major budgetary units, such as the food and beverage and housekeeping units. EOC functions depend on how the hotel GM chooses to use the group, the GM's style, and the structure of other management meetings in the hotel.

Distribution of Authority

Authority can be distributed throughout an organisation or held in the hands of a few select employees. The delegation of authority creates a chain of command, the formal channel that defines the lines of authority from the top to the bottom of an organisation. The chain of command specifies a clear reporting relationship for each person in the organisation and should be followed in both downward and upward communication. Following the chain of command enables each new employee, no matter what his or her position, to know exactly for whom and to whom he or she is responsible. When designing an organisational structure, managers must consider the distribution of authority. Decentralization is the process of distributing authority throughout an organisation. In a decentralized organisation, an organisation member has the right to make a decision without obtaining approval from a higher-level manager. Centralization is the retention of decision-making authority by a high-level manager. Traditionally, hotel and lodging management has been very centralized, probably due to its roots in small, owner-operated lodging.

As the hotel and lodging industry has expanded, decentralization has become a more frequent style of operation. Decentralization has several advantages. Managers are encouraged to develop decision-making skills, which help them advance in their careers. The autonomy afforded by this style of operation also increases job satisfaction and motivation. When employees are encouraged to perform well, the profitability of the organisation increases. Many hotel and lodging organisations have begun to empower employees and supervisors to make decisions that typically have been made by managers.

Staff Meetings

Big hotels increase communications through an elaborate structure of additional committees and meetings, including some or all of the following: operations, staff, sales forecast and marketing, departmental, subdepartmental, credit, safety, energy conservation, and employee meetings. The operations committee comprises the general manager, department heads, front office manager, manager on duty, and representatives from housekeeping, security, engineering, and food and beverage. The staff committee might include the GM, department heads, and all subdepartment heads who report to the department heads. The sales forecast and marketing committee might meet one to four times per month for several hours so the GM and department heads can review room demand for the coming 90 days and devise strategies to increase room nights (and thus bring in more revenue) and to increase average daily rates by up-selling potential guests to higher-rated rooms with perhaps more amenities or services. The departmental committee consists of the department head and his or her subdepartment heads, managers, and supervisors.

Meeting once or twice per month for an hour or so, the group reviews departmental issues.Similarly, subdepartment committees meet monthly for about an hour so the subdepartment head, managers, and supervisors can address issues unique to their subdepartment, such as the selection of a new type of floor cleaner by the housekeeping department or a more energy-efficient light bulb by the engineering department. The credit committee includes the general manager, the controller, sales, the front office, reservations, catering, and the credit manager. Meeting monthly for an hour, the committee reviews those guests and clients of the hotel who were granted credit but have not settled their account. The safety committee typically comprises representatives from human resources, food and beverage, housekeeping, and engineering. Meeting monthly for an hour or so, the committee reviews safety programs and safety records, addresses problems, and discusses the implementation of new safety regulations.

The future success of a hotel will be driven in large part by the ability to foresee and capitalize on change. As we go through global transitions, the successful hotel will examine the key factors that will not only define success but also the ability to survive in coming years. These key organisational trends must be acknowledged by the successful hotel organisation: visionary leadership, globalization, diversity, flexibility, flat structure, customer focus, zero defects, network orientation, and being in the information fast lane. The organisation must be able to respond to increasingly globalized sales, the movement to maintaining sales offices in many countries and hotel properties across the globe, and an increasingly globalized labor market.

Flexibility in the modern hotel organisation means assuring that systems, processes, and people can respond differently to different situations; fewer detailed rules and procedures; greater autonomy and encouragement of initiative; customizing employment relationships to include telecommuting and job-sharing; and lifetime employability rather than lifetime employment. The trend toward flatness in hotel organisations means fewer levels of management, workers empowered to make decisions, and fewer differences in responsibility. The organisation's employees need to believe in a sense of entrepreneurship that reacts proactively to market diversity. Traditional organisations that follow well-documented rules must give way to leaders who can balance a sense of discipline with one of flexibility. If the customer is king or queen in the 21st century, hotel organisaions will be best served by focusing less on their hotel assets as measures of success and more on their customers. This involves a fundamental shift from viewing the real estate asset as the wealth creator to seeing the customer as the key to building shareholder wealth.

A failing hotel organisation is overmanaged and underled. The networked hotel organisation can facilitate direct communication across unit and property boundaries, ignoring the chain of command; cross-unit team structures; outsourcing and downsizing; strategic alliances with competitors and others; customization; and decentralization. Being in the information fast lane is critical. The traditional role of information technology as a back office support for accounting and bookkeeping has clearly moved to front and center stage. Information technology today influences all aspects of business from corporate strategies to organisational structure. Technology was once viewed as a way to reduce costs by replacing people. That attitude has been firmly supplanted by the idea of seeking information technology support for the creative work all organisations must pursue. Information technology must enable organisations to react more speedily to market needs and, of course, produce the fulfillment of customer demands both quickly and accurately.

Technology and Organisational Changes

The organisation and business operations of hotel companies will be reshaped to satisfy the changing needs of constituents. This is due in part to rapid technological advances in information and communications, as well as a transformation of the capital base of the hotel industry. Customers and stakeholders will demand seamless access to hotel company business information and processes. Heightened business interdependencies between hotel companies, their suppliers, and marketing and service representatives, will undoubtedly blur corporate lines. Major changes will take place in the way the hotel industry accesses and deploys financing and venture capital. Nearly every business and most individuals in the United States have already entered the electronic age of information and communications. Laptop computers, cellular telephones, beepers and interactive communication devices have all become commonplace tools are heavily. Within the next few years, consumers will have unlimited direct access to most channels of market and business information and distribution. Consumers will want to handle daily activities and business transactions without leaving their homes or offices using their own personal computers.

Buying and selling goods and services, paying bills, researching topics of interest, handling banking transactions, and planning daily personal and business activities are all part of this change. What implications does this have for the hotel industry? Well, for starters, many individuals will want to book personally-tailored vacation packages and business itineraries using direct links through their own personal computers. This will require full access to on-line facility data bases and vacation catalogues, as well as price lists. Also, they will need direct access to hotel and airline rooms and seat inventory control systems. This alone could revolutionise the marketing and sales paradigm for the hotel industry.

Technological advances in information and communication will cause hotels to make dramatic chances in the way they serve and physically accommodate guests. Count on it, interactive computing and multimedia devices will be as commonplace in hotel rooms of the future as present-day remote control televisions and touch-tone telephones. Guests will want the option of avoiding interaction with hotel service and clerical personnel by using these devices. Just think, no more waiting in line to check in or out of your hotel room. No delay while waiting for the hotel operator or some other service clerk to answer the telephone to schedule your wake-up call, take your room service order or book your restaurant reservation. No need to call for additional towels, or to order a shoe shine or dirty laundry pick-up. You can do all of this by touching a few icons on your television screen.

Technological advancements may alter the physical design and space allocation of hotels in the future. Quite possibly, a computing and multimedia room will be required on every floor of every full-service hotel. Possibly, the amount and size of meeting rooms and auditoriums will change as guests wishing to participate in large conferences from the comfort and convenience of their guest rooms, may wish to use interactive video conferencing devices and remote response terminals, to participate. Another possibility is that the front desk area could be cut hack to a small greeting kiosk and the remainder of the space put to more productive use such as retail space.

Many new sources of revenues could result from these changes. Direct guest room linkups to a wide variety of online entertainment and informational networks will be a standard requirement in the future. This could mean large access fees for hotels. Rental or usage charges for peripheral devices could also mean big business. A number of hotel companies presently are focusing their attention on redesigning or participating in new global distribution systems. These will better link hotel companies, airlines, travel companies, and rental car companies to each other--but not directly to the consumer. Just think of the marketing opportunities that exist today for hotel companies to reach customers directly using international computer networks, on-line bulletin boards, and direct "E-mail" advertising. A few innovative hotel companies have already seized this opportunity.

Owners, investors, lenders and suppliers all want and are demanding more timely information on which to base their business decisions and monitor their business interests. Many hotel companies are finding that stakeholders particularly owners and lenders- want to check-in directly to the flow of business and financial information. Think about demands for information that might come up in the future. Hotel lenders may want on-line access to hotel treasury and cash management systems to daily sweep bank accounts and monitor compliance with covenants of loan agreements. Investors may want up-to-the-minute financial statement information to gauge investment performance and make daily investment decisions. Suppliers may want on-line access to perpetual inventory records to automatically trigger purchase orders and shipments. Already, travel agents, meeting planners and tour wholesalers want on-line access to room inventories and pricing information. To accommodate these needs, major changes in the business and accounting information systems of hotels and hotel companies will have to be implemented.

Sweeping organisational and operational changes will occur in the hotel industry. The need for large headquarters facilities with multiple departments and large technical support staffs will greatly diminish because of technological advancements in information and communications. In marketing and sales, huge competitive advantages can result from setting up state-of-the-art" customer databases with interactive communication linkups.

Through the use of wide area networks and other linkages, individuals will be able to share information and experiences between locations rapidly and set up multi-location workgroups to facilitate problem-solving. This will significantly reduce the need to cluster technical support staffs under one roof. The ability exists to link suppliers seamlessly with hotel companies using "E-mail" and knowledge management software. For the first time, outsourcing for a wide variety of technical and business support functions, such as payroll and personnel management, purchasing and new business development, is a viable option for most hotel companies. For hotels, the entire organisational and operational structure may change as a result of technological innovation. Front-office functions could be minimised or eliminated. Universal service representatives could tend to virtually every guest need from a single work station. Guests will likely be able to initiate many service functions directly using interactive guest room devices. This could change the service staffing requirements and mechanical resources to more productive activities such as better execution of guest requests. This also holds true for many back-office functions. Through better uses of technology, many hotels can approach elimination of many of the clerical functions presently performed in the back offices of hotels.

The shift in capital is expected to have a dramatic effect on the future underwriting of hotel loans and investments. No longer will the game be to convince the lender's credit committee or the investor's capital committee to do the deal. Now the game will be to convince the independent agencies rating the securities that the deal is good, since they are the ones that Wall Street investors rely on to rate the underlying securities. Underwriting parameters will continue to be tough in the future since virtually all loans will ultimately be sold in pools to investors as securities. Lenders will want to be sure that every loan meets the minimum underwriting criteria set by the investment bankers who sell the loans to investors. After the loan is made, a far greater amount of periodic business and financial information will be required from the borrower.

Hotel Organization of the Future

No hotel company operating today can be unaware of the swift pace of global change and its impact on every facet of the hospitality industry. With just five years left in this century, we can expect change to be the only constant. New business practices are evolving virtually as fast as our technologies, while resistance to change has become one of the primary causes of business failure. The specter of constant change raises fundamental questions as to the creation of shareholder wealth in a capital-constrained, highly competitive environment. How will hotel organizations build shareholder wealth, and what key drivers will result in success? What future products and services will be essential in a technology-driven, global environment marked by rising customer expectations? Moreover, what alternative approaches and skills must organizations develop to ensure market success?

The future success of hotel organizations will be driven in large part by the ability to foresee — and capitalize — on change. Beyond this truism, however, there is an urgent need to identify what will be required in the competitive environment of the future with its intense focus on serving customer needs. The hospitality industry — as is the case with business generally — is subject to deep currents of change set in motion as economic and social systems shaped in the industrial era evolve to a knowledge-based era driven by technology advances.

From an Asset to Customer Focus

Recognizing that the hotel industry has a somewhat split personality reflecting the inherent conflicts between its real estate and operational aspects, it is important to understand the industry's real estate origins and how they are shaping the challenges ahead.

The origins of the industry's real estate persona are embodied in the classic theory of location - "if we build it, they will come." As a result of this "building" complex, the industry has tended to have a real estate and asset orientation, rather than a customer focus. From the hotel company perspective — especially that of the brand-oriented "chain" — the varied interests of a diffused property ownership group can be quite different than the singular interest of the chain that operates and markets the properties.

Even when the ownership of geographically dispersed hotel properties is controlled by a single hotel organization, the financial structuring tends to be property-specific. Corporate financial strategies are frequently subjugated to the needs of the last property deal brought into the company's fold. Each property in a so-called "chain," is frequently the subject of a unique and distinctive ownership and financial structure. This phenomenon — quite common in the real estate sector, but unusual for business enterprises generally — makes for elusive economies of scale in the structuring and financing of property-driven expansion.

Collectively, these factors have produced low comparative returns in real estate, although criticism leveled at commercial real estate returns is somewhat less germane to the hotel industry, where management and franchise fees can produce high returns for those companies where property ownership is held by third parties. Nevertheless, average returns in the real estate industry in the United States, for example, are just over 10 percent, compared to small company stock returns at almost 20 percent and large company stocks at an average of about 15 percent.

While hotel chains have adopted traditional corporate frameworks, there are a number of predominantly real estate-driven, family-owned businesses in the hotel sector that continue to operate as relatively unstructured organizations. In meeting the future, these businesses will need plans, people and processes in order to establish viable corporate forms that can compete in tomorrow's marketplace and capitalize upon its opportunities.

In today's changed environment, the hotel organization must deal with a number of new realities. Investors in our industry are no longer satisfied with long-term capital appreciation and psychic income that heretofore were often the justification for otherwise seemingly uneconomic investments in hotel property or, indeed, hotel chains. The first reality is that there is a very specific and identifiable relationship between bottom line performance and value. Improvements in business operations raises values. It is not surprising, therefore, that the new owners attracted to this industry in recent years have new sets of demands. This transformation from an old-guard group of investors and owners to income and return-driven newcomers has meant that the once "quiet enjoyment" of operators in their management of hotels for third parties is being disturbed, interrupted and overturned.

These challenges all take place in an environment where capital has become extremely selective in markets that have little stability. A global shortage of capital will not remain a short-term problem, and future hotel organizations must have a stronger alignment to capital providers — a critical "customer" group. Hotel companies will need to compete by offering better returns and performance than in the past. Hotel chains have found their development timetables quashed in recent years, making it difficult to achieve goals of critical mass often required to improve performance. These factors are driving consolidation in the brand "sweepstakes." Capital markets, therefore, continue to favor well-established companies, a reality that must drive entrepreneurial organizations to meet the future now by planning for an evolving corporate context in which to operate.

Key Success Factors

Within this broad context, hotel developers, owners and

management companies will all need to develop new strategies, skills and processes that look forward to the competitive demands of the future. These ultimately must address issues related to vision and planning, as well as organizational skill sets and processes to attract and retain customers. To stake a claim in the future, current business practices should be examined in light of what can be expected to be the key success factors.

Embrace a Global Change Orientation

As the information age produces greater worldwide integration of business activities, a global knowledge base will become invaluable. Success in local and regional hotel markets will be shaped decisively by a global business environment that defines capital movement, customer expectations and applications of new technologies.

Focus on the Customer

If the customer is "king" in the 21st century, hotel organizations will be best served by focusing less on their hotel assets as measures of success, and more on their customers. This involves a fundamental shift in viewing the real estate asset as the wealth creator — to the customer as the key to building shareholder wealth. A customer focus must imbue business decisions at all levels of developing and operating a hotel organization. Pursuing such a course will inevitably impact shareholder wealth. To accomplish this, however, customers need to participate in the product development process.

Fully realizing a customer focus in the industry poses a significant challenge. The hotel industry must confront problems due to conflicts between operational needs and real estate goals. Quite simply, an operator must remain customer-focused, but the short-term strategies to meet these needs may be inconsistent with the long-term objectives of property owners. Balancing those goals will be essential. A customer. focus implies a significant shift in what drives hotel development — placing primary emphasis on the customer with the locations to follow. Nevertheless, a hotel organization with its large investment in fixed assets — the real estate — can never be as nimble as a consumer products company in adjusting products and services to match rapid shifts in the marketplace.

The Japanese taught us that the concept of "zero defects" in products and services can yield tremendous benefits. But today an even more rigorous standard dominates — quality that surprises. In practical terms, the hotel industry finds it extremely difficult to meet the standard of zero defects in service. Hotel services are based primarily on people, not computers or other equipment. Quality that surprises takes the concept of zero defects a step further. Yesterday's surprising product or service is today's status quo. Twenty years ago, a business executive did not expect a consistent and predictable level of service wherever he or she traveled in the world. Today that is a standard — not the exception — as is the expectation for sophisticated technology in hotel rooms to support business needs. With customer discrimination so acute, it is not surprising that brand loyalty is a diminishing "commodity" in the hotel industry.

Find the ingredients for visionary leadership. Today's hotel organizations need to recognize the need for visionary leadership. The ability to forecast the future — to anticipate change rather than react to it — will be one of the single greatest determinants of market dominance in the years ahead. The old "command and control" model of leadership is giving way to a focus on leadership in ideas, information, inspiration, vision and teamwork. Warren Bennis, an authority on leadership in the U.S., puts it this way — "For the most part, failing organizations tend to be over-managed and under-led. The leader sets the tone for the moral character, the vision, the corporate culture and the fiber of the institution."

While visionary leadership is essential, it must be linked to business operations and foster a risk bias, rather than a procedural bias. This will allow the organization to stretch and, in turn, change. And it must be shared by empowered professionals and staff throughout the organization, including those who meet the customer. Overcoming the resistance to change can be a daunting task, particularly in large hotel organizations in which diversions from the status quo may threaten established management lines. It suggests that a culture based on conformance may need to be replaced by an emphasis on flexibility, learning and cooperation. Management competencies will need to be aligned in order to achieve the desired result. For many organizations, this may mean a shift from traditional hierarchies typical of companies in an industrial era to a flatter organization with a more transparent interface between leadership, organizational functions and employees.

Create a Defensible Position through Corporate Strategy

For many of the industry's leaders, vision is driven by the strategic planning process, a function which has become critical for success. Strategic planning, however, has at times been a step-child in the hotel industry, and it is often the first to be cut when organizations are downsized. It is clearly in transition. There also has been a tendency to decentralize and simplify this function — both actions of potential benefit. Strategic planning must be led by the top people in the organization — the CEO and COO. On the other hand, it should be close enough to the customer to ensure that planners can "listen" to and be influenced by customer needs.

Empower Management

Beyond the ability to envision the future, core management capabilities will make the difference — they are essential. A clear vision without the management skills to support it cannot be a recipe for success. First and foremost, hotel management must have strategic development skills and the ability to integrate complex factors affecting success. Market volatility has become the norm, in part caused by the rapidly changing tastes of customers. Customers are increasingly approaching the hotel industry with widely different social, economic and political backgrounds, to say nothing of employees. Being able to deal with these diversities in a positive and constructive fashion that capitalizes on the differences, rather than working to find ways to mitigate them, is the clear path for successful management in the future.

The organization will also need to be imbued with a sense of entrepreneurship that reacts proactively to the market's diversity. Traditional organizations that follow well-documented rules must give way to leaders who can balance a sense of discipline with that of flexibility. Talent and resources must be marshaled and leveraged. In an industry with high fixed costs and labor intensity, the concept of leverage in the hotel business is an all-important one. Improving labor productivity through technology must be a goal for today's forward-looking hotel organization. Management must also be able to narrow the gap between the employer and the employee, forcing a flatter organization in the process. This will put management closer to the customer and speed the two-way communication process up and down the organization.

The traditional role of information technology (IT) as a back office support for accounting and bookkeeping has clearly moved front and center stage. IT today influences all aspects of business from corporate strategies to organizational structure — and from the very business processes it is designed to support to performance measurement. In a world where the customer is "king," IT must also deliver in two critical areas: sales and marketing and customer service. Technology was once viewed as a way to reduce costs by replacing people. That attitude has been firmly supplanted by one that seeks IT support for the creative work that all organizations must pursue. IT must allow organizations to react more speedily to market needs and, of course, produce the fulfillment of customer demands both quickly and accurately. To do this IT must operate on a decentralized basis. IT delivers, but it has to be the right information to the right people, and it needs to be done on a timely basis.

3

Developing a Hotel

Like many other businesses, hotels have been affected by shifts in emphasis among the living patterns. People and industry have moved from the so-called rust belt to the sun belt. The hotel business has been active in reborn and reconstructed central cities. The explosion of technology and information-based companies has concentrated human endeavor in technological corridors in California, Massachusetts,Washington, Texas, and North Carolina, to name a few such places. It can be safely said that where jobs are and major concentrations of economic activity occur, hotels will follow. Among other current and ongoing influencers of hotel design, construction, marketing, and operation are the following.

— *Demographics* play a major role and will continue to be influential in the foreseeable future. As the baby boom generation and its children mature, the population of the country will for many years be older, healthier, and better educated than previous generations. These facts will present new challenges and opportunities to all business managers.

— *Technology*—in the form of computers, communication, personal devices, and laborsaving mechanical equipment—has had and will have a major effect on the way in which hotels are managed and operated. The speed with which information is accumulated, stored, manipulated, and transferred is such that today most travelers expect that the hotel rooms they rent will allow them to be as productive as they are in the office or at home. Increasingly, with portable computing, personal data assistants (PDAs), wireless communication, and virtually everything somehow connected to the Internet, hotels must provide services and access that allow guests seamless transition from the business, travel, or home environment to that of the hotel. Increasingly, entertainment must be fused with communication and productive processes.

— The concept of market segmentation, or ever-increasingly finely tuned market definitions, will dictate hotel structures and organisations, and management tactics designed to address those market segments have become even more important to the management of hospitality service businesses. With the increased power in the information and data manipulation realm, hotels have available to them everexpanding databases about guests and are creating new products to attract those markets.

— One of the effects of the aging demographic is the emergence of *vacation re-sorts*—a modern incarnation of the timeshare properties of several decades ago. Because these are being developed and operated by name hotel companies and are marketed to the affluent, healthy, well-educated population segment, resort managers have had to absorb new managerial realities. The well-documented change in the complexion of the national economy from one that emphasises goods and, to a lesser extent, natural resources to one that emphasises services has kindled new ideas about the way in which we manage the design and delivery of these services. Hotels, restaurants, and travel services are now seen as unique entities that dictate special kinds of managerial techniques and strategies.

— Changes in people's *travel patterns* have altered the way we manage our hotel properties. Deregulation of the airlines has driven a change in the way millions of people travel each year, given the huband-spoke design of airline services. Many hotel companies are now locating major hotel properties adjacent to hub air transport facilities, taking advantage of the fact that business travelers may not need to travel to a central business district (CBD) to accomplish their purpose in a given area. Meetings and conferences can now be scheduled within a five-minute limousine ride from the air terminal, and the business traveler can be headed for his or her next destination before the day is over without having to stay overnight in a CBD hotel.

— New *patterns of investment* in hotel facilities have emerged in the last two decades, and more attention is now paid to achieving optimum return on investment. Be- cause people from outside the hotel industry are now participating in its financial structuring, hotel operations are no longer dependent on the vision of a single entrepreneur. Managers now must design tactics and strategies to achieve heretofore unanticipated financial goals. The same trend has also altered the complexion of management and organisation of the modern hotel. This is especially true of publicly owned hotel firms, where Wall Street stock analysts heavily influence stock prices through expectations of quarterly revenues and profits. This puts pressure on hotel companies and their operations managers to perform, on a quarterly basis, in a way contrary to many managers' instincts.

Most of the foregoing issues and influences still operate on the organisational structures and strategies of the modern hotel.

The cyclical nature of international economies has recently affected significantly hotels' ability to respond to changing circumstances. In early 1993, for instance, employment growth was stagnant; corporate profits were low; the expansion of the gross national product (GNP) was only a marginal percentage above previous years; and travel in most segments was down due to corporate restructuring, downsizing, or reorganising. Vast layoffs in the hundreds of thousands had been announced every month. While fuel prices continued to be relatively stable, consumer spending patterns and high employment growth had not materialised, particularly in light of corporate layoffs and the ongoing nervousness of consumers about whether or not their financial wherewithal was safe.

The terrorist attacks in New York and Washington, D.C., in 2001 changed the face of all business and travel, immediately and probably for the foreseeable future as well. Major airlines are in bankruptcy; hotels are struggling to achieve profitable occupancies; business travel is down; the high-tech stock market bubble burst; the country is at war in a number of locations; security has made travel more difficult, if not actually annoying; and people are nervous. Join this with an imbalance of trade, the outsourcing of jobs, and the largest federal deficits in history, and the face of the economy is challenging.This translates directly not only to business travel but personal and recreational travel as well. Finding ways to operate profitably in such an environment is the job of the next generation of hotel operators.

As surely as living patterns, economic cycles, and market segmentation have influenced the hotel industry, so will the change in ethnicity of the workforce.The cultural backgrounds that an increasingly diversified workforce will bring to hotel operations may be seen as a problem or a challenge—or both. To most operators, it will be seen as an opportunity to demonstrate to an increasingly diverse clientele that hotel companies are committed to hiring and training a workforce structure that mirrors society.

The legal and regulatory environments are increasingly important to all business managers, and hotel operators are no exception. Increasingly, operators must be aware of and alert to realms of risk that can engender lawsuits against them. Present-day security concerns also have significantly affected the ways in which hotels are operated. Awareness of the risk environment and the regulatory realm are factors that affect a hotel's ability to compete in the early part of the twenty-first century.

Hotel Development

The developer is the entrepreneur, the risk taker, who originates the idea for the hotel. Depending on the business structure selected, the developer often puts his or her personal wealth at risk when engaging in a hotel project. The developer, along with a small staff of people, networks with commercial real estate agents on the lookout for a suitable hotel site. Depending on the type of hotel to be developed, a site of at least two to four acres is required (for comparison, an acre is roughly the size of a football field).This property must be zoned by the city for a hotel, be visible from a freeway or major street arterial, and have city approval for such construction activities as curb cuts, lefthand turn lanes, and delivery truck access. Commercial realtors offer sites for the developer's consideration that include maps, aerial photos, and proof of hotel zoning. Sometimes the developer views potential sites by driving around the neighborhood within five miles of the site or touring multiple sites by helicopter, noting where the potential guests live and work and where potential competing hotels are located. The price per square foot of the land is considered. The higher the cost of land, the higher the rates the hotel will need to charge. Is the price too high for the average daily rate (ADR) in this particular market? Is it too low? Or is it acceptable? This is determined when the hotel financial pro forma budget document is created.

Feasibility Study

When the developer selects a site, a feasibility study is often commissioned to obtain an analysis of the site by an objective third party. Companies offer hotel feasibility studies for a fee and are experts in a particular market, or developers may use the consulting group of one of the major public accounting firms. The company retained to do the feasibility study can spend up to several months gathering detailed data to see if, in their opinion, it makes economic sense to build the hotel. Their conclusion offers an objective thirdparty opinion as to whether the project is feasible, hence the term *feasibility study*. Generally, the feasibility study considers, evaluates, and makes recommendations about the project based on the following variables:

The Site

— Proper zoning
— Size in square feet/acres
— Visibility from arterials/freeways
— Traffic counts/patterns
— Accessibility from streets, freeways, airports, train stations, etc.
— Proximity to where potential guests live, travel, or work
— Barriers that discourage competition coming into the market, if any

— How adjacent property and businesses are utilized
— Master area development plans
— Local permitting process and the degree of difficulty for that particular city
— Impact fees charged by the city

The Economy of the Area

— Major employers, government agencies
— Business trends for each employer/agency
— Hotel needs and the demand for each
— Leisure travel demand in the area
— Nearby tourist attractions
— Visitor counts
— Conventions, trade shows, and meetings history

The Hotel Market

— The competitors, both existing and planned
— Historical occupancy of hotels in the area
— Historical average rate
— Proprietary data on area travel

Identification of Which Hotel Market Segment to Serve

— Full service
— Limited service
— Extended stay
— Luxury
— Midprice
— Economy
— Budget

Selection of Appropriate Hotel Design

— High-rise
— Midrise
— Garden apartment style
— Hybrid design

Selection of Appropriate Hotel Brand

— Franchised (Marriott, Sheraton, Hyatt, etc.)
— Licensed (Best Western, Guest Suites, etc.)
— Independent
— Independent with strategic market affiliation (Luxury Hotels of America, Historic Hotels of America, etc.)

Ten-year Projection

— Occupancy projection by year
— ADR by year
— Estimated cash generated for debt
— Estimated cash generated for distribution to investors
— Estimated cash-on-cash return (after-tax income divided by equity invested)
— Overall projected yield
— Projected internal rate of return
— Net present value of the project over each of the next ten years

Once the feasibility study is completed, the developer is prepared to move forward with the project. Often, at this stage of the process, the developer purchases an option on the land to tie it up until the remaining development steps can be completed—and to prevent the competition from purchasing it.

Ownership Entity

An ownership entity (note that this is different than and separate from the development company) must be created to hold title to the land—and the hotel, once it's built. Considering the limitation of liability to the investors, tax consequences, estate implications for the investors, and potential requirements of the mortgage lender, a business structure is selected, normally in one of the following forms:

— Limited liability company (LLC)
— Limited partnership (LP)
— S corporation (formerly known as a Sub-S corporation)
— C corporation

Agreement

The newly formed entity now enters into a development contract with the development company to take the project to completion. The development company charges a fee, approximately 3 percent of the total project cost, for this service.The agreement generally covers such variables as:

— Selection of architect/engineers
— Selection and supervision of a general contractor
— Processing all building and occupancy permits
— Raising all the equity money from investors
— Securing a construction mortgage loan
— Selecting a franchise company
— Securing the franchise
— Selecting an interior designer that meets franchise company requirements
— Purchasing all opening furniture, fixtures, equipment

— Selecting a management company to operate the hotel
— Liability for cost overruns

Selecting Franchise

Depending on the type of hotel to be built (based on the feasibility study), the developer recommends a franchise company to the hotel owner. A major consideration is the best franchise brand for the market segment to be served. Each franchise company has different franchise fees, royalty fees, and marketing/ miscellaneous fees as part of its agreement structure with the operating company. Consideration must also be given to the brands already represented in the target market that may be available for franchise. The franchise company is approached and a franchise is requested, with the feasibility study offered as backup for the request.

The next step is for the franchise company to conduct an impact study of the market. This considers such matters as possible negative impact on existing hotels that carry the franchiser's flag. If the impact is judged to be insignificant, a franchise is usually granted to the ownership entity for a one-time fee of about $400 per room, depending on the franchise selected, with continuing royalty and marketing, usually based on a percentage of hotel revenue.

Selecting the Architect

Because the final product of this process is a building the operator has to run as a hotel, the architect's experience in designing hotels, his or her experience with the prototypical drawings of the franchise selected, the fee, and his or her on-time record must be considered. Architect fees can run up to 5 percent of the total project cost but are often negotiated down, if the project is big enough. The firm's experience and record on similar projects are critical. The architect does not have to operate the hotel when it is completed. The developer wants the architect to design a hotel that will be easy to operate and maintain.

Selecting General Contractor

Major consideration are the quality and reliability record of the general contractor and the firm's use of and relationships with the many subcontractors needed for a project as complex as a hotel. Again, experience in building the hotel type is important. It is hoped that the general contractor has learned from any mistakes made in building similar hotels. The general contractor and architect often bid the project as a team; this helps the developer determine the final cost. Often, up to a 10 percent contingency cost that allows for unforeseen circumstances is built into the project bidding process.

Financing

The following variables must be determined to qualify for financing:

— The cost of the land

— Design and construction cost of the building

— The cost of furniture, fixtures, equipment, and opening supplies

— Pre-opening marketing and labor costs

— A six-month operating capital cash reserve The sum of these constitutes the total cost of the project for purposes of securing financing.

With this information, the ten-year operating pro forma budget is updated to reflect actual costs. It's now time to go to the money markets for construction financing.The terms and conditions of a construction loan can vary widely depending on the individual lender. Important terms that can affect the cost of the loan include:

— Personal guarantees by developers and/or equity partners/investors
— Loan origination fees
— Interest rate
— Required loan-to-value ratio
— Terms of repayment
— A requirement that interest/taxes be held in reserve
— Required debt service coverage ratios
— Length of the construction loan; length and costs of extensions

These are only a few of the considerations that must be analysed when selecting a lender. The developer, on behalf of the owning entity, then approaches a number of lending institutions. The lending institutions analyse the deal and offer a proposed term sheet that answers all of the borrowers' questions. This allows the borrowers to select the lending institution with which they wish to work. The lender then commissions an appraisal of the project by an independent appraisal company such as Hospitality Valuation Services (HVS). Based on the appraisal, the lender issues a loan commitment for the project that usually offers up to 60 percent of the project cost.The balance must be raised as equity from investors.

With the bank committed to about 60 percent of the cost, the remaining 40 percent must be raised in equity commitments by investors. To pursue these, the developer prepares an offering solicitation document that meets current securities and exchange law. The nature of this document depends on the type of business entity that was formed. For limited partnerships or limited liability companies, a private placement offering circular and project description is prepared. For S or C corporations, stock offerings are prepared for sale consistent with applicable federal and state securities laws.

The developer now contacts money sources that have risk capital available to invest.

These can include:

— Individual investors
— Private asset managers
— Opportunity fund managers
— Venture capital fund managers

These potential investment sources are offered the opportunity to invest in the hotel. Based on their study and evaluation of the reports, documents, and studies detailed above, they decide whether or not to offer funding to the developer.

Once the loan is secured, the equity raised, and the building permit issued by the city, the land purchase option is exercised and the purchase is completed. Then the 12–16-month construction process begins. If the architect's plans work as intended, if the general contractor has no problems with subcontractors, unions, or permits, if all the furnishings, fixtures, and equipment arrive on time, if the weather cooperates, and if the employment market is such that human resources are sufficient to open a hotel, then congratulations!

Selecting Management Company

Often even before the construction activity commences, the owning entity selects an appropriate management company to manage the pre-opening, marketing and sales, selection and training of the opening staff, preparation of the operating budget, and day-to-day operations once the hotel is opened. Management companies charge 3–5 percent of revenue for this service.

In recent years, management companies have charged 3–4 percent of revenue and 2–3 percent of gross operating profit so they can be measured and evaluated on both sales and profitability. The franchise company may offer to provide management services to franchisees.

Marriott International, Inc., for example, manages about 50 percent of all hotels that carry the Marriott flag under 20-year contracts. Independent management companies manage the remaining hotels under long-term management contracts of up to ten years' duration, often with several five-year renewal options.

This is a largely linear explanation of the complicated process that a developer goes through in order to create a hotel. It has been described in a step-by-step process, but in reality, many of the steps are carried out concurrently to save time (and money).

Nevertheless, the hotel development process takes about three years from original concep-tion to first guest. It is important to remember that during the initial stages of the process, the developer can have as much as $1 million or more at risk in the process before a final go/no-go decision is reached. Only after the project is approved and all financing is in place can the developer start to recover upfront costs and collect development fees. Hotel development with its component parts of hotel feasibility studies, hotel appraisal, hotel real estate finance, and hotel management are all among the career opportunities available to hotel and restaurant administration graduates.

Story of an Extended-stay Hotel Development Project

The City Development Commission in a Pacific Northwest community purchased a 1.55-acre parcel of riverfront land in the downtown area.The land was previously contaminated with industrial pollutants that made the parcel unsafe for habitation and construction. The City Development Commission used state, local, and federal grants to have the land decontaminated, created a master plan for the area, and then offered the parcel for sale and development.

The City Development Commission issued a request for proposal (RFP) that outlined the asking price of $2,076,240 ($30/sq. ft.) for the land and the design requirements set down by the Commission for a building that would fit the intended look and feel of the area.The RFP was sent to many major hotel companies and commercial real estate brokers, asking prospective buyers to submit a purchase price bid along with a statement of the buyer's development history and ability to develop a hotel of the type envisioned by the Commission. It listed a closing date by which all bids had to be submitted.

An area commercial real estate broker contacted a hotel development and management company with a long history of developing and managing extended-stay hotels in the Pacific Northwest, including a property located in a similar setting to that being offered for sale.The commercial realtor offered to represent the developer in negotiations with the City Development Commission, which would be paying the real estate commission on the sale. An agreement was reached with the commercial real estate broker to represent the buyer to the seller, and the developer went to work in preparing a proposal.

The developer conducted a feasibility study to see all of the conditions in the marketplace that would be encouraging or discouraging to this development project.

Studies were conducted to estimate how many room-nights were being sold within a five-mile radius, how many extended-stay room-nights were available in the market, how many hotel rooms existed, and how many were being planned over the following five years. From this, the developer was able to estimate the number of extended-stay room-nights available needed to produce an 82 percent occupancy with an average daily room rate of $141 when the hotel achieved stabilisation three years after opening. That provided the basis for a ten-year revenue estimate.

The developer proposed a nine-floor, 258-suite extended-stay hotel with an indoor pool, spa, and exercise facility, a guest laundry, offices, meeting facilities, and a three-floor parking garage with parking for 193 automobiles, all at a total cost of $38 million, or $147,286 per suite.

The $38 million construction budget was broken down as follows:

Land	6.0%
Construction	66.0%
Office Equipment	1.4%
Furniture, Fixtures, Equipment	7.4%
Architecture/Engineering	2.8%
Permits/Fees/Environmental	2.8%
Appraisal/Legal/Tax/Insurance	1.3%
Pre-Opening Expenses	1.3%
Construction Loan Fee	1.1%
Developer Fee	2.8%
Construction Interest	2.8%
Working Capital	2.1%
Contingency	2.2%
Total	100%

The opening date for the hotel was projected at 27 months from the date of proposal acceptance.

The City Development Commission awarded the project to the developer, and work began.First, an ownership limited liability company (LLC) was formed as the ownership entity that would hold title to the hotel. The LLC, in turn, entered into a development and construction management agreement with the development company to manage the arrangements for financing and construction of the hotel.

The developer, as agent for the ownership LLC, also entered into a hotel management contract with a management company to manage the pre-opening marketing, preopening hiring and training, and the day-to- day operation of the hotel once it was opened.The arrangements called for the management company to be paid 3 percent of revenue and 2 percent of the net operating income for management services.

The ownership LLC then contacted a major hotel company and applied for a franchise to allow the development and operation of an extended-stay hotel. A 20-year franchise was granted with a fee of $400 per suite or, $102,800. This was to be followed by a 5 percent royalty and a 3 percent advertising fee once the hotel was open and operating. The developer, acting as agent for the owner, prepared a private placement memorandum document seeking investments from accredited investors.These investors were primarily defined as people with a net worth of $1 million, or those with an income in excess of $200,000 over the previous two years and expecting an income in excess of $200,000 in the current year.

The private placement memorandum offered $100,000 units of ownership to accredited investors, guaranteeing a 9 percent priority return on the investment and a combined 50 percent ownership in the hotel. A group of initial investors retained the other 50 percent in exchange for putting the project together.This effort was successful in raising 40 percent of the total cost of the hotel in anticipation that a lender would provide the remaining 60 percent in the form of a construction loan. In addition to the priority return, investors could expect to participate in any future capital gain realised should the hotel be sold.

The development company, continuing to function as agent for the owner, then sought a commercial bank to provide threeyear construction financing for the project. As $22,800,000, or 60 percent, of the $38 million development cost was to be borrowed, only major banks were considered as prospective lenders.The size of the construction loan was above the lending limits of most small regional banks. After a preconstruction appraisal by a third-party appraisal firm chosen by the lender confirmed the value at $38 million upon completion of construction, and for an origination fee of $400,000, a three-year construction loan was secured.The terms allowed the developer, as agent for the owner, to draw down the loan every 30 days after providing proof that funds had been properly disbursed in the construction process.The loan documents set an interest rate and also required that the ownership LLC seek a permanent mortgage prior to the three-year expiration date on the construction loan.

The development company then negotiated with and selected a general contractor with significant hotel construction experience who acted on behalf of the developer, as agent for the owner. The general contractor then selected design-build subcontractors and an interior designer to select colors, fabrics, furniture, fixtures, and equipment to meet the hotel franchise design requirements.

Building permits were applied for, and the building design was presented to the City Development Commission for its approval, along with other groups with a stake in the appearance of the finished building in relation to the area and neighborhood.With all of these approvals in place, construction commenced, and the hotel opened two years later.

Three years after the hotel opened, the ownership LLC had the obligation to secure permanent financing on the hotel to replace the construction loan. The September 11, 2001, terrorist attacks on the World Trade Center and the Pentagon slowed travel throughout the United States. As a result, the hotel did not achieve the projected occupancy or average daily rate during the three-year construction loan period. An appraisal that was primarily based on the hotel's trailing 12- month net operating income produced a value about $2 million below the original construction cost. The bank that had provided the construction loan notified the owners that they did not wish to provide permanent financing under these circumstances. The owners were forced to conduct a search for a new mortgage bank. They were able to find a mortgage, but only after buying down the loan by $2 million to bring the loan-to-value ratio back to 40 percent equity and a loan at 60 percent of the appraised.

This illustrates the risk that developers face when entering into a hotel project. However, as hotel values historically peak and decline on about a ten-year cycle, the owners look forward to the option of selling the hotel on the next peak, which will allow them to capture the original projected return through capital appreciation. Hotel development and ownership is a high-risk, highreward enterprise.

Changes in the Hotel Industry

Dramatic changes have affected the hotel industry over the past 30 years. These changes have had a disproportionately high bearing on the independent hotel owner, who, in the face of increasing pressure from large, wellfunded chains, struggles to maintain independence and to compete on the basis of distinctive hospitality and character.

Several organisations provide independent hotels and resorts with reservations and sales services. As competition has evolved and intensified, some of these organisations have modified their structure and enhanced their services to meet the changing needs of independent hotels and competitive market dynamics. Today, independent hotels may choose from among more than 20 such organisations delivering varying degrees of competitive advantage and ownership independence. In the new millennium, the face of the global hospitality market continues to change at a rate never before seen. Four factors contribute to this rapidly changing environment:

— *The broadening and diversification of the global consumer market.* Both the demographic and psychographic characteristics of the global consumer market are growing and changing radically.

— *The rapid advancement and availability of technology.* This includes internal hotel operating systems, revenue management, direct-to-consumer communications and booking technology (Internet), marketing technology (customer databases), and telecommunications and automated sales systems that enable central sales offices to become revenue producers.

— *The growth and importance of global brands.* Recognised brand names and brand attributes are important in reaching diverse customer segments and in creating customer loyalty.

— *Consolidation of multiple brands under a single global management.* The management and leveraging of multiple brands use similar technology platforms and shared sales and marketing infrastructures to consolidate and direct consumer demand.

Some established ways of doing business — long-term, high-fee management contracts and franchises, a focus on traditional distribution channels, and traditional hospitality industry marketing techniques—are no longer effective in the new consumer-focused market. More and more hospitality marketing budgets are being directed toward technologyenabled customer booking and communication; this shift away from traditional hospitality marketing techniques is expected to evolve over several years and involve millions of U.S. dollars in telecommunication, e-commerce, data warehousing, and one-to-one marketing investment. The independent hotel or resort and many small branded management companies may not be able to fund this requirement. However, this shift will not affect all independent hotels and resorts simultaneously.

The first wave of change will hit the global business and city hotel market. This is primarily because of brand competition and the fact that the business travel distribution network is more structured and driven by multinational corporations desiring lower and more predictable costs. The second wave will affect the leisure market, and the changes could follow quickly. Leisure travel content, including packaging on the Internet, will increase rapidly as the presently fragmented leisure travel distribution network becomes more unified and efficient through consolidation. The emergence of e-commerce modes in the hospitality industry is not eliminating the intermediary and empowering the individual property, as once thought; instead, it is creating new, more powerful intermediaries. Some of these evolve from the hospitality industry, while others are opportunistic e-commerce companies.

Management Contract

In the 1970s, hotel chains continued to evolve as the need for capital to invest in additional properties restricted growth opportunities. This pressure bolstered the proliferation of the *management contract*, whereby the chain offers the hotel owner the rights to use its brand name and established facility and service standards as well as trained operations management and reservation and marketing services—for a significant fee, usually a percentage of gross sales. The pressure to grow also fostered the development of the franchise concept and franchise system in North America. The franchise differs from the management contract in that the owner is responsible for operations, including meeting the franchise standards. The growth of management and franchise contracts has been remarkable, and today, according to a recent study, 75 percent of the hotel rooms in North America are covered by some form of branded franchise or professional management agreement.

These new business structures continued to threaten the traditional independent owner by accelerating the growth of the chains' share of the lodging market. In response, the marketing/ referral organisations formed in the 1960s began to offer a wider range of services.

While these additional offerings leveraged linkages to the global distribution systems and led to strong relationships with travel agents, the consumer was largely ignored, and the organisations did little to generate consumer brand awareness. In the United States, strong consumer branded operators are attracting increasing amounts of capital to fund their growth at the expense of unbranded operators.

Brand Development

As the consumer market became more diverse and the hospitality product more segmented, branding became increasingly important. By the late 1980s, without a recognised brand affiliation or a close relationship with the lending community, owners/developers found it difficult to obtain permanent financing on a new hotel or resort. Lenders, believing that an established brand provided greater economies of scale and established infrastructure, opted for the lower-risk alternative.

In this brand-driven environment, the independent hotels' distinctive style and character became a competitive advantage, but only if they were able to meet recognised standards. As a result, the need for independent hotels to be associated with a clearly defined, trusted brand became more critical than ever. In the late 1990s, independent hotels, particularly those in Europe, began to face the daunting costs of upgrading their technological infrastructure and facilities to accommodate changing consumer needs. Such upgrades as new property management systems, highspeed Internet access, two-line phones, inroom faxes, and leisure and health facilities became critical to maintaining competitiveness. When coupled with ever-increasing costs of consumer marketing, these costs put unprecedented strains on independent hotels' finances. As a result, these hotels became increasingly focused on leveraging greater returns from their reservation affiliation.

Reservation Affiliations

The relationship of independent hotels and resorts to reservation affiliations has been long and generally successful. These relation-ships operated best in a market environment that was stable, somewhat homogeneous in terms of demographic market segmentation, and where travel influencers played a dominant role in transient business, group, and leisure travel. Reservation affiliations are most effective in regional hospitality markets that do not have multiple brand competition and when the goals and objectives of the reservation organisation are in alignment with the goals of the independent hotel owners. A contributing element to the attractiveness of reservation affiliations has always been the networking and camaraderie opportunities for the professional management at independent hotels.

Reservation affiliations focus on traditional channels of distribution. Access to the Global Distribution Systems (GDS) is no longer a competitive advantage; the GDS is a universal pipeline. The new competitive playing field is proprietary distribution channels leveraged by consumer segmentation, e-commerce technology and partners, and innovative customer management programs.

In the new technology-driven and consumer-empowered global market, the strength and effectiveness of reservation affiliations are challenged by new market and operating imperatives. The cost to compete against chains will grow exponentially.As competition intensifies, it is probable that local and regional market share at independent hotels and resorts will be drawn off by local and regional licensees of strong global brands. Independent hotels, therefore, need to draw more national and international business to fill occupancy gaps.This requirement runs counter to the established business model and capabilities of reservation affiliations.

The average room-night contribution of reservations companies to affiliated inde-pendent hotels is less than 5 percent of available rooms.

At least four emerging factors are challenging the effectiveness of traditional reservation organisations:

1. The growing demographic and psychographic complexity of the global consumer market requires significant new expertise and resources in the area of segmentation and analysis.
2. The emergence of consumer direct-booking Internet technology requires significant new and ongoing investment.

3. The new marketplace requires innovative global brand management together with resources to establish and maintain a brand in the face of intense competition. To be competitive, a brand must attract new development and must therefore be strong enough to convince lenders to commit to permanent financing. Brand management also includes loyalty program management and the development of regional and global partners to strengthen and extend the effectiveness of the brand.
4. The corporate objectives and governance policies of traditional reservation organisations are influenced by the need to grow and meet shareholder profit requirements. These goals for growth can be at odds with the goals and expectations of independent hotel and resort members.

The traditional reservation affiliations must change not only their focus but also their structure if they want to succeed in this new competitive world.

The traditional reservation organisation must be prepared to respond to competitive challenges by expanding resources and skills necessary to increase average room-night contribution to affiliated independent hotels to 15 percent—an average growth per member hotel of at least 200 percent over present performance levels. In response to this competitive environment and the need for more cooperative and focused business relationships, a new hospitality business structure is evolving for all scales of hotels: the branded distribution company.

Branded Distribution Organisation

The ideal branded distribution organisation is a conventional equity company with ownership shared (in some cases) by the individual hotel owners, who have direct input into the corporation through an elected board of directors. This ownership structure creates a true operating partnership and a sharing of energies toward the common goal of creating value through increased brand awareness and room sales. Corporate profits must be adequate to maintain technical and managerial leadership and to support the shareholders' investment.

Unlike a reservations and representation company, a branded distribution corporation owns and builds a branded distribution network asset that, in turn, provides services as set out in the diagram below.The sole focus is performance for the affiliated independent hotels and resorts.

Joining such an organisation is appropriate for independently owned and managed hotels and resorts that want to keep owner control but require effective and low-cost distribution, global consumer brand awareness, and group purchasing benefits without the encumbrances and costs of a traditional hotel chain franchise or management contract. Above all, it promises the independent hotel awareness of, and access to, their target consumer and rapidly emerging technology through cooperative ownership.

This new business structure is attractive from an owner's or a developer's standpoint for a number of reasons, including:

— *Costs:* First, it requires less up-front cash; second, ongoing fees and reservation commissions are significantly lower than with either a pure franchise or management agreement. For example, a 9 or 10 percent franchise fee in many cases equals 50 percent of gross profits.

— *Contract terms*: The terms are typically shorter, easier to negotiate, and allow for substantial owner control over the operation, style, and character of the hotel.

As a result, conflicts can be avoided, and the branded distribution contract can be completed and signed in as few as 45 days.

— *Marketing*: It frees hotel management from the daunting and increasingly expensive task of acquiring profitable new customers and allows them to focus their attention and operating skills on the de- livery of an exceptional hospitality experience.

— *Common objectives*: Both the owner and the branded distribution company enter into the agreement with the same primary objective: revenue. The branded distribution company receives no revenue if it does not deliver to the hotel or resort.

This shared goal strengthens and energises the relationship between the two partners. From a branded distribution company's standpoint, this structure allows the brand to expand faster because capital is not used to subsidise additional construction or to support an older business model. Instead, funds are used to build and maintain an up-todate global distribution network and infrastructure composed of telecommunications, commerce functions, reservations software, data warehousing capability, and sales and marketing. The efficiency of the operation is assured by a focus that is almost entirely on the most important part of this business relationship—the generation of brand awareness and measurable room-night revenue for each affiliated hotel or resort.

Unlike hard flags, which focus primarily on hotel operations and asset management such as the Marriott or the Westin, and reservation affiliations, which focus on professional camaraderie and traditional distribution channels such as the Best Western, the branded distribution company is primarily marketfocused; its full attention is on customer and travel influencer communication, relationship technology, and revenue streams.

In contrast, asset management, profitability, and operating efficiency are the major concerns of management companies, which tend to be public companies with stockholder expectations that must be met. It is often the case that strategic asset management concerns conflict with day-to-day tactical operating needs. This is evident in Marriott's recent move to separate its ownership and operating divisions, to the benefit of both.

The same conflict can arise between the independent owners of a hotel property, who are focused on real estate concerns, and the management company they hire. Such misunderstandings can sour what should be a mutually supportive relationship. The fact that management contract fees are charged and collected, even when the cash flow is negative, does not create owner confidence in the partner. A franchise relationship can cause a similar conflict and put a financial and operating burden on an owner.

In contrast, participation of independent owner/operators as shareholders in a branded distribution company enables them to move beyond these concerns and focus on their operation and the consumer—the source of their revenue and the basis of their success.

The owners of property within a branded distribution company must relinquish a minimal amount of control and decision making, mainly in the areas of branding and quality assurance. In certain cases, member proper-ties may have to adopt and maintain specific quality standards. In addition, they may also be required to demonstrate their affiliation with the branded distribution company through using its logo on marketing materials as well as participating in e-commerce and inventory management initiatives.

However, these drawbacks can actually enhance a hotel's operations and market positioning while allowing the hotel to maintain independent ownership and management.

Independent hotels face significant risk in today's marketplace. Given the advances in technology and the profitability pressures put upon chain hotels by shareholders, competition for customers is intensifying. Keeping in step with competitive chain hotels presents a significant challenge to independent owners.

To address this, they currently have several options outside of the branded distribution company, including representation firms, reservations services, flagged chains, and franchise management companies. However, given the economic, societal, and technological trends that are dramatically changing the hospitality industry, many of these oldeconomy options can offer only short-term solutions to long-term competitive pressures. A branded distribution company has an inherent advantage going into this new competitive arena. Its sole focus is on customer acquisition and management, achieved through the development of new technologies. This competitive advantage extends to the independent hotel aligned with a branded distribution company. By providing the independent owner with a global brand and the technology and expertise to acquire profitable new customers, the branded distribution company enables the hotel management to focus its attention on the delivery of exceptional service and profits to the owners. This separation of skills, expertise, resources, and operating cultures in a cooperative business relationship provides a model and formula for success.

Independent hotels and resorts that align themselves with a branded distribution company will not only continue to operate profitably in the new global marketplace, but will also flourish.

4

Operating a Hotel

If you ever have the chance to be involved with opening a hotel, jump at the opportunity. Opening a hotel is one of the most rewarding jobs in the hospitality industry despite its frustrating and exhausting aspects. Walk into any hotel, anywhere, and look around. Everything you see, hear, and feel, every detail, involved many people and countless decisions.

The operations project manager (OPM) is the third person hired, after the general manager and the director of marketing. The role of an OPM is to pull together the visions of the architect, interior designer, owner, operator, and others. When these visions are successfully melded, the hotel guest satisfied, the owner makes money, and the architect and interior designer can add the project to their list of successful accomplishments. The OPM oversees the following aspects of a project:

— Reviewing blueprints and specifications for the entire building

— Assisting with the creation of a model room

— Developing the pre-opening staff plan

— Developing and managing the pre-opening budget

— Developing the operational supplies and equipment budget (OS&E)

— Overseeing the purchasing, warehousing, delivery, and installation of the OS&E

— Developing the interior graphics package

— Coordinating the installation of thirdparty vendors

Responsibilities of OPM

The OPM's responsibilities start with the architectural blueprints.The focus is to ensure a good flow for guests, staff, and goods. The bellperson bag storage room should be located between the porte cochere (entry) and the elevators and contain 1 square foot of space for each guest room. If valet parking is offered, ensure that a convenient cashier's station is located near the porte cochere. Arrange for a key rack to hold the keys for each valet parking stall.

Given a 10,000-square-foot ballroom, the catering department can sell functions for 800_ for dinner.This requires 80 6-foot round tables, 800 chairs, a dais for the head table, a dance floor, and staging for the band. If sold for a 700-guest all-day meeting, the classroom setup requires 1,400 linear feet of narrow tables and 700 chairs. A short theater meeting setup for 1,000 requires 1,000 chairs, a podium, staging, and audio visual equipment. The same space accommodates a cocktail reception for 1,400 guests; this requires cocktail tables, portable bars, buffet stations, and so on. This all boils down to ensuring ample storage space for equipment not being used—at least 1,500 square feet.

Moving goods from the back of the house to the front requires careful planning to ensure that precious labor dollars are used efficiently. Are the rollaway beds, cribs, and high chairs stored near an elevator for quick delivery? The housekeeper closets should be centrally located on guest room floors to cut down on access time. A 6-foot, 2-cubic-yard garbage cart will not work if the elevator is only 5 feet deep.

If ice machines are offered for guest selfservice, they must produce an ample supply (10 pounds per room per 24-hour period) for the number of guest rooms on that floor or floors. The ice machine room requires the proper utilities, including electricity, plumbing, lighting, and HVAC. Don't forget the sign on the outside of the room, which must meet ADA standards!

Build a typical king and double/double guest room close to the site so you can review every single item in them. Are ample electrical and telecom outlets placed exactly where the TV, lamps, clock radio,mini-bar, coffeemaker, hair dryer, Internet access, and telephones are located so the cords are hidden? Are spare outlets offered for guest use (computer, iron, etc.)? Is the closet rod hung so the ironing board organiser and iron board fit in the closet? Is the thermostat location convenient for guest access?

Are the case goods (dresser, nightstands, headboards, chairs, etc.), designed for commercial heavy-duty use? Will they hold up to abusive use? Do they have sharp corners that will snag guest clothing? Does the bedskirt hang ½ inch off the floor? Do the bedside lamps give off enough lumens so guests can read in bed? Does the room meet or exceed every operator brand standard?

These model rooms serve as sales tools for the sales and marketing staff selling group rooms up to three years before opening.

Pre-opening Staffing

The pre-opening staffing begins with an organisational

chart with all positions. Once the titles and staff counts by position are finalised, then spreadsheets are created to include the position titles, start dates, pay rates, bonus, transfer allowances, and number of full-time equivalents (FTEs) for all positions.

The pre-opening staff plan is a comprehensive document that states who is hired, when they start, how much they are paid, and whether or not they are allocated a relocation allowance and benefit costs. Each of these pieces is used to build the pre-opening staff plan budget. If hiring has already begun and the opening date changes, the budget must be amended. Hiring a position that does not conform to the plan, such as bringing on a renowned chef one month earlier than planned, also requires the budget be modified.

Pre-opening Budget

The OPM develops and manages the preopening budget.This budget typically consists of three major categories; labor cost (40 percent), sales and marketing efforts (40 percent), and miscellaneous (20 percent).

The labor cost is taken directly from the pre-opening staff plan. Sales and marketing activities comprise advertising, collateral, public relations, and travel to see clients. Rounding out the budget are all of the miscellaneous items. These include office space rental before moving into the hotel, utilities (power, water, Internet, and telephone), human resources recruitment (ads, headhunters, drug testing, etc.), training materials, association dues, and licenses and permits (business, liquor, sales tax collection, etc.). If the hotel opening date is delayed for any reason, the pre-opening budget is affected. Additional costs include labor, office rent, utilities, and marketing efforts. If the opening date changes within three weeks of the original plan, major costs are encountered, as most of the staff is already hired.

Operational Supplies and Equipment

The largest and most complex aspect of the OPM's responsibility is specifying, quantifying, and budgeting for the operational supplies and equipment (OS&E) list.This budget typically pencils out to $8,000 to $10,000 per guest room for a typical four-star property. The list of goods typically exceeds 2,500 line items. Add a little more for a full-service resort; deduct a little for an in-city business hotel.

The OS&E comprises all of the items that are not nailed down, with the exception of the furniture, fixtures, and equipment (FF&E). The FF&E is typically specified and ordered by the interior designer.

Typical guest room items include bedding (frames, box springs, mattresses, mattress pads, sheets, pillows, pillowcases, towels, etc.), clock radios, hangers, laundry bags, laundry tickets, iron, ironing board, ironing board organiser, luggage rack, guest amenities (soap, shampoo, lotion, etc.), hair dryer, shower curtains, and shower curtain hooks.

Housekeeping equipment includes vacuums (guest room and wide-area units), carpet shampooers,, carpet extractors, housekeeper carts, laundry bins, garbage trucks, valet delivery carts, and shelving, to name a few of many items. Housekeeping must also keep an inventory of guest request items including humidifiers, dehumidifiers, cribs, high chairs, rollaway beds, bedboards, spare pillows, towels, amenities, refrigerators, laundry soap, and so on.

Food and beverage front-of-the-house items include flatware (knives, forks, and spoons), hollowware (serving trays, serving utensils, chafing dishes, sugar bowls and sauce boats, punch bowls), glassware, table linen, napkins, skirting, salt and pepper shakers, china, plate covers, espresso machines, menu covers and the list goes on and on.

Banquet items include all of the above plus tables, chairs, staging, staging steps and railings, dance floors, carts, carving boards, ice carving trays, flags, podiums, portable bars, ice bins, pianos, and tray jack stands.

The largest purchase order—typically over 100 pages long—is for a full-service kitchen and includes everything a chef needs to produce the menus being sold at the hotel.

Every utensil, pot, pan, dish, and glass rack, warewashing chemicals, mops and buckets, specialty items (roller-docker, anyone?) must be reviewed by the chef, purchased, and delivered the day before the chef starts burning in the kitchen.

On the hotel administration side, the OPM specifies the office desks, chairs, cork and dry-erase boards, conference tables, filing cabinets, safes, bullet-proof window for the general cashier's office, fax machines, copiers, currency and coin trays, and a set of flags for the exterior flagpoles.

Before quantifying uniform needs, many questions are asked. Do we need summer and winter uniforms? Will the uniforms be laundered by the hotel or the hotel associates? How many extra servers are needed for a capacity dinner function in the ballrooms? Is the intent to have a large percentage of parttime staff? Which uniforms need custom embroidery (restaurants, culinary, engineering, etc.)? What percentage of spare uniforms are needed in reserve?

Once these questions are answered, then the selection process begins. Operations and the interior designer review the look and feel the options available. Each position (housekeeper, bellperson, etc.) or similar position (front desk clerk/concierge) has different requirements. Housekeepers and bellpersons require durable uniforms that breathe and can handle lots of bending and stretching.The uniforms of the culinary and engineering staffs are often stained and must hold up to numerous launderings.

The uniform order is placed 90 to 120 days before the first uniformed staff is hired. To quantify the sizes required, a typical bell chart sizing curve is used for the particular country or region of the hotel. The uniforms are delivered and sorted prior to the individual fitting process. On the line staff's second day on the job, each individual is measured for uniforms. An army of seamstresses then takes the pants, jackets, and dresses and alters each piece for each associate. The fitted uniforms are issued a few days before opening day.

In an ideal process, the 500 purchase orders are issued beginning six months prior to opening. Each order is tracked to ensure it is delivered to the proper location on the desired date. Most goods are delivered to a local warehouse and pulled for delivery to the site as the general contractor completes construc-tion and turns over areas. Some goods are shipped directly to the site to eliminate double handling. These large orders include bed sets (21 40-foot shipping containers for the Kona project), televisions (3 containers), banquet chairs (2 containers), banquet tables (3 containers), and guest room safes (1 container).

The linen order for guest rooms and F&B are shipped to an off-site laundry facility for initial washing.

Once the goods are on site, they are typically staged in the largest ballroom for unpacking and distribution. The unpacking process requires a plethora of workers. For example, each clock radio must be unpacked, the electrical twist tie removed, the 9-volt battery installed, and the time set. Then the unit is placed in a guest room on the nightstand. For the 525-room Kona project, this task required two people for three eight-hour days.

Once they completed this task, they spent the next five working days installing the 7,000_ shower curtain hooks, 525 shower curtains, and 525 shower liners. Then they unboxed 30,000 glasses and placed them in glass racks for washing.These kinds of tasks must be carried out for each of the 2,500 line items.

Once receiving and distribution begins on site, another element comes to the forefront: garbage. During the five-week Kona installation process, over 3 tons of packing material were generated *every day!* Making friends with the local waste-hauling service is a priority.

Interior Graphics Package

The project manager reviews the interior graphics package for errors and omissions. This package includes every sign needed to direct guests and staff in front and back of the house areas. The recent Kona project included 1,600 signs, 98 percent of which were one of a kind.The text must be correct, the directional arrows must point the correct way, and most are required to include raised Braille text, per the ADA. The OPM works with the marketing department to develop the identity for the unique areas within a property.These include the restaurants, bars, pools, spa, and retail areas. These logos are incorporated into the signage package, collateral (cocktail napkins, menus, check presenters, etc.), and uniforms.

Third-party Vendors

Many third-party vendors must have access to the property prior to opening. The project manager schedules and directs all of these vendors, including the soft-drink vendor (who installs soda guns for the bars and vending machines for the guest floors), the coffee company (which must install and test equipment), the pay-per-view TV vendor (who must connect every television in the building and test the signal strength), the warewashing chemical vendor (who must install and calibrate the dishwashing machines), and the office furniture installer (who must assemble all office equipment). Among the other vendors are those dealing in copier services, postage machines, telephones, fitness center equipment, security systems, and first aid supplies.

These vendors are constantly informed when they can install their equipment based on the general contractor's completion dates. When the construction schedule changes, vendors must be updated so they show up when the area they need access to is ready.

Human Resources Management

The OPM assists the human resources personnel during the last two months of preopening so that they have all of the tools they need to recruit and hire the staff. On average, the HR department interviews at least five applicants for every position. This works out to over 1,000 applicants for a typical 300-room four-star hotel. This process is referred to as the *mass hire*. The mass hire is typically conducted over a two- or three-day period six weeks before opening. To interview this many job seekers, HR requires office space, reception space for up to 200 at one time, rest rooms, and break rooms for the interviewers. The OPM coordinates all of these details so that the operations team can focus on the recruitment.

Once the offer letters are accepted, all line associates start work about three weeks out. The first few days on the job are dedicated to group training, operational philosophies, code of conduct, and other general policies. On day three, divisional training takes place. In the second week of training, the staff is broken out into departmental or job-specific duties.

Departmental training includes teaching staff to make beds, clean a room, cook every menu item, the most efficient route to each guest room, and what to tell the guest en route to the room.

Online Pricing

The importance of electronic hotel-distribution routes has grown substantially in recent years. According to statistics quoted in the Horwath Worldwide Hotel Industry Studies, direct reservations fell from approximately 39 percent in 1995 to 33 percent in 1999, with the shift in sales going almost exclusively to electronic channels.

While hotels continue to make extensive use of travel-agent-oriented global distribution systems (GDSs), consumer adoption of the Internet as a reliable and secure commerce medium has prompted a change in the way in which hotel rooms are being distributed. The Internet has dramatically changed the way people communicate, research information, and buy goods and services. Travel products in particular have proven to be suitable for sale on line. The typical Internet user—an affluent, frequent traveler who spends more than the average on leisure and entertainment—is an attractive market for travel suppliers.

Furthermore, from a consumer's perspective purchasing travel products on line has, in many instances, become faster, easier, and more convenient than contacting a travel agent or telephoning a supplier directly. As a result, on-line travel-related revenues are forecast to grow sharply. For example, according to a recent report by Jupiter Media Metrix, on-line travel sales will more than triple in the next five years—from US$18 billion in 2002 to US$64 billion in 2007.

Booking volumes are also forecast to climb. The Travel Industry Association of America (TIAA) estimated that by the end of 2002 between 6 percent and 10 percent of all travel reservations would originate on the web. If Jupiter's 2007 prediction comes true, travel will be the biggest selling on-line product, with a volume nearly double that of the current leading product, PC hardware.

Price is key to selling successfully on line. Studies by Internet analysts Gomez and PhoCusWright, and also a study by TIAA, all identified price as being one of the key motivating factors that encourages consumers to purchase travel on line. For example, the PhoCusWright study found that competitive pricing is the best way to attract customers. When travelers who haven't bought on line were asked what would encourage them to do so, 64 percent said that saving money would make them more interested. No other benefit—whether saving time, getting bonus loyalty-club points, more control, or obtaining better information came close to this level of response.

Yesawich, Pepperdine, and Brown found in a 2000 study that almost six out of ten leisure travelers now actively seek the "lowest possible price" for travel services. Similarly, a 2001 Forrester Research study found that 66 percent of all buyers had used an on-line discount in the previous 12 months to buy travel on line, and a study by the Joint Hospitality Industry Congress found a real expectation among consumers that Internet prices would be lower than those available in the "bricks and mortar" world.

Such a perception has developed for several reasons. First, many of the best-known Internet retailers initially competed with traditional outlets based, to a large extent, on price. Second, savvy consumers are aware that webbased distribution costs are lower than those of other channels. As Jack Geddes, Radisson Hotels Worldwide's managing director, sales and marketing Asia, has pointed out: "Consumers now understand that suppliers are cutting costs through this channel and expect savings to be passed on to them, as well as being rewarded for making the booking themselves". Such expectations are being reinforced by the budget-airline sector, which offers substantial discounts for online bookings.

Companies such as EasyJet, RyanAir, and Buzz estimate that by avoiding telesales and travel agents, they can achieve savings of up to 30 percent—which they pass on to customers in the form of lower fares. Many hotels (and airlines) use the web to sell last-minute deals—packages at relatively low prices but with short lead times. While such promotions can help dispose of unsold inventory, they have also resulted in the public's associating rooms sold over the Internet with lower prices.

These factors have combined to make consumers associate on-line booking with good value, which in the consumer's mind translates into low prices. However, in the case of hotel brands' own web sites, industry practice frequently seems to be the opposite of theory. In a 1999 survey, for instance, it was found that rates obtained from the web site were usually substantially higher than those obtained by contacting the central reservations office. That study was limited, however, in that it focused only on direct sales over hotel chains' own branded web sites. Electronic distribution is rapidly evolving for hotels, and a large number of other on-line consumerfocused channels are now available, with most chains using multiple routes to reach the consumer.

The availability of numerous points of sale poses some interesting questions. Foremost among these is: Is there consistency between the room availability and prices being offered over each of the channels? Unlike in the physical world, where a potential customer would have to telephone or visit several suppliers, comparison shopping on the web can generally be accomplished relatively quickly. Research has shown that consumers shopping for travel on line almost always check more than one site before purchasing.

Both the range of channels through which hotels can be booked and the complexity of such channels have grown. The majority of hotel brands now use simultaneous, multiple electronic channels of distribution, making their rooms available to a relatively wide audience.

While the use of CRS-based reservations has fallen slightly, there has been a growth in the availability of hotel companies' own web sites, and make their rooms available for sale in this manner. The differences between this study's findings and earlier published research indicate a major expansion in hotel chains' use of the web as a direct-sales medium, perhaps accompanied by a realisation of the web's benefits in comparison with other, more traditional, electronic channels of distribution. Most companies offer multiple rates to customers over each channel. It is interesting to note, however, the large number of companies that now offer consistent pricing across all channels.

It is clear that for those with a taste for upscale products, the hotel brand's own web site is not the place to shop, as better value can be obtained in most cases through other channels. More interesting, however, is the fact that, in general, prices have become more or less equal across many of the channels investigated, and by implication, across many other electronic distribution channels as well. It is well established that time is a valuable commodity in today's society. Since the number and variety of ways that a consumer can book a hotel room has become undeniably manifold, the cost associated with searching through even a small number of the many consumer-focused channels currently available in the marketplace in an attempt to find a low price has increased. Given that this study has found that many of the rates being offered over alternative channels are more or less the same for many hotels, customers should reconsider whether all that time and energy searching for the lowest rate is actually worthwhile.

The implications for the hotelier are more pressing. My findings suggest that many hotel chains are not actively managing the room rates being offered in their portfolio of electronic distribution channels. Most companies offer multiple rates on each channel, which, as discussed earlier, can be beneficial as it gives a choice to the customer. Displaying too many rates, though, can be counterproductive, if the customer becomes overwhelmed. Presenting a small number of tightly defined rates would be the most appropriate solution. However, most companies currently display about five rates in response to a customer inquiry, with others showing significantly more, usually with little or no apparent product differentiation.

In addition, there appears to be inconsistency in terms of the rates being offered over electronic channels. In many cases, no clear or logical pricing strategy is apparent. The lowest prices are offered on channels with the highest transaction costs, and vice versa. A small number of companies offer consistent pricing irrespective of the channel being used to make the booking. Informal follow up with those companies revealed that they follow this strategy as they believe in the principle of one "correct" price for each customer. In this way, they do not have to address the issue of customer dissatisfaction as a result of a person's being quoted a lower price for a room on a different channel after having already made a booking. However, such an approach ignores the issue of the cost of processing a booking over a particular channel. Such costs vary greatly depending to a large extent on the number of intermediaries between the supplier and the customer. The greater the number of intermediaries, the greater the transaction cost and processing fees—and therefore the greater the distribution cost.

This would seem to argue for having high rates on the channels that have high-cost structures and low prices on those with lowcost structures. Coupled with this matter is the fact that customers have become more knowledgeable about and comfortable with e-commerce issues in general, are more aware that distribution costs are lower in the virtual world than the bricks-and-mortar one, and thus increasingly expect to find the cheapest prices over electronic, and particularly direct electronic, routes. Put simply, when they go to a hotel company's web site, they expect to find the best value there.This study has shown that in many cases this is simply not the case, given that luxury hotels in particular tend to offer their highest rates over direct channels — and (ironically) their cheapest rates over the most expensive on-line intermediaries. Informal follow up to the study revealed that this may be due to the proactive approach of the on-line companies in contacting hotel companies on practically a daily basis and encouraging them to reduce their rates in return for better positioning on their search listings. In contrast, the rates on hotel companies' web sites go largely unmanaged, in many cases being set far in advance and not adjusted to reflect changing supply and demand.

Irrespective of its root cause, the behavior of hotel companies is driving Internet shoppers into the arms of the waiting on-line intermediaries, where in addition to consistently low prices, they also find wide product choice. Because of this, it's likely that many hotels are losing potential bookings to competitors as a result of consumers' migration toward the on-line travel sites that offer relatively low rates from many different hotel chains. Instead of being presented with a list of a chain's properties on a company's web site, prospective guests see a much wider variety of options from the on-line intermediary and may be tempted to book a competitor's room (especially if price becomes an issue).

Once consumers conclude that they will usually find better prices on a third-party channel, they will make Expedia or Travelocity, for example, their first port of call for future bookings—threatening brand loyalty, driving up transaction fees, increasing reservation leakage, and strengthening the third parties' power to demand "special rates" or commission overrides for a company to gain premium positioning (or even inclusion) in their search listings. Hotel companies need to take urgent action if they are not to lose control over the sale of their own product. At the very least, this means offering consistent prices over all channels, but more probably means providing customers the lowest rate over their own web site. This would decrease guests' motivation to book on alternative electronic channels, would help build web-site traffic, and should help to decrease distribution costs.

Organising the Hotel

The success of hotel organizations will be driven in large part by the ability to foresee—and capitalize – on change. Beyond this truism, however, there is an urgent need to identify what will be required in the competitive environment of the future with its intense focus on serving customer needs. The hospitality industry—as is the case with business generally—is subject to deep currents of change set in motion as economic and social systems shaped in the industrial era evolve to a knowledge-based era driven by technology advances. In this period of global transition, it behooves hotel organizations to examine the key factors that will not only define success, but the ability to survive in coming years. Its mission was to identify the characteristics needed to lead successful businesses in the next century. These executives offer a number of compelling messages regarding the key success factors of the future. Customers will have the strongest influence on the corporation in the year 2000. Indeed, these executives believe that the customer will be "king" in the new century. Exceptional leadership was by far the attribute most frequently cited by CEOs and senior executives; the consensus appears to be that successful companies in the year 2000 will be led by corporate visionaries.

A strategic planning focus is not only essential, but must embody a concept of planning for the future that anticipates change, rather than being based exclusively on historical models. In structuring organizations for the future, companies must build management capabilities to deal with one of the most critical challenges—diversity in the marketplace. Employing information technology to drive business success in this information-driven era is not only the path of least resistance, but vital to virtually every aspect of operations. Recognizing that the hotel industry has a somewhat split personality reflecting the inherent conflicts between its real estate and operational aspects, it is important to understand the industry's real estate origins and how they are shaping the challenges ahead.

The origins of the industry's real estate persona are embodied in the classic theory of location - "if we build it, they will come." As a result of this "building" complex, the industry has tended to have a real estate and asset orientation, rather than a customer focus. From the hotel company perspective—especially that of the brand-oriented "chain"—the varied interests of a diffused property ownership group can be quite different than the singular interest of the chain that operates and markets the properties. Even when the ownership of geographically dispersed hotel properties is controlled by a single hotel organization, the financial structuring tends to be property-specific. Corporate financial strategies are frequently subjugated to the needs of the last property deal brought into the company's fold. Each property in a so-called "chain," is frequently the subject of a unique and distinctive ownership and financial structure. This phenomenon—quite common in the real estate sector, but unusual for business enterprises generally—makes for elusive economies of scale in the structuring and financing of property-driven expansion. Collectively, these factors have produced low comparative returns in real estate, although criticism leveled at commercial real estate returns is somewhat less germane to the hotel industry, where management and franchise fees can produce high returns for those companies where property ownership is held by third parties.

While hotel chains have adopted traditional corporate frameworks, there are a number of predominantly real estate-driven, family-owned businesses in the hotel sector that continue to operate as relatively unstructured organizations. In meeting the future, these businesses will need plans, people and processes in order to establish viable corporate forms that can compete in tomorrow's marketplace and capitalize upon its opportunities. In today's changed environment, the hotel organization must deal with a number of new realities. Investors in our industry are no longer satisfied with long-term capital appreciation and psychic income that heretofore were often the justification for otherwise seemingly uneconomic investments in hotel property or, indeed, hotel chains. The first reality is that there is a very specific and identifiable relationship between bottom line performance and value. Improvements in business operations raises values. It is not surprising, therefore, that the new owners attracted to this industry in recent years have new sets of demands. This transformation from an old-guard group of investors and owners to income and return-driven newcomers has meant that the once "quiet enjoyment" of operators in their management of hotels for third parties is being disturbed, interrupted and overturned. These challenges all take place in an environment where capital has become extremely selective in markets that have little stability. A global shortage of capital will not remain a short-term problem, and future hotel organizations must have a stronger alignment to capital providers—a critical "customer" group. Hotel companies will need to compete by offering better returns and performance than in the past.

Hotel chains have found their development timetables quashed in recent years, making it difficult to achieve goals of critical mass often required to improve performance. These factors are driving consolidation in the brand "sweepstakes." Capital markets, therefore, continue to favour well-established companies, a reality that must drive entrepreneurial organizations to meet the future now by planning for an evolving corporate context in which to operate. Hotel developers, owners and management companies will all need to develop new strategies, skills and processes that look forward to the competitive demands of the future. These ultimately must address issues related to vision and planning, as well as organizational skill sets and processes to attract and retain customers. To stake a claim in the future, current business practices should be examined in light of what can be expected to be the key success factors in the year 2000.

As the information age produces greater worldwide integration of business activities, a global knowledge base will become invaluable. Success in local and regional hotel markets will be shaped decisively by a global business environment that defines capital movement, customer expectations and applications of new technologies. If the customer is king in the 21st century, hotel organizations will be best served by focusing less on their hotel assets as measures of success, and more on their customers. This involves a fundamental shift in viewing the real estate asset as the wealth creator—to the customer as the key to building shareholder wealth. A customer focus must imbue business decisions at all levels of developing and operating a hotel organization. Pursuing such a course will inevitably impact shareholder wealth. To accomplish this, however, customers need to participate in the product development process.

Fully realizing a customer focus in the industry poses a significant challenge. The hotel industry must confront problems due to conflicts between operational needs and real estate goals. Quite simply, an operator must remain customer-focused, but the short-term strategies to meet these needs may be inconsistent with the long-term objectives of property owners. Balancing those goals will be essential. A customer focus implies a significant shift in what drives hotel development—placing primary emphasis on the customer with the locations to follow. Nevertheless, a hotel organization with its large investment in fixed assets—the real estate—can never be as nimble as a consumer products company in adjusting products and services to match rapid shifts in the marketplace.

Hotel services are based primarily on people, not computers or other equipment. Quality that surprises takes the concept of zero defects a step further. Yesterday's surprising product or service is today's status quo. Twenty years ago,.a business executive did not expect a consistent and predictable level of service wherever he or she traveled in the world. Today that is a standard—not the exception—as is the expectation for sophisticated technology in hotel rooms to support business needs. With customer discrimination so acute, it is not surprising that brand loyalty is a diminishing "commodity" in the hotel industry. Find the ingredients for visionary leadership. Today's hotel organizations need to recognize the need for visionary leadership. The ability to forecast the future—to anticipate change rather than react to it—will be one of the single greatest determinants of market dominance in the years ahead. The old "command and control" model of leadership is giving way to a focus on leadership in ideas, information, inspiration, vision and teamwork. "For the most part, failing organizations tend to be over-managed and under-led. The leader sets the tone for the moral character, the vision, the corporate culture and the fiber of the institution."

While visionary leadership is essential, it must be linked to business operations and foster a risk bias, rather than a procedural bias. This will allow the organization to stretch and, in turn, change. And it must be shared by empowered professionals and staff throughout the organization, including those who meet the customer. Overcoming the resistance to change can be a daunting task, particularly in large hotel organizations in which diversions from the status quo may threaten established management lines. It suggests that a culture based on conformance may need to be replaced by an emphasis on flexibility, learning and cooperation.

Management competencies will need to be aligned in order to achieve the desired result. For many organizations, this may mean a shift from traditional hierarchies typical of companies in an industrial era to a flatter organization with a more transparent interface between leadership, organizational functions and employees. Create a defensible position through corporate strategy. For many of the industry's leaders, vision is driven by the strategic planning process, a function which has become critical for success. Strategic planning, however, has at times been a step-child in the hotel industry, and it is often the first to be cut when organizations are downsized. It is clearly in transition. There also has been a tendency to decentralize and simplify this function—both actions of potential benefit. Strategic planning must be led by the top people in the organization—the CEO and COO.

Beyond the ability to envision the future, core management capabilities will make the difference—they are essential. A clear vision without the management skills to support it cannot be a recipe for success. First and foremost, hotel management must have strategic development skills and the ability to integrate complex factors affecting success. Market volatility has become the norm, in part caused by the rapidly changing tastes of customers. Customers are increasingly approaching the hotel industry with widely different social, economic and political backgrounds, to say nothing of employees. Being able to deal with these diversities in a positive and constructive fashion that capitalizes on the differences, rather than working to find ways to mitigate them, is the clear path for successful management in the future.

The organization will also need to be imbued with a sense of entrepreneurship that reacts proactively to the market's diversity. Traditional organizations that follow well-documented rules must give way to leaders who can balance a sense of discipline with that of flexibility. Talent and resources must be marshaled and leveraged. In an industry with high fixed costs and labour intensity, the concept of leverage in the hotel business is an all-important one. Improving labour productivity through technology must be a goal for today's forward-looking hotel organization. Management must also be able to narrow the gap between the employer and the employee, forcing a flatter organization in the process. This will put management closer to the customer and speed the two-way communication process up and down the organization.

5

Human Resource Administration

Hotel managers are being asked more and more often to assume responsibility for management of the sales staff. It is a job for which they have received little training and for which they have a number of challenges. Five years ago, when demand was high and the sales function was relegated to answering the phone and taking the order, it was relatively easy for managers to keep an eye on things in the sales department. Unemployment was at historic lows and in order to keep positions filled, we were reluctant to expect too much or discipline an under performing employee. There was a tendency to keep the chair warm rather than let a position go unfilled. Times have changed both in terms of demand of demand and the employment pool but often the attitudes of management have not. Sales people represent a distinct management challenge. The good ones are bright, aggressive, able to sell their managers as well as their clients but they are also very human. They like most other employees will take the path of least resistance, need to have expectations made clear and have objective standards of performance by which they are evaluated.

Hotel managers have a particular challenge in that they work long hours and very closely with their sales staffs. It is difficult to maintain an objective and professional distance that allows for the kind of management that gets results. There are a few simple steps you can take to make your monitoring of the sales effort more effective. They may also make the sales effort more effective. There has to be a line of familiarity that you don't cross. It negates your ability to lead and manage effectively. Have regular sales meetings with a fixed agenda. It should occur at least once a month, preferably once a week at a time when it does not interfere with Prime Selling Hours. This provides a structured environment in which you can ask the 'tough' questions without sounding picky and irrational. To a sales person, if you just casually ask a question about an account or ask for numbers, they are likely to feel that you are just in a bad mood and it will pass. Take a course in sales. If you come from another discipline in the industry, learn about basic sales. Read a book, take a course—take a course in sales not related to the industry. There are many fine resources for hotel sales available especially now when that function has become so challenging. Sales people who have worked on commission 'get it'.

Set realistic goals and involve them in the process. Goal setting should be an objective process. When you let them know what they need to produce and why, then involve them in figuring out how they are going to get there, they understand and ideally buy into the plan. Be supportive but expect results! Your head is on the line here too!. If your sales staff is making a ton of calls but producing few results, it could be a skills problem. Offer them some training. When a reasonable amount of time and training effort has passed, don't be afraid to make the tough decision. The fact of the matter is they are uncomfortable at their non-performance and may be happier and more satisfied in another position. A comfortable room, good food, and a helpful staff can make being away from home an enjoyable experience for both vacationing families and business travellers. While most lodging managers work in traditional hotels and motels, some work in other lodging establishments, such as camps, inns, boardinghouses, dude ranches, and recreational resorts. In full-service hotels, lodging managers help their guests have a pleasant stay by providing many of the comforts of home, including cable television, fitness equipment, and voice mail, as well as specialised services such as health spas. For business travellers, lodging managers often schedule available meeting rooms and electronic equipment, including slide projectors and fax machines. Lodging managers are responsible for keeping their establishments efficient and profitable. In a small establishment with a limited staff, the manager may oversee all aspects of operations. However, large hotels may employ hundreds of workers, and the general manager usually is aided by a number of assistant managers assigned to the various departments of the operation. In hotels of every size, managerial duties vary significantly by job title. For example, general managers have overall responsibility for the operation of the hotel. Within guidelines established by the owners of the hotel or executives of the hotel chain, the general manager sets room rates, allocates funds to departments, approves expenditures, and establishes expected standards for guest service, decor, housekeeping, food quality, and banquet operations. Managers who work for chains also may organise and staff a newly built hotel, refurbish an older hotel, or reorganise a hotel or motel that is not operating successfully. In order to fill entry-level service and clerical jobs in hotels, some managers attend career fairs.

Resident managers live in hotels and are on call 24 hours a day to resolve problems or emergencies. In general, though, they typically work an 8- to 10 hour day and oversee the day-to-day operations of the hotel. In many hotels, the general manager also is the resident manager. Executive housekeepers ensure that guest rooms, meeting and banquet rooms, and public areas are clean, orderly, and well maintained. They also train, schedule, and supervise the work of housekeepers, inspect rooms, and order cleaning supplies.

Front office managers coordinate reservations and room assignments, as well as train and direct the hotel's front desk staff. They ensure that guests are treated courteously, complaints and problems are resolved, and requests for special services are carried out. Front office managers may adjust charges posted on a customer's bill. Convention services managers coordinate the activities of various departments in larger hotels to accommodate meetings, conventions, and special events. They meet with representatives of groups or organisations to plan the number of rooms to reserve, the desired configuration of the meeting space, and the banquet services.

During the meeting or event, they resolve unexpected problems and monitor activities to ensure that hotel operations conform to the expectations of the group. Assistant managers help run the day-to-day operations of the hotel. In large hotels, they may be responsible for activities such as personnel, accounting, office administration, marketing and sales, purchasing, security, maintenance, and pool, spa, or recreational facilities. In smaller hotels, these duties may be combined into one position. Assistant managers may adjust charges on a hotel guest's bill when a manager is unavailable. Computers are used extensively by lodging managers and their assistants to keep track of guests' bills, reservations, room assignments, meetings, and special events. In addition, computers are used to order food, beverages, and supplies, as well as to prepare reports for hotel owners and top-level managers. Managers work with computer specialists to ensure that the hotel's computer system functions properly. Should the hotel's computer system fail, managers must continue to meet the needs of hotel guests and staff. Because hotels are open around the clock, night and weekend work is common. Many lodging managers work more than 40 hours per week. Managers who live in the hotel usually have regular work schedules, but they may be called to work at any time. Some employees of resort hotels are managers during the busy season and have other duties during the rest of the year. Lodging managers sometimes experience the pressures of coordinating a wide range of functions. Conventions and large groups of tourists may present unusual problems. Moreover, dealing with irate guests can be stressful. The job can be particularly hectic for front office managers during check-in and check-out time. Computer failures can further complicate an already busy time.

Lodging managers held about 69,000 jobs in 2002. Self-employed managers-primarily owners of small hotels and motels-held about 50 percent of these jobs. Companies that manage hotels and motels under contract employed some managers. Hotels increasingly emphasise specialised training. Postsecondary training in hotel or restaurant management is preferred for most hotel management positions, although a college liberal arts degree may be sufficient when coupled with related hotel experience. Internships or part-time or summer work are an asset to students seeking a career in hotel management. The experience gained and the contacts made with employers can greatly benefit students after graduation. Most bachelor's degree programmes include work-study opportunities. Community colleges, junior colleges, and some universities offer associate's, bachelor's, and graduate degree programmes in hotel or restaurant management. Combined with technical institutes, vocational and trade schools, and other academic institutions, over 800 educational facilities have programmes leading to formal recognition in hotel or restaurant management. Hotel management programmes include instruction in hotel administration, accounting, economics, marketing, housekeeping, food service management and catering, and hotel maintenance engineering. Computer training also is an integral part of hotel management training, due to the widespread use of computers in reservations, billing, and housekeeping management. Additionally, over 450 high schools in 45 States offer the Lodging Management Programme created by the Educational Institute of the American Hotel and Lodging Association. This is a two-year programme offered to high school juniors and seniors, which teaches management principles and leads to a professional certification called the "Certified Rooms Division Specialist". Many colleges and universities grant participants credit towards a post-secondary degree in hotel management.

Lodging managers must be able to get along with many different people, even in stressful situations. They must be able to solve problems and concentrate on details. Initiative, self-discipline, effective communication skills, and the ability to organise and direct the work of others also are essential for managers at all levels. In the past, many managers were promoted from the ranks of front desk clerks, housekeepers, waiters, chefs, and hotel sales workers. Although some employees still advance to hotel management positions without education beyond high school, postsecondary education is preferred.

Restaurant management training or experience also is a good background for entering hotel management, because the success of a hotel's food service and beverage operations often is important to the profitability of the entire establishment. Graduates of hotel or restaurant management programmes usually start as trainee assistant managers. Some large hotels sponsor specialised on-the-job management training programmes that allow trainees to rotate among various departments and gain a thorough knowledge of the hotel's operation. Other hotels may help finance formal training in hotel management for outstanding employees. Newly built hotels, particularly those without established on-the-job training programmes, often prefer to hire applicants who have hotel management experience.

Large hotel and motel chains may offer better opportunities for advancement than small, independently owned establishments, but relocation every several years often is necessary for advancement. The large chains have more extensive career ladder programmes and offer managers the opportunity to transfer to another hotel or motel in the chain or to the central office. Career advancement can be accelerated by the completion of certification programmes offered by various associations. These programmes usually require a combination of course work, examinations, and experience. For example, outstanding lodging managers may advance to higher level manager positions.

Employment of lodging managers is expected to grow more slowly than the average for all occupations through 2012. Additional job openings are expected to occur as experienced managers transfer to other occupations or leave the labour force, in part because of the long hours and stressful working conditions. Job opportunities are expected to be best for persons with college degrees in hotel or restaurant management. Increasing business travel and domestic and foreign tourism will drive employment growth of lodging managers.

Managerial jobs are not expected to grow as rapidly as the hotel industry overall, however. As the industry consolidates, many chains and franchises will acquire independently owned establishments and increase the numbers of economy-class rooms to accommodate bargain-conscious guests. Economy hotels offer clean, comfortable rooms and front desk services without costly extras such as restaurants and room service. Because there are not as many departments in these hotels, fewer managers will be needed. Similarly, the increasing number of extended-stay hotels will temper demand for managers because, in these establishments, management is not required to be available 24 hours a day. In addition, front desk clerks increasingly are assuming some responsibilities previously reserved for managers, further limiting the employment growth of managers and their assistants. Additional demand for managers is expected in suite hotels, because some guests-especially business customers-are willing to pay higher prices for rooms with kitchens and suites that provide the space needed to conduct meetings.

Leadership

The hotel you just walked into has a certain crispness to it; a certain feeling. You get a sense of it all around you from the moment you arrive at the front desk. It isn't just that this place is spotlessly clean, though it is. It isn't just that everyone seems friendly and on their toes, though, that certainly is obvious. It isn't just that the hotel employees seem to genuinely care about meeting or exceeding your expectations, though that also is happening at every turn you make. No, it's something else; something intangible, yet unmistakably obvious. This is a hotel that exudes quality. But how did it get there? Why do you notice it here, and not somewhere else? The answer rests in the matter of Leadership. If something in a hotel environment leads you to the conclusion that you are in the midst of quality, it is because Leadership brought the organisation into that state. For sure, quality doesn't happen on its own. Someone made it happen and brought others with him or her to ensure that quality would endure.

The mark of a good manager isn't how well things run when you're there. It's how well things run when you're not there. Managers must hire the right people; people who care and show a willingness to care for others—that's what hospitality means. Then, they must train their employees in the rudiments of the job and later, coach them to do their job well in a positive environment that inspires and motivates teamwork. Training and coaching are not the same things. Training teaches skills. Coaching teaches the application of those skills; and training must always precede coaching. Finally, the manager needs to get out of the way and let people do their job. Delegate tasks, authority and decision making, but don't abdicate them. Hold people accountable for their actions. Cultivate and nurture key players and you will develop winners along the way. The manager who works seven days a week to make sure things get done right has missed this important attribute of leadership. On the other hand, managers who are never around while the department is in a state of chaos have equally missed the point. People do what they do because of what they get after they do it. People behave within an organisation a certain way because that is what is being culturally reinforced. Culture is nothing more than the collective attitudes of those who hold power. Managers who are not leaders and leadership that does not preside has abdicated power, but power will still be held by someone within the organisation, and usually by tenured employees with lower standards than their customers.

Leadership's role is to use its authority as a means to influence behaviour. Reward is the only thing that initiates lasting changes in behaviour and in order for reward to succeed, it must be positive, immediate and certain. Giving reward is a Leadership behaviour that acknowledges someone for having done something correctly. Unfortunately, many managers see their role as correcting behaviour only when it is wrong. We've all worked for the manager that was always on our case when we made a mistake, was slow to give praise for having done something right and rarely said, "Good job." Good Leadership is always noticing when someone does something right and makes mention of it. Reward need be nothing more than a smile and a few kind words, but given routinely and as soon as a positive act is observed, it will set the culture moving in the right direction. Do it. Do it right. Do it right now. Leaders act. Leaders get it right the first time. Leaders take action the moment it is required and inspire others to do the same. If you've ever had a complaint, then explained the complaint to a frontline clerk only to be told that you'll have to see the manager, you might understand the importance of this Axiom. There probably is no more important place in a hotel where this Axiom is needed than in the Sales office.

A hotel where leadership has a certain operational intensity and sense of urgency about getting things done has embraced this philosophy, which is a hallmark of good Leadership. The attitude of any staff reflects the attitude of their leader. If a front desk crew is friendly and vivacious, their leader is, too. If a restaurant delivers outstanding service, you can bet that the leader exhibits the same attitude toward serving the customer. Leaders, by their very attitude, set the standard by which others will behave. Leadership sets an expectation, creates an environment where that expectation is routinely met and ensures that it will endure over time. This means managers have to be willing to deal with the nitty-gritty and the fundamentals of their department. Every service encounter that an employee will make and every expectation that Leadership has must be communicated and reinforced. You can grow, or you can be comfortable, but you cannot do both at the same time. Leadership isn't a state that is suddenly attained, at least not for most of us. And while it is true that great leaders are born, they still have to learn an awful lot about channelling their innate ability to become great leaders.

Leadership is a path of continual enlightenment that occurs over a lifetime. That path is often difficult. Hotel managers don't have an easy job, but any level of discomfort may well be precisely because that path has been taken. All leaders reach certain plateaus in the course of their development: that's called experience. But learning never stops and it's never very easy. Managers who rest in their comfort zone will eventually fail because the world all around them isn't static. The market isn't; the competition isn't; customers aren't and neither are employees. Leaders must continually challenge themselves to compensate for the changing environment and learn new ways to gain market share, beat the competition, find new customers and retain good employees. People don't always do what you expect. They'll do what you inspect. Checking behind your crew doesn't mean you don't trust them; it just means you accept your Leadership role. General Managers in particular should never stop checking rooms and you can almost always tell the hotels where they have.

At the heart of business is the need to be fiscally healthy and it is Leadership's responsibility to guide the organisation toward that state. Junior managers in particular sometimes lose site of the fact that their decisions, on an hour-by-hour basis, are having financial impact on the hotel, both good and bad. Yes, put people before money and recognise that the organisation deals with human issues every day; Leadership must always be caring and compassionate. But absent financial success, the business will fail, and then, all human conditions fall prey to unfortunate and often unsavoury outcomes: lay-offs, litigation, foreclosure or take-over.

Managing Human Resource

Over the last decade, human resource management has come to be viewed as the dominant paradigm within which analyses of the world of work have been located. Common perceptions of management practices in the hotel industry typically include work intensification, high labour turnover, lack of training and poor career prospects, and casualised terms and conditions of employment. Primary influences on managerial decision-making in the hotel industry are no different from the primary influences affecting decision-making elsewhere, countering the argument that mainstream management theories are inapplicable within the hotel industry. Furthermore, where hotels emphasise the importance of service quality enhancement and where they introduce HRM as an integrated, mutually supporting package of practices, a strong relationship between HRM and organisational performance is proposed.

The human resources management function includes a variety of activities, and key among them is deciding what staffing needs you have and whether to use independent contractors or hire employees to fill these needs, recruiting and training the best employees, ensuring they are high performers, dealing with performance issues, and ensuring your personnel and management practices conform to various regulations. Activities also include managing your approach to employee benefits and compensation, employee records and personnel policies. Usually small hotel managers have to carry out these activities themselves because they can't yet afford part- or full-time help. However, they should always ensure that employees have — and are aware of — personnel policies which conform to current regulations. These policies are often in the form of employee manuals, which all employees have.

Job Design

Staffing is one of a hotel's most important management functions, is an ongoing challenge because of the high rate of employee and manager turnover. Full-service hotels can experience annual turnover rates in excess of 100 percent in certain employee classifications. Some managers consider an annual employee turnover rate of 33 percent low. At this rate, the entire hotel must be completely restaffed every three years. The higher the turnover rate, the larger the number of employees who must be replaced. In an attempt to reduce employee turnover, hotel and lodging businesses are giving increasing attention to job design, seeking to enhance those job characteristics that give the employee the greatest satisfaction and motivation.

Good job design must take into account the needs of employees as well as the demands of the job. Well-thought-out job design begins when management conducts a job analysis-that is, a thorough evaluation of the specific tasks performed for a particular job and the time required to perform them. Job analysis is an ongoing process, as many jobs change with improvements in technology and pressure to improve product quality. The job analysis is the basis for the job description and job specification. A job description includes the job title, pay, a brief statement of duties and procedures, working conditions, and hours.

The job specification is an outline of the qualifications necessary for a particular job. In response to the limits of specialization, organisations can redesign jobs to improve coordination, productivity, and product quality while responding to an employee's needs for learning, challenge, variety, increased responsibility, and achievement. Such job redesign often involves job rotation, the systematic movement of employees from one job to another; job enlargement, an increase in the number of tasks an employee will do in the job; job enrichment, the attempt to give the employee more control over job-related activities; and flextime, a flexible work schedule that permits employee input in establishing work schedules. In team-driven job redesign, a concept similar to job rotation, employees can transfer back and forth among teams that provide different services or products.

Hotels recruit employees from a variety of sources. Newspapers and employee referrals are used to recruit nonskilled hourly employees. Supervisory and management employees generally are recruited through colleges and universities, promotions from within, professional associations, and management recruiters. Hotels that take more time in making their selections are more successful in retaining employees. Discussions of employee training and development often concentrate on training techniques without giving a full explanation of what a hotel is trying to accomplish. As training and development impart job skills and educate employees, supervisors, and managers, they also improve current and future employee performance, which affects the bottom line.

Effective training includes problem solving, problem analysis, quality measurement and feedback, and team building. Performance evaluation, also called performance appraisal, is the systematic review of the strengths and weaknesses of an employee's performance. The major difficulty in a performance appraisal is quantifying those strengths and weaknesses. The performance of some jobs is easy to quantify, while for others it is more difficult. An important part of the appraisal process is a well-established job description, so that the employee and the supervisor have similar expectations. Compensation includes the monetary and nonmonetary rewards that managers, supervisors, and employees receive for performing their jobs. In order to set compensation levels, the human resources department must periodically conduct job evaluations, which determine the value of the job to the hotel. Knowledge of the value of the job to the organisation and of wage rates for each job classification allows the hotel to establish a fair compensation policy. There are several activities involved in staffing a housekeeping operation. Executive housekeepers must select and interview employees, participate in an orientation program, train newly hired employees, and develop employees for future growth.

Employee Selection

Each region has its own demographic situations that affect the availability of suitable employees for involvement in housekeeping or environmental service operations. For example, in one area, an exceptionally high response rate from people seeking food service work may occur and a low response rate from people seeking housekeeping positions may occur. In another area, the reverse may be true, and people interested in housekeeping work may far outnumber those interested in food service. Advertising campaigns that will reach these employees are the best method of locating suitable people. Major classified ads associated with mass hirings will specify the need for food service personnel, front desk clerks, food servers, housekeeping personnel, and maintenance people. Such ads may yield surprising results. If the volume of response for housekeeping personnel is insufficient to provide a suitable hiring base, the following sources may be investigated:

- Local employment agencies
- Flyers posted on community bulletin boards
- Local church organizations
- Neighborhood canvass for friends of recently hired employees
- Direct radio appeals to local homemakers

— Organizations for underprivileged ethnic minorities, and mentally disabled people

If these sources do not produce the volume of applicants necessary to develop a staff, it may become necessary to search for employees in distant areas and to provide regular transportation for them to and from work. If aliens are hired, the department manager must take great care to ensure that they are legal residents of this country and that their green cards are valid. More than one hotel department manager has had an entire staff swept away by the Department of Immigration after hiring people who were illegal aliens. Such unfortunate action has required the immediate assistance of all available employees to fill in. Whether you are involved in a mass hiring or in the recruiting of a single employee, a systematic and courteous procedure for processing applicants is essential.

The efficient handling of lines of employees, courteous attendance, personal concern for employee desires, and reference to suitable departments for those unfamiliar with what the hotel or hospital has to offer all become earmarks for how the company will treat its employees. The key to proper handling of applicants is the use of a control system whereby employees are conducted through the steps of application, prescreening, and if qualified, reference to a department for interview. Even though an employee may desire involvement in one classification of work, he or she may be hired for employment in a different department. Also, employees might not be aware of the possibilities available in a particular department at the time of application or may be unable to locate in desired departments at the time of mass hirings. Employees who perform well should therefore be given the opportunity to transfer to other departments when the opportunities arise. According to laws regulated by federal and state Fair Employment Practices Agencies (FEPA), no person may be denied the opportunity to submit application for employment for a position of his or her choosing. Not only is the law strict on this point, but companies in any way benefiting from interstate commerce may not discriminate in the hiring of people based on race, color, national origin, or religious preference. Although specific hours and days of the week may be specified, it is a generally accepted fact that hotels and hospitals must maintain personnel operations that provide the opportunity for people to submit applications without prejudice.

A carefully planned, concerned, and informational orientation program is significant to the first impressions that a new employee will have about the hospital or hotel in general and the housekeeping department in particular. Too often, a new employee is told where the work area and restroom are, given a cursory explanation of the job, then put to work. It is not uncommon to find managers putting employees to work who have not even been processed into the organization, an unfortunate situation that is usually discovered on payday when there is no paycheck for the new employee. Such blatant disregard for the concerns of the employee can only lead to a poor perception of the company. A planned orientation program will eliminate this type of activity and will bring the employee into the company with personal concern and with a greater possibility for a successful relationship. A good orientation program is usually made up of four phases: employee acquisition, receipt of an employee's handbook, tour of the facility, and an orientation meeting.

Once a person is accepted for employment, the applicant is told to report for work at a given time and place, and that place should be the personnel department. Preemployment procedures can take as much as one-half day, and department managers eager to start new employees to work should allow time for a proper employee acquisition into the organization. At this time it should be ensured that the application is complete and any additional information pertaining to employment history that may be necessary to obtain the necessary work permits and credentials is on hand. Usually the security department records the entry of a new employee into the staff and provides instructions regarding use of employee entrances, removing parcels from the premises, and employee parking areas. Application for work permits, and drug testing, will be scheduled where applicable. All documents required by the hotel's health and welfare insurer should be completed, and instructions should be given about immediately reporting accidents, no matter how slight, to supervisors.

For new facilities, access to the property should be gained within about one week before opening, and many new employees can be taken on a tour simultaneously. It is possible for employees to work in the hotel housekeeping department for years and never to have visited the showroom, dining rooms, ballrooms, or even the executive office areas. A tour of the complete facility melds employees into the total organization, and a complete informative tour should never be neglected. For ongoing operations, after acquisition, the new employee may be turned over to a department supervisor, who becomes the tour director. An appreciation of the total involvement of each employee is strengthened when a facilities tour is complete and thorough. If necessary, the property tour might be postponed until after the orientation meeting; however, the orientation activity of staffing is not complete until a property tour is conducted.

Employee orientation meetings that are scheduled too soon fail to answer many questions that will develop within the first two weeks of employment. The meeting should be held in a comfortable setting, with refreshments provided. It is usually conducted by the director of human resources and is attended by as many of the facility managers as possible. Most certainly, the general manager or hospital administration members of the executive committee, the security director, and the new employees' department heads should attend. Each of these managers should have an opportunity to welcome the new employees and give them a chance to associate names with faces. All managers and new employees should wear name tags. In orientation meetings, a brief history of the company and company goals should be presented. Although the new employee will be gaining confidence and security in the position as training ends and work is actually performed, informal orientation may continue for quite some time. The formal orientation, however, ends with the orientation meeting. Finally, it should be remembered that good orientation procedures lead to worker satisfaction and help quiet the anxieties and fears that a new employee may have. When a good orientation is neglected, the seeds of dissatisfaction are planted.

Training of Employees

Employees, regardless of past experiences, always need some degree of training before starting a new job. Small institutions may try to avoid training by hiring people who are already trained in the general functions with which they will be involved. However,most institutions recognize the need for training that is specifically oriented toward the new experience, and will have a documented training program. Some employers of housekeeping personnel find it easier to train completely unskilled and untrained personnel. In such cases, bad or undesirable practices do not have to be trained out of an employee. Previous experience and education should, however, be analyzed and considered in the training of each new employee in order that efficiencies in training can be recognized. If an understanding of department standards and policies can be demonstrated by a new employee, that portion of training may be shortened or modified. However, skill and ability must be demonstrated before training can be altered. Finally, training is the best method to communicate the company's way of doing things, without which the new employee may do work contrary to company policy.

First training of a new employee actually starts with a continuation of department orientation. When a new employee is turned over to the housekeeping or environmental services department, orientation usually continues by familiarizing the employee with department rules and regulations. Many housekeeping departments have their own department employee handbooks. Training may be defined as those activities that are designed to help an employee begin performing tasks for which he or she is hired or to help the employee improve performance in a job already assigned. The purpose of training is to enable an employee to begin an assigned job or to improve upon techniques already in use. In hotel or hospital housekeeping operations, there are three basic areas in which training activity should take place: skills, attitudes, and knowledge.

Skills training

A sample list of skills in which a basic housekeeping employee must be trained follows:

— *Bed making*: Specific techniques; company policy

— *Vacuuming*: Techniques; use and care of equipment

— *Dusting*: Techniques; use of products

— *Window and mirror cleaning*: Techniques and products

— *Setup awareness*: Room setups; what a properly serviced room should look like

— *Bathroom cleaning*: Tub and toilet sanitation; appearance; methods of cleaning and results desired

— *Daily routine*: An orderly procedure for the conduct of the day's work; daily communications

— *Caring for and using equipment*: Housekeeper cart; loading

— *Industrial safety*: Product use; guest safety; fire and other emergencies The best reference for the skills that require training is the job description for which the person is being trained.

Attitude guidance

Employees need guidance in their attitudes about the work that must be done. They need to be guided in their thinking about rooms that may present a unique problem in cleaning. Attitudes among section housekeepers need to be such that, occasionally, when rooms require extra effort to be brought back to standard, it is viewed as being a part of rendering service to the guest who paid to enjoy the room.The rooms are there to be enjoyed. Positive relationships with various agencies and people also need to be developed. The following is a list of areas in which attitude guidance is important:

— The guest/patient

— The department manager and immediate supervisor

— A guestroom that is in a state of great disarray

— The hotel and company

— The uniform

— Appearance

— Personal hygiene

The most important task of the trainer is to prepare new employees to meet standards. With this aim in mind, sequence of performance in cleaning a guestroom is most important in order that efficiency in accomplishing day-to-day tasks may be developed. In addition, the best method of accomplishing a task should be presented to the new trainee. Once the task has been learned, the next thing is to meet standards, which may not necessarily mean doing the job the way the person has been trained. There is a need to conduct ongoing training for all employees, regardless of how long they have been members of the department. There are two instances when additional training is needed:

— the purchase of new equipment, and

— change in or unusual employee behavior while on the job.

When new equipment is purchased, employees need to know how the new equipment differs from present equipment, what new skills or knowledge are required to operate the equipment, who will need this knowledge, and when. New equipment may also require new attitudes about work habits. Employee behavior while on the job that is seen as an indicator for additional training may be divided into two categories: events that the manager witnesses and events that the manager is told about by the employees. Events that the manager witnesses that indicate a need for training are frequent employee absence, considerable spoilage of products, carelessness, a high rate of accidents, and resisting direction by supervisors. Events that the manager might be told about that indicate a need for training are that something doesn't work right, something is dangerous to work with, something is making work harder. Although training is vital for any organization to function at top efficiency, it is expensive. The money and man-hours expended must therefore be worth the investment. There must be a balance between the dollars spent training employees and the benefits of productivity and high-efficiency performance.

A simple method of determining the need for training is to measure performance of workers: Find out what is going on at present on the job, and match this performance with what should be happening. The difference, if any, describes how much training is needed. If the employee could not do the job even if his or her life depended on the outcome, there is a deficiency of knowledge (DK). If the employee could have done the job if his or her life depended on the outcome, but did not, there is a deficiency of execution (DE). If either deficiency of knowledge or deficiency of execution exists, training must be conducted. The approach or the method of training may differ, however. Deficiencies of knowledge can be corrected by training the employee to do the job, then observing and correcting as necessary until the task is proficiently performed. Deficiency of execution is usually corrected by searching for the underlying cause of lack of performance, not by teaching the actual task. There are numerous methods or ways to conduct training. Each method has its own advantages and disadvantages, which must be weighed in the light of benefits to be gained. Some methods are more expensive than others but are also more effective in terms of time required for comprehension and proficiency that must be developed.

On-the-Job Training

Using on-the-job training (OJT), a technique in which "learning by doing" is the advantage, the instructor demonstrates the procedure and then watches the students perform it. With this technique, one instructor can handle several students. In housekeeping operations, the instructor is usually a GRA who is doing the instructing in the rooms that have been assigned for cleaning that day. The OJT method is not operationally productive until the student is proficient enough in the training tasks to absorb part of the operational load.

OJT requires progress toward daily production of ready rooms, simulation requires that the model room not be rented. In addition, the trainer is not productive in cleaning ready rooms. The advantages of simulation training are that it allows the training process to be stopped, discussed, and repeated if necessary. Simulation is an excellent method, provided the trainer's time is paid for out of training funds, and clean room production is not necessary during the workday.

Modern trends in training

Many hotels use training aids in a conference room, or post messages on an employee bulletin board. Aside from the usual training aids such as chalkboards, bulletin boards, charts, graphs, and diagrams, photographs can supply clear and accurate references for how rooms should be set up, maids' carts loaded, and routines accomplished. Most housekeeping operations have films on guest contact and courtesy that may also be used in training. Motion pictures speak directly to many people who may not understand proper procedures from reading about them.

Many training techniques may be combined to develop a well-rounded training plan. It is possible to have two students sitting side by side in a classroom, with one being trained and the other being developed. Recall that the definition of training is preparing a person to do a job for which he or she is hired or to improve upon performance of a current job. Development is preparing a person for advancement or to assume greater responsibility. The techniques are the same, but the end result is quite different. Whereas training begins after orientation of an employee who is hired to do a specific job, upon introduction of new equipment, or upon observation and communication with employees indicating a need for training, development begins with the identification of a specific employee who has shown potential for advancement.

Training for promotion or to improve potential is in fact development and must always include a much neglected type of training -supervisory training. Many forms of developmental training may be given on the property; other forms might include sending candidates to schools and seminars. Developmental training is associated primarily with supervisors and managerial development and may encompass many types of experiences. Development of individuals within the organization looks to future potential and promotion of employees. Specifically, those employees who demonstrate leadership potential should be developed through supervisory training for advancement to positions of greater responsibility. Unfortunately, many outstanding workers have their performance rewarded by promotion but are given no development training.

Development of new growth in the trainee becomes difficult when the training instructor or coordinator is not only developing a new manager but is also being held responsible for the production of some aspect of housekeeping operations. Whether you are conducting a training or a development program, suitable records of training progress should be maintained both by the training supervisor and the student. Periodic evaluations of the student's progress should be conducted, and successful completion of the program should be recognized. Public recognition of achievement will inspire the newly trained or developed employee to achieve standards of performance and to strive for advancement. Once an employee is trained or developed and his or her satisfactory performance has been recognized and recorded, the person should perform satisfactorily to standards. Future performance may be based on beginning performance after training. If an employee's performance begins to fall short of standards and expectations, there has to be a reason other than lack of skills.

The reason for unsatisfactory performance must then be sought out and addressed. This type of follow-up is not possible unless suitable records of training and development are maintained and used for comparison. Although evaluation and performance appraisal for employees will occur as work progresses, it is not uncommon to find the design of systems for appraisal as part of organization and staffing functions. This is true because first appraisal and evaluation occurs during training, which is an activity of staffing. Once trainees begin to have their performance appraised, the methods used will continue throughout employment.

As a part of training, new employees should be told how, when, and by whom their performances will be evaluated, and should be advised that questions regarding their performance will be regularly answered. Initial employment should be probationary in nature, allowing the new employee to improve efficiency to where the designated number of rooms cleaned per day can be achieved in a probationary period (about three months). Should a large number of employees be unable to achieve the standard within that time, the standard should be investigated. Should only one or two employees be unable to meet the standard of rooms cleaned per day, an evaluation of the employee in training should either reveal the reason why or indicate the employee as unsuitable for further retention. An employee who, after suitable training, cannot meet a reasonable performance standard should not be allowed to continue employment.

Evaluation of staff is an attempt to measure selected traits, characteristics, and productivity. Unfortunately, evaluations are generally objective in nature, and raters are seldom trained in the art of subjective evaluation. Initiative, self-control, and leadership ability do not lend themselves to measurement; therefore such characteristics are estimated. How well they are estimated depends to a great extent on the person doing the estimating. Certain policies on the use of evaluations should be established so that they are understood by both the person doing the evaluating and the person being evaluated. These policies must be established and disseminated by management. Evaluation should be used at the end of a probationary period, and the employee must understand at the beginning of the period that he or she will be observed and evaluated. Each item, as well as what impact the evaluation will have on future employment, should be explained to the employee. People undergoing periodic evaluations, such as at the end of one year's employment, should also know why evaluations are being conducted and what may result from the evaluation. In both situations, the evaluation should be used for counseling and guidance so that performance may be improved upon or corrected if necessary. Certainly, strong points should be pointed out.

6

Front Office Operations

The front office is the nerve center of a hotel property. Communications and accounting are two of the most important functions of a front desk operation. Effective communications-with guests, employees, and other departments of the hotel-are paramount in projecting a hospitable image. Answering guest inquiries about hotel services and other guests, marketing and sales department requests for information on guest room availability, and housekeeping department inquiries concerning guest reservations are but a few of the routine tasks performed almost constantly by a hotel front desk in its role as communications hub. Accounting procedures involving charges to registered and nonregistered hotel guest accounts are also important in the hospitality field. Itemized charges are necessary to show a breakdown of charges if a guest questions a bill. Services for which fees are charged are available 24 hours a day in a hotel property. Moreover, because guests may want to settle their accounts at any time of the day, accounts must be current and accurate at all times. Keeping this data organized is a top priority of good front office management.

Whatsoever system and setting the hotel might use, it should reflect easy access to the equipment, forms, and supplies necessary. Moreover, the setting shall reflect position flexibility. Rather, they shall be stored in drawers or slots located under or away from the front desk. For, this would ensure security and safety of guests. Front desk designed alternatives:

— *Circular or semi-circular structure*: this very structure provides an effective service to more guests and appears more modern and innovative but since guests will approach the front desk from all angles, more staff is needed.
— *Traditional straight desk*: Under this very design, fewer staff is needed, but fewer guests can be served at the same time.
— *Deskless environment*: Under this design, there is no front desk at all. This is usually replaced by a hostess, or steward welcoming the guest, seating him or her on a chair/sofa, and conduct registration activities there while, for example, having a cocktail or a drink.

Functions of Front Office Manager

The front office of a hotel is responsible fotr the following management functions.

Planning

At the planning stage, the front office manager shall determine the department's goals. Later, the front office manager shall use these goals as a guide for planning more specific and measurable objectives. Lastly, the front office manager shall determine the strategies and tactics to reach these objectives.

Organisation

The front office manager shall organise the work to be done through dividing it among staff members. While doing so, the work shall be distributed fairly and shall be completed in a timely manner.

Coordination

Involves bringing together and using the available resources to attain planned goals. In its most basic form, a hotel is two or more people working together to reach a goal. Whether a hotel is highly bureaucratic or changing and self-organizing, the organization must exist for some reason, some purpose, some mission — or it isn't a hotel at all. The hotel must have some goal. Identifying this goal requires some form of planning, informal or formal. Reaching the goal means identifying some strategies, formal or informal. These strategies are agreed upon by members of the hotel through some form of communication, formal or informal. Then members set about to act in accordance with what they agreed to do. They may change their minds, fine. But they need to recognize and acknowledge that they're changing their minds. This form of ongoing communication to reach a goal, tracking activities toward the goal and then subsequent decisions about what to do is the essence of management coordination. It needs to exist in some manner — formal or informal.

Staffing

Staffing involves finding the right people, with the right skills, abilities, and fit, who may be hired or already working for the hotel.

Leadership

Involves overseeing, motivating, training, disciplining, and setting an example for the front office. One can categorize the exercise of leadership as either actual or potential:

— *actual* - giving guidance or direction, as in the phrase "the emperor has provided satisfactory leadership".

— *potential* - the capacity or ability to lead, as in the phrase "she could have exercised effective leadership"; or in the concept "born to lead".

In both cases, as a result of the constancy of change some people detect within the late 20th and early 21st centuries, the act of learning appears fundamental to certain types of leading and leadership. When learning and leadership coalesce, one could characterize this as "learnership". Leadership can have a formal aspect (as in most political or business leadership) or an informal one (as in most friendships). Speaking of "leadership" (the abstract term) rather than of "leading" (the action) usually implies that the entities doing the leading have some "leadership skills" or competencies.

Controlling

Control in one of the managerial functions like planning, organising, staffing and directing. It is an important function because it helps to check the errors and to take the corrective action so that deviation from standards are minimised and stated goals of the organisation are achieved in desired manner. According to modern concepts, control is a foreseeing action whereas earlier concept of control was used only when errors were detected. Control in management means setting standards, measuring actual performance and taking corrective action.

Evaluation

Determines the extent to which planned goals are, in fact, attained. Moreover, it involves reviewing and, when necessary, revising or helping to revise front office goals. Evaluation is carefully collecting and analyzing information in order to make decisions. There are many types of evaluations in organizations, for example, evaluation of marketing efforts, evaluation of employee performance, program evaluations, etc. Evaluations can focus on many aspects of an organization and its processes, for example, its goals, processes, outcomes, etc.

Room Rates Establishment

The front office manager shall assign to each room category a rack rate. In accordance, front office employees are expected to sell rooms at rack unless a guest qualifies for an alternative room rate. While establishing room rates, management shall be careful about its operating costs, inflationary factors, and competition. Generally, there are three popular approaches to pricing rooms:

Market condition approach

Under this very approach, management shall look at comparable hotels in the geographical market, see what they are charging for the same product, and "charge only what the market will accept". Some drawbacks of this approach are that it does not take into consideration the value of the property, and what a strong sales effort may accomplish.

Rule of thumb approach

In this very approach, the rate of a room shall be $ 1 for each $ 1,000 of construction and furnishing cost per room, assuming a 70% occupancy rate. This approach, however, fails to take into consideration the inflation term, the contribution of other facilities and services towards the hotel's desired profitability, and assumes a certain level of occupancy rate.

Hubbart formula approach

This very approach considers operating costs, desired profits, and expected number of rooms sold (i.e. demand). The procedure of calculating a room rate is as follows:

— Calculate the hotel's desired profit by multiplying the desired rate of return (ROI) by the owner's investment.

— Calculate pre-tax profits by dividing the desired profit by 1 minus hotel's tax rate.

— Calculate fixed charges and management fees. This calculation includes estimating depreciation, interest expense, property taxes, insurance, amortisation, building mortgage, land, rent, and management fees.

— Calculate undistributed operating expenses. This includes estimating administrative and general expenses, data processing expenses, human resources expenses, transportation expenses, marketing expenses, property operation and maintenance expenses, and energy costs.

— Estimate non-room operating department income or loss, that is, F&B department income or loss, telephone department income or loss.

— Calculate the required room department income which is the sum of pre-tax profits, fixed charges and management fees, undistributed operating expenses, and other operating department losses less other department incomes.

— Determine the rooms department revenue which is the required room department income, plus other room department direct expenses of payroll and related expenses, plus other direct operating expenses.

— Calculate the average room rate by dividing rooms department revenue by the expected number of rooms to be sold.

Forecasting Room Availability

Forecasting room availability is forecasting the number of rooms available for sale on any future date. This type of forecasting helps manage the reservation process, guides the front office staff for an effective rooms management, and can be used as an occupancy forecast, which is, further, useful in attempting to schedule the necessary number of employees for an expected volume of business. In order to forecast room availability, the following data are needed:

Number of expected

1. room arrivals
2. room walk-ins
3. room stayovers
4. room no-shows
5. room understays
6. room check-outs
7. room overstays

These data help the front office in conduct various daily operational ratios such as:

— No-shows percentage = (number of no-show rooms)/(number of rooms reserved)

— Walk-ins percentage = (number of walk-in rooms)/(total number of rooms arrivals)

— Overstays percentage = (number of overstay rooms)/(number of expected check-outs)

— Understays percentage = (number of understay rooms)/(number of expected check-outs)

The forecasted number of rooms available for sale for any future date can be tracked using the following formula:

Forecasted number of rooms available for sale = total number of guest rooms - number of out of order rooms - number of stayovers rooms - number of reserved rooms + number of no-show rooms + number of understay rooms - number of overstay rooms

Under non-automated and semi-automated systems, number of rooms available for sale forecasts are calculated upon demand and need and vary from three-day to ten-day forecasts. However, under fully automated systems, forecasts can be done at any moment for any future period of time. For, computers run forecasts on a room count considerations, hence eliminating tedious labour work and human error margins.

Budgeting

At least once per year, hotels shall prepare annual budgets, which are profit plans that address all revenue sources and expense items for the following calendar year. Moreover, the hotel annual operating budget represents standards against which management can evaluate actual results of operations. In the annual budget preparation process, close coordination efforts of all management personnel is vital. The hotel's annual operation budget is commonly divided into monthly plans, which in turn are divided into weekly and even daily plans, for better control over actual results. While preparing the front office department annual budget, the front office manager shall coordinate with the accounting department as to estimate only rooms revenue and related direct expenses. The hotel controller and the general manager, then, shall revise this very budget.

— *Forecasting room revenue*: In order to forecast room revenue, the front office manager might consult historical financial information such as past room revenue, past number of rooms sold, past average daily rate, and past occupancy rates.

— *Forecasting direct expenses*: Due to the fact front office manager is responsible only for his/her department direct expenses, the front office manager can, also, consult historical financial data depicting variable cost to room revenue ratios, in order to estimate department expenses.
— *Refining budget plans*: Sometimes, if external uncontrollable factors change significantly, in an unexpected way, then the actual operating budgeted figures shall be revised.

Room Reservation

Prior to computerization era, the main function of the reservation process is only to determine basic room availability. That is to say, the reservation clerk can only tell the potential guest that a room is reserved for him/her. However, the reservation clerk can not tell you the type of the room, rate honored. Nowadays, with the wide use of reservation software package programmes, it is now possible to reserve a room by room type, rate, and to accommodate all the possible special requests of the guest. Therefore, the selling function shifted from the front office to the reservation department. Hence, projections of room revenues and profitability analysis became one of the basic functions of the reservation department. In parallel, reservation department and reservation agents should have sales goals to achieve which might focus on number of room nights, average room rate, and/or booked room revenue.

Types of Reservations

Guaranteed reservation

Insures that the hotel will hold a room for the guest until a specific time following the guest's scheduled arrival date.

On return, the guest shall guarantee his/her reservation of room unless reservation is properly canceled. In order to guarantee a reservation, guests might opt for one of the following methods:

a) Prepayment guaranteed reservation

b) Credit card guaranteed reservation

c) Advance deposit or partial payment

d) Travel agent guaranteed reservation

e) Voucher or Miscellaneous Charge Order [MCO]

f) Corporate guaranteed reservation

Non-guaranteed reservation

Insures that the hotel agrees to hold a room for the guest until a stated reservation cancellation hour (Usually 6 p.m.) on the day of arrival. Reservation agents shall make sure to encourage their guests to guarantee their reservations especially in the high season.

Central Reservation Systems

The majority of lodging properties belongs to one or more central reservation systems. A central reservation system is composed of a central reservation office, member hotels connected together via communication devices, and potential guests. Central Reservation Office [CRO] offers its services via a 24-hours toll free telephone numbers. Hotel members of the central reservation system shall provide and exchange accurate room availability data to central reservation offices. To illustrate, central reservation offices and member hotels shall communicate (on real time) any reservation transaction. This is possible, nowadays, with the sophisticated communication equipment available. These very equipment shall be provided by central reservation offices to its member hotels. Such equipment may range from Teletype, telex, facsimile machines, to personal computers, Internet connections. On return, central reservation offices charges a fee for the utilization of its services which might take the form of a flat fee and a variable fee, or a flat percentage of potential room revenue, actual room revenue, and/or rooms division gross profit.

Central reservation offices are divided into two:

a) *Affiliate reservation network*: This very network is referred to as the hotel chain's reservation system. In fact, it is composed of a CRO, and hotels, which are members of the same chain. The main advantages of affiliate reservation network are:

   a) Streamline the process of reservation
   b) Reduce overall system costs
   c) Attract business for or refer business to another chain property
   d) Affiliate reservation networks might serve, in addition to its main function, other duties like:
      — Serve as an inter property communication network
      — Serve as an accounting transfer tool
      — Serve as a destination information center
      — Serve as a connection with Global Distribution Systems [GDS]. System including several Central Reservation Offices connected to each other

b) *Non-affiliate reservation network*: A non-affiliate reservation network is composed of a central reservation office, potential guests, and member independent hotels.

Intersell agencies are special types of central reservation offices contracting to handle reservation for more than one Product line.

Group Reservations

Conducting a reservation request for a group shall be treated differently than accommodating a reservation of individual guests. The main reason, is that individual reservation requests are treated by the reservation department, while group reservations are initiated by the sales and marketing division, and finalized through a careful coordination of the reservation from one hand and the marketing from the other.Below is a detailed procedure of how group reservation, in a typical hotel, is conducted:

1. A group representative, a member of the travel agency or the tour operator, not individuals, shall communicate group reservations' request to the hotel's marketing department
2. Upon availability, the hotel's reservation department shall block the requested number of rooms for this very group
3. The Hotel shall give a deadline for the group, in order to receive their final list. That deadline is called cut-off date
4. After receiving the final list, the reservation department shall change the desired number of rooms' status from blocked to booked (or reserved) rooms, and release the remaining rooms (if any left) as vacant
5. If the hotel did not receive the final list by the cut-off date, then the reservation department has all the right to cancel the group reservation and release all the initially booked rooms into vacant rooms.

Reservation Availability

After receiving a reservation request, the hotel might accept it, as it is, if there is room availability. If not, the reservation department should suggest alternative room types, dates, and/or rates, to the potential guest. If, however, the potential guest insists on his/her previous request, the hotel should suggest an alternative hotel. That's one of the main reasons why we need to maintain good relation-ships with nearby competing hotels.The reservation department should always compare historical reservation volumes against actual arrivals. The main reason is to cope with overbooking, which a situation occurring when the total number of rooms reserved for a certain period of time exceeds the total number of rooms available for sale, for the same period of time. In order to cope with the overbooking problem, some statistical and historical data should be stored and processed by the hotel and should be continuously updated. Such data should include:

a) Number of rooms reserved for a specific date
b) Number of rooms occupied by stayovers
c) Forecasted no-shows percentage
d) Forecasted understays percentage
e) Forecasted overstays percentage
f) Forecasted cancellation percentage
g) Number of out of order rooms for a specific date

In order to function properly, the reservation department shall maintain control books, wall charts, and/or a computerized system. Whatsoever system chosen, the reservation department shall maintain and update that system to include any reservation transaction. Below is a description of the three commonly used sets of equipment to track room availability under the manual, semi-automated and fullyautomated systems:

— *Control books*: Control books are standard three-ring, loose-leaf binders with a tally Page assigned to each day of the year. Under this very system, when a potential guest calls to have a reservation, the reservation clerk shall check the cells corresponding to rooms.

— *Wall charts*: These are charts stapled on the wall depicting days of the month versus hotel rooms. Moreover, upon need and convenience, these charts might be customized to track appropriate room Numbers, rates, and codes, hence, is advantageous to control books. Moreover, in this very system, different colors are used to differentiate between different reservation transactions, types of guest reserving. Lastly, wall charts eliminates the erasures and rewriting associated with control book, hence lees errors might occur.

— *Computerized systems:* Computerized systems are by far the best systems that track room availability. In fact, these very systems control room availability data and automatically generate many reservation-related reports in an accurate manner. Moreover, computerized systems can itemize room availability for future periods by open dates, closed dates, versus special event dates. Lastly, this very system can forecast room availability for any reservation horizon needed in the future.

Reservation Recording

Each reservation department shall prepare a reservation record, which depicts the various personal and financial data of guests, for each reservation transaction. The aim is to identify guests and their occupancy needs before guest's arrival. Moreover, the hotel can personalize or customize guest services and better schedule staff accordingly. In order to create a reservation record, the following items are needed:

a) Guest name

b) Guest's home or billing address

c) Guest's telephone number, including area code

d) Name, address, and telephone number of guest's company, if appropriate

e) Name of and pertinent information about the person making the reservation, if not the guest

f) Number of people in the group, and perhaps ages of any children

g) Arrival date and time

h) Number of nights required or expected departure date, depending on how the system is programmed

i) Reservation type

j) Special requirements

k) Additional information, if needed

At the reservation process, reservation agents shall keep in mind that a rate quoted and confirmed must be honored. Moreover, reservation clerks should be aware of the following:

a) Supplementary charges for extra services or amenities

b) Minimum stay requirements in effect for dates requested

c) Special promotions in effect for dates requested

d) Applicable currency exchange rates, if quoting rates to an international tourist

e) Applicable room tax percentages

f) Applicable service charges or gratuities

The hotel should communicate guests by telephone, telex, mail, or e-mail a letter of confirmation, which confirms the important points of the reservation agreement. This very letter might be shown at the registration process in order to accelerate the pace of registration and prove that the guest has the right to have a room at the hotel.

The hotel shall send a confirmation letter to all reserved potential guests, whether their reservations are guaranteed or non-guaranteed. Below are the main points that should be communicated in a confirmation letter:

a) Name and address of the guest
b) Date and time of arrival
c) Room type and rate
d) Length of stay
e) Number of persons in a group, if any
f) Reservation type
g) Reservation confirmation number
h) Special requests, if any.

Hotels shall communicate meaningful confirmation numbers to their potential guests. These numbers shall have statistical meanings, which might help the hotel in maintaining an efficient historical database. Here is an example: 32 02 G JC 63

a) 32: Guest's scheduled arrival date on Julian dates calendar.
b) 02: Group reservation. In this very system, 01 might mean Frequent Independent Traveler.
c) G: means that the reservation is guaranteed. If N is written, it means non-guaranteed.
d) JC: are the initials of the reservation agent who processed the reservation.
e) 63: Consecutive numbering of all reservation confirmation numbers issued in the current year.

Registration Activities

In the semi and fully automated systems, most of the registration activities are handled at the pre-arrival stage while in the manual system they are conducted at the arrival stage. Registration encompasses the following major activities:

1. Creating the registration record
2. Assigning the room & rate
3. Fulfilling special requests

Pre-registration Activities

At the semi and fully automated systems, guests with reservations experience experience a more rapid check-in due to the information collected by reservation clerks during the reservation process. However, at the manual system, it is inconvenient to pre-register guests at the exception of VIP's and groups. For, VIP's, even under the manual system, need to feel different than other guests. Moreover, group reservations, even though time consuming, might create time benefits at the arrival stage. Lastly, whatsoever operating system the hotel opts for, all walk-ins shall be registered at the arrival stage of the guest cycle.

Registration Record

The registration record is a collection of important personal and financial guest information. A typical registration record includes:

a) Guest name and surname
b) Guest address and telephone number
c) Company affiliation
d) Expected arrival date
e) Planned departure date or length of stay
f) Required room rate
g) Required room type

h) Room number
i) Method of payment
j) Special requests
k) Signature

Rate Assignment

The hotel shall identify and allocate an available room from a specific required room category. That's why, under semi and fully automated systems, reservation and check-in clerks shall be sales minded while negotiating room and rate assignment with guests. This fact applies for registration clerks under the manual system. Moreover, while assigning rooms, check-in clerks shall keep an eye on hotel's future reservation commitments and not assign a room to a guest, while that very room is preassigned to some other guests at the same period of time.

While pricing rooms, the hotel shall keep in mind that rate should be between a minimum (determined by cost structure) and a maximum (determined by competition structure) boundary as depicted below:

Minimum (Hurdle Rate) < Room Rate < Maximum (Rack Rate)

Cost Structure < Room Rate < Competition Structure

Front office department shall finalize room rates with guests during the registration process. Moreover, rack rates shall only be applicable for walk-ins especially during the high season. Lastly, room rates might be affected by:

a) Seasonality
b) Variations in the number of guests assigned to rooms
c) Service level
d) Room location
e) Type of Guest and/or usage.

At registration, check-in clerks shall contact the housekeeping department to be informed about the last status of hotel rooms so that they can assign only clean and available for sale rooms to their guests. That's why, the Front office, Housekeeping and Reservation department shall maintain a high degree of collaboration between them. In order to be sales minded and convince potential guests to accept the highest priced rooms, the front office clerk shall be aware of the characteristics of each room type, the differences within the same room category.

Method of Payment

Guests, at the registration stage, shall communicate or confirm their intended method of payment. Below are the common methods of payments accepted by hotels:

— *Cash*: Guests intending to settle their accounts by cash shall have no in-house charge privileges and, hence, all their purchases should be paid in advance (i.e. PIA status), which means that as guests purchase any kind of service or product, they shall pay for it immediately. In accordance to cash payment, registration clerks shall prepare lists of PIA guests and communicate them to all Point of Sales outlets. On the other hand, paying immediately might not suit some guests, that's why hotels might give guest charge privileges, at the condition they provide an imprint of a valid card or an approved direct billing privilege at registration.

— *Personal checks*: Nowadays, very few hotels still accept personal checks as a method of payment due to the high probability of fraud associated with this method. In fact, in order to accept personal checks, most hotels necessitates that these very checks be supported by a credit card with a check-cashing guarantee, that the amount to be cashed against checks shall be within the hotel's established limit, and preferably accept personal checks only during standard business hours where banks are open. If personal checks are to be accepted, front office personnel shall imprint the credit card on the backside of the guest personal check and record the Guest ID card or driving license certificate along with the guest's address and telephone number on the face of the check.

— *Credit Cards*: Credit cards, nowadays, become a preferable method of payment for guests and hotels. In accordance to this very method of payment, front office clerks should check the following items before accepting the credit card as a method of payment:

  — Expiration date
  — *Invalid credit card*: This can be checked either by on-line authorization systems, or comparing the card across some cancellation bulletins
  — Credit card floor limit.

Direct Billing

Some guests do not prefer to wait at checkout queues like other guests before departure. They, rather, prefer, only to sign their guest folios, go to their homes, later receive a certain invoice detailing their charges while they were staying at the hotel to be settled by payment to hotel bank accounts. In order to satisfy the needs of this category of guests, hotels created the direct billing process. To be eligible for a direct billing privilege, guests shall at pre-arrival stage or maximum at the arrival stage fill a hotel credit application form along with the provision of an imprint of a valid credit card. This very form is sent to the Front Office manager, or Rooms Division manager for approval. If not approved, guests are requested to pay with any of the other methods of payments.

Issuing Room Keys

With the issuing of room keys, the rooming process gets to an end. However, concerning room keys, front office clerks shall respect hotel's written policies governing guestroom key control. As an illustration, front desk agents shall only handle the room key to the guest without announcing and/or spelling out the room number. This is a vital requirement to protect and ensure guest safety and privacy. After guest is handed his/her room key, front office clerks shall offer bellboy assistance.

Fulfilling Special Requests

The front office department shall watch for any guest special requests and try promptly to satisfy them. This way creates a good and professional relationship with the guests and increases the probability that the hotel will receive these guests for another time in the future (i.e. repeat guests). Guests' requests are usually grouped under the following categories:

a) Room type

b) Bed type

c) View

d) Location

e) Amenities

Some of the following innovations are nowadays commonly used while registering a guest:

a) Eliminating the front desk structure (i.e. deskless environment)

b) Having a hotel greeter register guests at a special lobby location

c) Creating a unique & separate registration area for VIP guests

d) Simplification of room process for corporate gatherings, tour , and convention groups Self registration (i.e. self check-in terminals)

Front Office Accounting

The front office accounting system is responsible for:

— Creating and maintaining an accurate accounting record for each guest or non-guest in the hotel

— Tracking all financial transactions throughout the guest cycle

— Ensuring internal control over cash and non-cash transactions

— Recording settlement for all goods & services provided

The front office accounting system shall be customised and tailored to track each hotel's needs. Therefore, no two hotels have exactly the same front office accounting systems.

Generally Accepted Accounting Principles (GAAP) are the following:

— *Unit of Measurement*: Companies operating in a specific country shall use that country's local currency as a unit of measurement.

— *Historical Cost*: The principle of historical cost states that the value of merchandise or services obtained through business transactions should be recorded in terms of actual costs, not current market values.

— *Going Concern*: The principle of going concern (also known as continuity of the business unit) requires financial statement to be prepared under the assumption that the business will continue indefinitely and thus carry out its commitments. Normally, a business is assumed to be a going concern unless there is objective evidence to the contrary.

— *Conservatism*: The principle of conservatism guides the decisions of accountants in areas that involve estimates and other areas that may call for professional judgement. Therefore, the principle of conservatism provides accountants with a practical alternative for situations that involve doubt. In these very situations, the solution or method shall be the one that does not overstate assets or income.

— *Objectivity*: This very principle states that all business transactions must be supported by objective evidence proving that the transactions did in fact occur.

— *Realisation*: Under the realisation principle, revenues resulting from business transactions are recorded only when a sale has been made and earned, when a hotel receives cash from a guest served in the dining room, for example.

— *Matching*: The matching principle states that all expenses must be recorded in the same accounting period as the revenue that they helped to generate. When expenses are matched with the revenue they helped to produce, external and internal users of financial statements can make better judgements about the financial position and operating performance of the hospitality business. There are two accounting methods for determining when to record results of a business transaction: cash accounting and accrual accounting.

— *Consistency*: The generally accepted accounting principle of consistency states that, once an accounting method has been adopted, it should be followed consistently from period to period. This way, accounting information can be comparable.

All guest folios shall be created during the pre-arrival or arrival stage of the guest cycle. Moreover, folios might be either placed in front desk folio tray [i.e. posting tray, folio well, or bucket] or stored as an electronic guest folios in fully automated systems. As far as walk-ins are concerned, all their guest folios are created at the arrival stage!

Record Keeping Systems

— *Non- automated systems*: Ensured through a series of columns listing individual debit and credit entries accumulated during the occupancy stage after which and establishment of an ending outstanding balance is needed.

— *Semi-automated systems*: Under this very system, all guest transactions should be printed sequentially on a machine-posted folio. Later, the front office clerk needs to come up with the folio outstanding balance. It is extremely important here to mention that, under this very system, each account's previous balance shall be re-entered each time a transaction is posted to the folio.

— *Fully-automated systems*: All guest charges are automatically posted to an electronic folio

Guest Charge Privileges

Potential guests who would like to have guest charge privileges shall present an imprint of an acceptable credit card or direct billing authorisation at registration. Failing to do so, guests would have to pay, in full, all their charges through cash, hence called Paid-in-Advance [PIA] guests and have, hence, have no post status.

Credit Monitoring

In order to monitor and control charge privileges, the front office clerk should check whether the total net purchases are less than the minimum of floor Limit (i.e.: credit card company's limit) and house limit (i.e. hotel's limit). At least, each day, lists of guests with high risk or high balance accounts shall be communicated to all point of sale outlets. This is vital since, failing to do so, will let point of sales outlets continue giving charge privileges to a point that eventually the credit card company refuses to pay the amount of money exceeding its limit. This will cause very serious financial losses to the hotel.

Tracking Transactions

Under the manual and semi-automated systems, tracking transactions is ensured through an intensive use of vouchers. On the other hand, Under fully automated systems, tracking transactions is ensured through on-line electronic transfer of transactional information from remote points of sale to the front office main frame terminal. In accounting, a transaction is an exchange of goods and services for cash or a promise to pay. Under this very assumption, "nothing happens until a transaction occurs". This means that front office clerks shall first of all have a transaction, its supporting documents to be able later to debit or credit certain accounts. In hotels transactions might have the form of:

— *Cash payment*: In this very transaction, front office clerks shall post cash payment as a credit in the guest folio. Moreover, cash vouchers shall be used as a transaction-supporting document.

— *Charge purchase*: Charge purchases represent deferred payment transactions that increase the outstanding balance of a folio account. In this transaction type, front office clerks shall use charge vouchers as a transaction-supporting document.

— *Account correction*: Account correction is used to resolve a posting error in a folio detected at the day the error is made (i.e. before the closing of the business day). In this transaction, front office clerks shall use correction vouchers as a transaction-supporting document.

— *Account allowance*: Account allowances occur because of two reasons:

— Either as compensation of poor service, or as rebates for coupon discounts. That way, guest outstanding balance decreases.

— As to correct a posting error detected after the closing of the business day.

Internal Control

In the hotel industry, the main purpose of internal control is to track transaction documentation, verify account entries and account balances, and to identify vulnerabilities in the accounting system. The keyword to internal control is auditing, which is the process of verifying front office accounting records for accuracy and completeness. Below are some forms that are of extreme importance to internally control, one of the most vital assets in the hotel:

— *Front office cash sheet*: The front office cash sheet lists each cash receipt or disbursement in order to reconcile cash on hand at the end of a cashier's shift with the documented transaction that occurred during the same shift.

— *Cash, house banks or petty cash*: Petty cash is the amount of cash assigned to a cashier so that he/she can handle the various transactions that occur in a particular work shift. At the beginning of each shift, all cashiers must sign their cash banks and at the end of the shift, shall deposit all cash, checks, and other negotiable instruments in the general cashier's safe deposit box. Moreover, at the end of each shift, cashiers should watch out for cash discrepancies.

Cash discrepancies might have the form of cash overages, shortages, or due backs. Lastly, cashiers might come up with the net cash receipt, which is: Amount of all cash, checks, and other negotiable instruments in cashier's drawer—amount of the initial cash bank + all paid outs

— *Audit control*: Along with the fact that hotels might employ internal control auditors, at least once in a year, to get use of external certified public accountants responsible for approving hotel's accounts.

Accounts Settlement

One of the responsibilities of front office clerks is to settle guest accounts, which means the eventual collection of payment for outstanding account balances. This is usually ensured either by full cash payment, transfer to an approved credit card, personal check, special programme, or direct billing account. Checkout and settlement describe the activities associated with the final stage of the guest cycle (i.e. departure). The major activities, which are conducted at departure, include:

— Resolving outstanding guest account balances
— Updating room status information
— Creating guest history records

Departure Procedures: At checkout, front office clerks shall:

— Check for mails, messages, and faxes
— Check for safe deposit box, or in-room safe keys
— Post all outstanding charges
— Verify account information
— Inquire about additional recent charges
— Present the guest folio for guest signature
— Verify the method of payment

— Process the account payment
— Update the room status

Methods of Settlement

— *Full cash payment*: the front office clerk shall destroy the guest's credit card voucher
— *Personal check payment*: the front office clerk shall shift the credit from guest ledger to personal check account, which is a sub-account of the city ledger and the guest shall only sign a personal check voucher
— *Credit card payment*: the front office clerk shall shift the credit from guest ledger to credit card account, which is a sub-account of the city ledger and the guest shall only sign a credit card voucher
— *Special programme payment*: the front office clerk shall shift the credit from guest ledger to special programme account, which is a sub-account of the city ledger and the guest shall only sign a special programme voucher
— *Direct billing payment*: the guest shall sign only his/her folio, and depart. Later, he/she, upon receipt of hotel invoice, shall deposit a certain amount of money in the hotel bank account.
— *Combined settlement method*: In this case, depending on which combination, front office clerk shall proceed by preparing different kinds of vouchers!

Sales minded cashiers: As guests tends to depart from the hotel, the cashiers shall approach them in the following way:

— Provide them comment cards and encourage them to use these very cards
— Thank the guest for choosing the hotel and wish him/her a safe trip

— Ask the guest whether he/she is considering returning to the property on any return trip to the area. Cashiers might sometimes accept future reservations!

Late check out: Late check out refers to the situation where guests check out after the hotel's established check out time. Late check out shall not be considered as a guest right, rather a privilege which might be honoured by the front office manager upon room availability whether free of charge or charged a late check out fee. There are a lot of innovative ways to check out apart from the traditional way. Below are two commonly used check out options:

— *Express check out*: This is usually convenient for guests who decide to check out very early in the morning. In fact, at night, bellboys (for example) shall slip the guest folio under the expected departed guestroom. When the guest wakes up, he/she shall sign the gust folio, and the credit card voucher, leave the room, give back the room key to the bellboy, and departs.

— *Self check out*: Guests might check out using self check out terminals situated at public areas or in their rooms if in-room check out systems are integrated with front office main frame.

Unpaid Account Balances: Unpaid account balances occur because of the following reasons, most of which are because hotels do not operate fully-automated systems:

— A departing guest honestly forgetting to settle his/her account

— Late charges

— Skippers

In order to minimise late charges, front office clerks shall:

— Post transactional vouchers as soon as they arrive at the front desk

— Survey front office equipment, voucher and folio racks

for non-posted charges before the front office clerk checks a guest out

— Ask departing guests whether they have incurred any charge purchase or placed long distance telephone calls, which do not appear on their final folio

Account Collection

All unpaid account balances shall be transferred to city ledger accounts, which might have the form of:

— Credit card billing
— Direct billing
— Travel agency accounts
— Bad check accounts
— Skipper accounts
— Disputed bills accounts
— Guaranteed reservation accounts
— Late charge accounts
— House accounts

In order to receive all their city ledger accounts, hotels shall devise effective and efficient account receivables billing procedures.

Expense Accounting

In the accounting terminology, expense is an income statement account representing the cost of items consumed in the process of generating revenue or that expires due to the passage of time. Expense cannot be mixed with expenditure. For, Expenditure represents the purchase amount of a certain asset. In the hotel industry, expenses are divided into two main categories:

Direct expenses

These are the expenses that vary with the level of production. For example, in the Food and Beverage department, the Cost of Food Sales is a direct expense. For, the more dishes we serve, the more cost of Food Sales the Hotel incurs. Moreover, in the Telephone Department, the Cost of Calls is a direct expense. For, the more we connect guests to whatever destination wanted, the more cost of calls the hotel incurs. At this very stage a bracket would be opened to explain that there is a primordial difference between revenue generator departments.

In fact, revenue generator departments are classified into two: Service Type departments versus merchandising departments. Service type departments are revenue generators making money from solely providing services. On the other hand, merchandising departments ensure revenue by getting use of certain raw material, processing it, and than sell the final product. Therefore, only merchandising departments have a direct expense called Cost of Sales.

The various types of Rooms Division department direct expenses include:

— *Commissions expenses*: This account includes payments by the hotel to authorised agents that bring room business to the hotel. Usually at the end of each month, hotels sit with these agents in order to reconcile their monthly sales figures and authorise commission payment.

— *Reservation expenses*: This expense account represents any payment to various agents contracting to bring potential room revenue business to the hotel.

— *Contract cleaning expenses*: This expense account represents payment to contracting outside cleaning agencies. Some hotels might opt for contract cleaning because of its attractive financial implications. If this is the case, these hotels might not be forced to have a housekeeping department, or might keep housekeeping staff to minimum. Such expenses should be determined in light of the contract signed between both parties.

— *Laundry and dry cleaning expenses*: This cost applies to outside laundry and dry cleaning costs for the Rooms Division department. In most of the cases, such contracts are signed to benefit more than one revenue generator. In this case, the rooms division department shall report the laundry and dry cleaning expenses related only to the Rooms Division department.

– *Guest transportation expenses*: These expenses include the cost of transporting guests from and to the hotel via various means of transportation. If the guest transportation's volume business, staff, and costs are significantly high, then a separate department might be established.

— *Linen expenses*: This specific expense account includes the allocation of a portion of linen expenditure for a specific period of time. This practice goes along with one of the accounting principles: the matching principle. Some sub-accounts of linen expense might be:

— Towels expenses

— Blankets expenses

— Facecloth expenses

— heets expenses

— Pillow expenses

— *Guest supplies expenses*: This account includes the various guest supplies provided free of charge to guests in their rooms. Some sub-accounts of guest supplies expenses might include:

  - Newspaper expenses
  - Guest stationary expenses
  - Shoe cloth expenses
  - Coffee expenses
  - Writing supplies expenses
  - Toilet requisites expenses
  - Flowers expenses
  - Hangers expenses
  - Matches expenses
  - Ice expenses
  - Candy expenses
- *Cleaning supplies expenses*: Such an account includes the cost of Rooms Division's cleaning supplies. Some sub-accounts of guest supplies expenses might include:
  - Brooms expenses
  - Soaps and polishes expenses
  - Cleaning cloths expenses
  - Mops expenses
  - Cleaning chemicals expenses
  - Dusters expenses
  - Brushes expenses
  - Insecticides expenses
  - Dustpans expenses
  - Pail expenses
  - Disinfectants expenses
  - Cleaning accessories expense
- *Printing and stationary expenses*: This expense account includes printed formats, office supplies, printed manuals and guidelines for the use of the Rooms Division employees.

— *Uniforms expenses*: This expense account includes the allocation of a portion of uniforms asset for a certain period of time along with the expense of repairing, and cleaning them. If the hotel rents uniforms rather than purchasing them, then the uniform expense shall include the renting cost, usually predetermined in light of the contract linking the hotel and the uniform renting company.

Indirect expenses

These are the expenses that do not vary with the level of production, or variable costs that can not be feasibly distributed to various Financial Reporting Centers. In the hotel industry, indirect expenses are, hence, divided into two different categories:

Fixed Charges: Examples might include rent, insurance, property taxes, and interest expense. For, these very expenses are incurred for the benefit of the hotel as a whole not for the benefit of each single department. To illustrate, if a hotel insures itself against fire, theft and burglary, and one day some valuable equipment has been stolen, from any department whatsoever, the insurance company will indemnify the hotel.

Undistributed Expenses: Examples might include electricity, energy, and water expenses. For, usually the hotel receives a total energy bill to be paid. In the old days, some hotels went for allocating this amount according to certain factors. However, this practice proved to be misleading, since it might under-allocate energy expenses for some departments and over-allocate it for others.

Other Responsibilities

The work of a receptionist involves spending a lot of time

dealing with guest enquiries of all descriptions. The ability to answer guest enquiries accurately and promptly is the key to good customer service. While it may not be possible to know all the answers, to all questions, all the time, there are steps you can take to ensure that each guest enquiry is dealt with satisfactorily.

Enquiry

The type of enquiry you can expect to get on reception usually falls into three categories:

— *Reservation*: to deal with enquiries about reservations either over the telephone or in person, the receptionist must have on hand up-to-the-minute information of room status, the advance reservation chart, and the hotel directory and room rates/tariffs.
— *Information for the guest*: guests have come to expect reception staff to have all sorts of information at their fingertips. Enquiries can range from the cost of sending a postcard to Europe, to car rental facilities, to information on places of interest in the locality.
— *Information regarding guests:* enquiries about guests should be handled with caution and discretion. All guests are entitled to a measure of privacy and protection and any person requesting information about a guest, for example, the name and room number of a resident, should be referred to a supervisor or manager.

Receptionists are right if they believe that the customer expects them to know everything. Of course you cannot know everything, but it should be in your power to satisfy the guest's need, whatever the nature of the enquiry. As this is the service that is most likely to be in demand from reception or the information desk, you should build up your knowledge, particularly of the most frequently asked questions. These may include information on:

— the hotel facilities and services
— the locality—geographic location
— the locality—places of interest
— local services, e.g. transport, places of worship, airline offices, etc.
— entertainment—restaurants, theatre, etc
— additionally, foreign visitors may request information on local customs, cultural issues and language.

So while it may not be possible for the receptionist to have the answers to all questions, it is important to know where to get the answer and how. Every effort should be made to assist the guest with his enquiry. To do so promptly and accurately will require you having access to a range of information directories. You should have:

— a list of all the facilities and services in the hotel, with details such as opening times
— a list of names of members of staff, their job titles and telephone extensions
— details of what is happening from day-to-day throughout the hotel
— a good idea of what goes on in the locality so that you can inform guests looking for details of church services, entertainment and so on
— good reference sources to hand, such as local papers, telephone and trade directories, relevant street maps and so on
— timetables of local transport services
— tourist guide book of the region

Having the information on hand is of no use unless you know how to use the reference material you have. Make sure you find out how to use the reference books in the hotel to get the information you need—know how to use the index system, read timetables and interpret the postal tariffs. Adopt a simple general procedure to deal with standard enquiries:

— Greet the customer with a smile.

— Listen carefully to find out the requirements.

— Make a note of the relevant details if necessary.

— To avoid misunderstandings, repeat the main points back to the customer. Take special care if the enquiry is complicated, or the person has difficulty hearing.

— Ask further questions if you still are unclear.

— Deal with the enquiry immediately.

You should always try and deal with a guest enquiry yourself as it is very annoying for the guest if he has to ask several different staff members the same question. However there will be times when you cannot answer the enquiry and will have to direct the guest elsewhere. You should know what type of enquiries it is better not to try to answer but to pass on to the appropriate person. Some examples of these may include:

— What special discounts can be given to a group booking—refer to the front office manager or another senior manager

— Whether the hotel can accommodate a wedding on a particular day- refer to the banqueting manager

— Can the receptionist book an airline seat—refer to the local travel agent

Handling of Emergency Situations

You should be aware of enquiry situations, which could be regarded as emergencies, requiring an immediate and urgent response, for example, and a request for medical attention. Each hotel will have its own procedure for dealing with these situations and you should familiarise yourself with the practice in your hotel. Very often the principle will remain the same:

— Ascertain the facts

— Repeat and confirm the essential details

— Action immediately—it is usual in emergency situations to contact the supervisor or manager immediately

— Record the incident in the reception log book

In cases of emergency the essential points to remember are:

— *Remain calm and act immediately*: Remember that the most important part of the enquiry process is communication. Effective communication—with guest, colleagues and interdepartmental is essential to ensure a high level of customer service and guest satisfaction.

Keep this checklist with you as a useful reminder of what you should do not should not do when dealing with guest enquiries.

Handling Mail and Messages

When handling mail and messages it is important to process them promptly and efficiently. This is good customer relations practice where the principles of speed, accuracy and professionalism are all key to "getting the job done" to the highest possible standard. The range of mail and messages you are likely to be dealing with are:

— *Incoming mail*: Received via the postal system, mail may arrive for various departments in the hotel, hotel guests and staff. With the arrival of new technology it is now possible to receive "letters" by Facsimile (the fax machine) or via the computer terminal, which is known as electronic mail or e-mail.

— *Outgoing mail*: Letters and packages for posting.

— *Messages*: Telephone and personal messages for your own and other departments in the hotel and hotel guests.

It is necessary to have a procedure for receiving, recording and distributing all types of incoming mail both for guests and the hotel to ensure that the right message gets to the right person with the minimum delay. A simple and efficient procedure would involve:

— Time/date stamp all mail as soon as is received.

— Record in the mail register.

— Sort into appropriate batches—internal and guest.

— Distribute promptly.

Guest mail may fall into four categories and therefore it is important to know how to handle each type efficiently. The following procedures are suggested:

— Mail for guests in residence

  — Sort alphabetically.

  — Check against the alphabetical guest list and write the room number on the envelope.

  — Place in the appropriate pigeonhole in the letter rack. Large envelopes, packages, and registered mail will need to be stored in a separate place.

  — Notification may be sent to the guest to tell him that mail has arrived, for example, if the hotel has a telephone message light system this might be activated.

  — Alternatively, the hotel may operate a delivery system where standard mail is delivered to the guest room by the porter/bellboy.

  — A notification memo is placed in the pigeonhole in the letter rack asking the guest to collect it if a registered letter or package is received at the reception or information desk.

— *Mail for departed guests*: Many guests will leave a forwarding address, filling in a mail forwarding form. These are kept on file for a specified length of time. Once the expiration date passes, the cards should be removed. Any mail arriving after that date, or if no forwarding address was left, is returned to sender via the post office.

— *Mail for future guests*: Mail for guests yet to arrive is sorted into alphabetical order and kept to one side. The advance reservation list is checked for the guest's arrival date, a note made in the hotel diary that mail is being held, and on the appropriate date it is placed in the letter rack. Hotels with a computer system can check the guest records and leave a message on the computer for the guest at check-in.

— *Mail for which no record of a guest can be found*: This mail should be held over for a specified number of days and checked daily against the arrivals list in case a guest arrives who did not have a reservation or there was a misspelling in the guest name originally. If after the specified number of days the name can still not be found then the mail is returned to sender via the post office.

Registered mail and special delivery services, for example DHL, must be signed for by the person accepting delivery and in turn must be signed for by the guest on collection. The recommended procedure for handling deliveries of this sort is:

— Enter into a logbook with date, time of arrival, and receipt number

— Place under lock and key or in a safe

— A notification memo is placed in the letter rack or the message light is switched on asking the guest to collect.

— The logbook is signed by the guest to confirm that they have taken delivery

However, you should always check the hotel policy and procedure regarding this and follow the guidelines accordingly.

If reception is responsible for dealing with any outgoing mail then a procedure is necessary to ensure that this mail is dispatched with the minimum delay. A standard procedure might be:

— Set a deadline for receipt of mail to be mailed that day.
— Make regular collections from the various departments throughout the day.
— Sort and weigh to ensure the correct postage is affixed.
— Post office receipts for registered mail should be attached in a special book kept for that purpose.

Handling messages

Messages are normally conveyed in writing or verbally. Many of which will need to be passed on by the receptionist to another person who may be:

— A member of staff
— A customer, guest, conference delegate, visitor, friend, relative or colleague of a customer
— A potential customer

If you receive a message for someone else verbally it is always a good idea to write it down rather than pass it on verbally, especially if the message is complicated or the person to receive it is not available straight away.

Procedure for taking messages:

— Establish who the message is for

— Write message down accurately with all the relevant details:

  — Make sure the facts are correct

  — Think what the recipient needs to know

  — Be concise

The most common mistakes when taking down messages over the phone are:

  — Missing out a figure from a telephone number

  — Forgetting to ask the caller's name

  — Not taking the callers telephone number

— Repeat the message back to caller

— Pass on the message immediately or as soon as possible.

— Check if possible that the recipient has understood.

Messages may also be conveyed to guests via an in-house paging system. The system may vary in each hotel but the common methods are:

— *Paging board*: A page or bellboy walks through the lobby and public areas usually ringing a small bell to get the attention of guests, carrying a board with the name of the guest prominently displayed. This system alerts all guests that there is a message for someone and the onus is on the guest to check if the message is for him.

— *Public address*: An announcement can be made over a public address system requesting the guest by name to identify him for a message or telephone call.

Reception frequently sells postage stamps to guests as a service to them. It is important to be familiar with the postal rates and know how to look up postal charges on the postal tariff list. As this task involves the handling of cash, some form of control procedure should be in place to keep a record of sales and cash. Post cards may also be available and a similar control procedure should be in place.

Evaluation of Front Office Operations

A successful front office manager shall continuously evaluate the results of department activities on a daily, monthly, quarterly, and yearly basis. While evaluating, the following items and tools shall be used:

1. *Daily operations report*: It is also known as the manager's report, the daily report, and the daily revenue report. This very report contains a summary of the hotel's financial activities during a 24-Hour period. Moreover, it serves as to reconcile cash, bank accounts, and revenue and accounts receivable, and as an important data that must be input to link front and back office computer functions.
2. *Occupancy ratios*: Occupancy ratios measure the success of the front office in selling the hotel's primary product (i.e. guestrooms). Some common ratios used in the front office department are given below:
   — *Occupancy percentage* = (number of rooms occupied)/ (total number of rooms available for sale)

   — *Multiple occupancy percentage* = (number of rooms occupied by more than one guest) / (total number of rooms occupied)

   — *Average guests per rooms sold* = (total number of guests)/ (total number of rooms sold)

   — *Average daily rate* = (total rooms revenue) / (total number of rooms sold)

   — *Average rate per guest* = (total rooms revenue) / (total number of guests)

3. *Rooms revenue analysis*: One main report to enhance control over room revenue is the room rate variance report, which is the one that lists those rooms that have been sold at rates other than their rack rates. Another form is the yield statistic, which is the ratio of the actual revenue to the total possible potential revenue if all rooms are sold at rack rates.
4. *Hotel income statement*: This very statement provides important financial information about the results of hotel operations for a given period of time
5. *Rooms division income statement*: The rooms division income statement shall be referenced on the hotel's income statement. Moreover, the rooms division schedule shall be prepared by hotel's accounting division not the hotel's front office accounting staff.
6. *Rooms division budget reports*: These reports are monthly budget forms that compare actual revenue and expense figures against budgeted amounts depicted both in dollar values and percentage variances
7. *Operating ratios*: Operating ratios assist managers in evaluating the success of front office operations. Moreover, for ratios to be meaningful they should be compared against proper standards such as prior period's, competitor's, and/or budgeted ratios.

7

Customer Relationship Management

Customer Relationship Management (CRM)—a managerial philosophy that enables a firm to become intimately familiar with its customers—is currently gaining widespread popularity in many industries. Firms that embrace CRM strive to provide consistent and personal customer service over time and across multiple touch points. At first glance, the lodging sector, with its emphasis on customer service and multiplicity of customer touch points, seems ideally positioned to take advantage of CRM initiatives.We believe, however, that the current structure of the lodging industry gives rise to a "data-ownership dilemma," which appears to be limiting the adoption of a comprehensive CRM approach.

The three parties typically involved in running a hotel—the owner, the management company, and the brand (*Brand* refers to the franchiser that flags a given property, e.g., Hilton, Marriott, Six Continents)—have partially misaligned interests and, as a result, often resist sharing customer data, a prerequisite for successful CRM.

Customer Relationship Management (CRM) is currently one of the hottest topics in the fields of business strategy, information technology, and marketing management. Put simply, CRM is a management philosophy that calls for the reconfiguration of the firm's activities around the customer.

CRM can be the single strongest weapon you have as a manager to ensure that customers become and remain loyal. CRM is the single strongest weapon you have, even before your people. Sound like heresy? Let us explain what we mean.

Great employees are, and always will be, the backbone of any business. But employee performance can be enhanced or hampered by the strategy you set and by the tools that you give employees to get the job done. Done right, CRM is both a strategy and a tool, a weapon, if you will. In your hands, and in the hands of your employees, CRM comes to life, keeping you and your team on course and able to anticipate the changing landscape of the marketplace. With CRM, loyal customers aren't a happy accident created when an exceptional customer service representative, salesperson or product developer intuits and responds to a customer need. Instead, you have at your fingertips the ultimate advantage-customer intelligence: data turned into information and information turned into acustomer-satisfying action.

Implementing CRM is a nonnegotiable in today's business environment. Whether your customers are internal or external, consumers or businesses, whether they connect with you electronically or face to face, from across the globe or across town, CRM is your ticket to success.

Customer Relationship Management is a comprehensive approach for creating, maintaining and expanding customer relationships. Let's take a closer look at what this definition implies.

First, consider the word "comprehensive." CRM does not belong just to sales and marketing. It is not the sole responsibility of the customer service group. Nor is it the brainchild of the information technology team. While any one of these areas may be the internal champion for CRM in your organization, in point of fact, CRM must be a way of doing business that touches all areas. When CRM is delegated to one area of an organization, such as IT, customer relationships will suffer. Likewise, when an area is left out of CRM planning, the organization puts at risk the very customer relationships it seeks to maintain.

The second key word in our definition is "approach." An approach, according to Webster, is "a way of treating or dealing with something." CRM is a way of thinking about and dealing with customer relationships. We might also use the word strategy here because, done well, CRM involves a clear plan. In fact, we believe that your CRM strategy can actually serve as a benchmark for every other strategy in your organization. Any organizational strategy that doesn't serve to create, maintain, or expand relationships with your target customers doesn't serve the organization. Strategy sets the direction for your organization. And any strategy that gets in the way of customer relationships is going to send the organization in a wrong direction. You can also consider this from a department or area level. Just as the larger organization has strategies-plans-for shareholder management, logistics, marketing, and the like, your department or area has its own set of strategies for employee retention, productivity, scheduling, and the like. Each of these strategies must support managing customer relationships.

CRM is about the entire customer cycle. When you implement your CRM strategy, you will capture and analyze data about your targeted customers and their targeted buying habits. From this wealth of information, you can understand and predict customer behavior. Marketing efforts, armed with this customer intelligence, are more successful at both finding brand new customers and cultivating a deeper share of wallet from current customers. Customer contacts, informed by detailed information about customer preferences, are more satisfying. Are you a manager whose area doesn't deal with external customers? This part of the definition still applies.

First, you and your team support and add value to the individuals in your organization who do come into direct contact with customers. Again and again, the research has proven that external customer satis- faction is directly proportional to employee satisfaction. That means that the quality of support given to internal customers predicts the quality of support that is given to external customers.

Second, consider your internal customers as advocates for your department or area. For you and your team, CRM is about growing advocates and finding new ways to add value.

Finally, what do we mean by "customer relationships" in today's economy, where we do business with individuals and organizations whom we may never meet, may never want to meet, much less know in a person-to-person sense? CRM is about creating the feel of high touch in a high tech environment. Consider the success of Amazon.com. Both of us are frequent customers and neither of us has ever spoken to a human being during one of our service interactions. The CRM tools that support customer relationship strategy allow to:

— Add value to customer transactions by identifying related items with their "customers who bought this book also bought" feature, in much the same way that a retail clerk might suggest related items to complete a sale.

— Reinforce a sense of relationship by recognizing repeat shoppers and targeting them with thank you's ranging from thermal coffee cups to one-cent stamps to ease the transition to new postal rates.

In short, customers want to do business with organizations that understand what they want and need. Wherever you are in your organization, CRM is about managing relationships more effectively so you can drive down costs while at the same time increasing the viability of your product and service offerings.

CRM differs from traditional marketing initiatives in that, while the latter take predominately a short-term, transaction approach, CRM focuses on maximising revenue from each customer over the lifetime of the relationship by getting to know each one intimately. CRM is also, by definition, a crossfunctional philosophy that calls for substantial business integration. Thus, to implement CRM successfully, a very different mindset is needed: The firm no longer markets to customers, but it fosters a relationship with them through programs that span marketing, operations, information systems, accounting, and other organisational functions.

One of the questions most often asked about CRM is, "why bother?" Changing an organisation's philosophy and methods of operation is troublesome; developing and maintaining in-depth customer databases is expensive and the benefits of the approach are not guaranteed. Day, Dean, and Reynolds neatly summarise the benefits of using CRM.

First, by developing a closer relationship with customers, the firm may gain a competitive advantage and, through increased switching costs, may be able to defend it. Over time individual customers typically educate a company about their individual needs, wants, and preferences—a costly process that they are reluctant to repeat with a rival. Thus, getting to know customers intimately creates a barrier to imitation of the leader's strategy.

Second, effective CRM can lead to increased customer satisfaction. Properly implemented, the customer-company dialogue facilitates the tailoring of products and services closely to individual needs, and the development of new products and services to meet changing needs or even anticipate future needs.

Third, using CRM techniques contributes to decreasing overall marketing expenditure. Acquiring new customers is estimated to be more expensive than keeping existing ones. Figures of between five and seven times as much have been quoted. And, last, developing a closer relationship with customers is thought to increase customer loyalty, and loyal customers are thought to stay with the firm longer, buy more from it, and buy more often. An oft-quoted statistic is that companies can improve profitability by between 25 and 85 percent by reducing customer defections by 5 percent. While the value of loyalty is currently being debated, for some time now lodging firms have been fostering loyalty through frequenttraveler programs and CRM may be seen as the logical next step.

CRM leads to higher profitability due to increased sales, declining customer acquisition costs, and increasing profitability of customers willing to pay a premium for "better" service. Substantial investments in CRM are not right for everyone. In a small or niche business, for example, it is relatively easy to keep in touch with customers' preferences.But because of the significant increase in the amount of information that must be managed as the firm's scale and scope increase, successful CRM requires significant investments in technology, process redesign, and people. An airline or a major international hotel chain must manage substantially larger amounts of data than does a small inn to achieve a similar relationship with its customers. However, information technology (IT)—used appropriately can help mitigate the problem.

Between 1990 and today, the world has seen enormous transformations in the extent to which organisations can deploy computer power. IT allows customer data to be collected, consolidated, manipulated, and analysed on an unprecedented scale, and IT has been identified by many authors as one of the key success factors for CRM implementation. IT allows increased reach into new markets without high incremental entry costs, and facilitates specifically tailored customer marketing and increased responsiveness.

The role of IT in CRM efforts is so important that some writers, and many practicing managers and vendors, associate CRM with the technology that is used to support the approach.Many use the term in the highly specific sense of database marketing, where a range of demographic, lifestyle, and purchasing activities are recorded and tracked, and subsequently used as the basis of targeting differentiated products to selected customer groups. In turn, their response to each marketing contact is tracked and used to further refine the approach.

However, CRM is a broader concept than just technology. For example, CRM has been defined as "an enterprise- wide commitment to identify your named, individual customers and create a relationship between your company and these customers so long as that relationship is mutually beneficial".

This definition highlights several key CRM concepts —that the company will actively seek out the right customers (and, by implication, will not target those that will not do business with them), will develop a long-term, mutually beneficial relationship with each customer by starting and maintaining a two-way dialogue, will strive to satisfy customers' needs and solve customer problems, and will support customers throughout the life cycle of their interactions with the firm.

This approach to CRM demands more than computer systems and information technology. The customer must become the focal point of the organisation. All members of the organisation must understand and support the shared values required for CRM, its philosophy must encompass not just marketing but the entire organisation, and it must be used to manage all aspects of the customer relationship in a coordinated way.

Although limited research about the effectiveness of CRM has been published to date, most observers agree that successful CRM is predicated on the ability to effectively capture exhaustive data about existing and potential customers, profile them accurately, identify their individual needs and idiosyncratic expectations, and generate actionable customer knowledge that can be distributed for ad-hoc use at each point of contact. The objective is to achieve a comprehensive view of customers, and be able to consistently anticipate and react to their needs with targeted and effective activities at every customer touch point.

CRM requires the firm to keep track of the information produced through each interaction so that it can "learn" on a continuous basis, get to know each guest better, and enrich its database of individual customer knowledge. Godin has likened CRM to "dating a customer," in that it is a long-term process that requires an investment of time, information, and resources by both parties. The result is an active, participatory, and interactive relationship between customer and supplier.

Lastly, CRM is about customisation, or the ability to consistently treat different customers differently. Relationships differ as they develop. We do not treat old friends in the same way as new friends or good friends in the same way as casual acquaintances. Such consistent personalised interaction requires integration and synchronisation of many organisational functions, from marketing to accounting to operations and information systems. Failure to understand the scope, essence, and magnitude of CRM is likely to result in problems, rather than its promised benefits.

Power of CRM

The past several years have witnessed an explosion in CRM tools, especially software applications. Your CRM strategy should drive your organizational structure, which should in turn drive choices around technology implementation. Yet, individuals and organizations become enamored of the technology applications and forget that that they must start with a CRM strategy. The language confusion doesn't help. Countless articles and reviews of CRM tools and technologies never mention strategy. They imply, or even come right out and say, that the only thing you need to do to have effective CRM is buy the right application. Yes, the right application is critical. But it is your CRM strategy that informs which application will be right for you. The power of CRM comes from the clarity of your approach. Think for a moment about your personal planner and organizer.

Lodging-industry participants face an increasingly competitive market. In addition, the basis of competition is changing. Location, a key driver of business, is fixed in the short and medium term, and attracting and retaining customers based on facilities and amenities is becoming increasingly difficult as they have become increasingly standardised across competing brands. Price competition is unattractive, even more so as consumers are able to easily find and compare prices over the Internet. As a consequence consumers are increasingly displaying less brand loyalty, and CRM is becoming increasingly attractive as a way for hotel companies to differentiate themselves from their competitors.

The lodging sector is ideally suited to applying the principles of CRM. In few other industries is there such potential to build up a comprehensive and accurate picture of the client. In few other industries do customers provide the significant amount of information hotel guests divulge when making a reservation and during their hotel stay. Every interaction between the guest and the customer is an opportunity to refine knowledge about her or him and to further build a relationship. By methodically collecting, consolidating, and analysing both guest preferences and transactional data, hotel chains have the potential to develop a deep understanding of each customer's needs and preferences, provide substantially improved service levels, individually tailor the customer experience, and generally offer more personalised service.

Providing outstanding personal service is certainly not a new concept in the hotel sector. Companies such as Rits-Carlton and the Savoy group historically maintained extensive manual guest-history systems recording guest preferences in an effort to better serve their best customers. However, when oper- ated manually, such systems are expensive to maintain, are frequently inaccurate, and can only be used to track a limited number of clients at individual properties.

Developments in information and communications technologies have enabled automation and efficiencies in these processes, reducing costs, increasing accuracy, and allowing comprehensive knowledge about each customer to be shared on a global basis. As a result, many companies are turning to technology to improve customer service by implementing large-scale CRM programs.

Analysis of the lodging sector shows that, driven in most cases by pressure from the marketing function, many of the dominant hotel chains are in the process of deploying (or have already deployed) the technological infrastructure to support CRM. A recent study by Arthur Andersen and New York University found that over one-third of U.S. hotel chains had a data warehouse in 2000, with another 50 percent planning to install one in the near future. Many chains have introduced information systems to improve the targeting of marketing and sales efforts. Such systems can help the firm to assess the value of each customer as well as their propensity to respond to various offers, and to market to them individually.

While important, such initiatives do not imply that the company has adopted CRM. In most cases, such developments focus solely on marketing objectives and lack the integration among functional areas that characterises a CRM initiative. Only where the company reconfigures its operations to deliver a comprehensive view of the customer and to support consistent, highly personalised service at every customer touch point could it truly be regarded as CRM. Few companies in the lodging sector appear to have progressed to such an advanced stage. Given the geographic dispersion of hotel properties and the role of brands in marketing and distribution, large-scale CRM initiatives seem most justifiable at the brand level.

Implementing CRM at this level would help to increase consistency and personal service throughout the chain and at each customer touch point. However, to achieve this, consistent and comprehensive information must be captured from all properties within the brand and then consolidated, analysed, interpreted, and subsequently disseminated to each property in time to influence the next customer interaction.

Two barriers currently prevent that from happening—a lack of standardisation and ITsystem integration within each franchise, and the fact that at any one time there may be up to three parties holding a stake in the operations of a particular property.The two issues are largely interconnected as the industry's generally reactive attitude toward IT has been exacerbated by its structural characteristics. The technical challenge is subsiding due to recent developments in technology, including the emergence of the application service provider (ASP) model.

Effective CRM Implementations

Once you've decided to invest in a CRM application, the next steps include a well-developed strategy that is effectively communicated, well-defined business objectives, a well-planned approach, identified data sources and verified data quality. This article describes the right order for effective CRM, and points out some classic mistakes that lead to failed CRM implementations.

The most typical approach to CRM has companies developing point solutions, something that solves one particular problem, out of acute necessity. However, whether you use a consulting firm to help you implement the point solution or you go it alone, you should be sure that the key questions around direction, integration, processes and people are being asked.

Generally speaking, the questions are a lot more easily asked than answered, which leads most companies back to the need for an overarching strategy and the realization that CRM really is a way of running the business, not just the program du jour. Additionally, CRM is a way to increase revenues and/or reduce costs. Not understanding the fact that this is a bottom line strategy could lead you to make the wrong decisions in establishing your strategy.

Everyone wants to be a CRM Hero — the desired outcome. No one wants to be a CRM Zero — the career-limiting option. Allow us to offer five words of advice: don't start by picking software. In addition, it would be prudent to watch for these classic mistakes:

1. *Thinking that CRM is, at its heart, technology-based.* The best example of this is the client who told us, "We need to get a CRM." That makes no sense, for it is not the technology that makes you a hero, it is the recognition and belief by your organization that CRM is a way to operate the company. To accomplish this,

the CRM Hero must demonstrate the leadership necessary to develop a CRM strategy and get the rest of the company to come along for the ride. At the risk of stating the obvious, too many companies we've seen have adroitly demonstrated that they have no clue where their CRM program is going – but, wow, look at all that data! Never mind that they will soon be another case study in failed expectations. However, with a well-conceived strategy that highlights all aspects of the customer relationship, they would be able to clearly articulate the specific changes, tools and techniques that must be employed over time within their organization to deliver measurable results.

2. *So I've made a strategy, let's go get the software.* Not so fast. With clear articulation comes the second step: communicating the strategy to the rest of the company and your guests. Not much new technology is needed for this step, either. However, you are guaranteed to fall short of your CRM goals without effective communication throughout the company. Meanwhile, the CRM Hero grows ever more frustrated that people don't "get it." Yet, people are the most vital, and the most frequently overlooked, part of the equation. As service providers, we all know that our frontline people have the power to make or break the relationships we enjoy with our guests, but it is stunning to note that occasionally this basic truth gets forgotten. If our people don't understand the importance we are suddenly placing on effective relations with our guests, those relations will be anything but effective.

4. *OK, we've got everybody jazzed about this CRM thing; let's get some technology in here to help them.* Sounds great, but help them do what? The same things they did before you got them the technology? While those things worked really well for you under your old way

of managing the business, remember that this is a new way of thinking you're trying to impart. With new thinking must come new ways of working, which means you will need to lead the way in helping your company look at things the same way your guests look at things. These guest-centric business processes are simple in concept, but much more difficult to get your people to design. Some companies have taken the radical step of inviting customers into their process design meetings to be sure they're taking a customer-centric approach.

4. We know what we're trying to do, everybody's on board and our processes are aligned with the desired guest experience – now all I need is a new POS system, a data warehouse, a campaign management tool, new call center software for my reservations agents, a good PMS built on the latest platform and a new yield management tool. It's finally time for technology, but if you follow this approach your systems integrators will be happy, though your IT shop won't be when they have to keep all of these balls in the air. Integration is the key – single points of data collection, techniques for data cleansing and easy ways of getting the right information to the right people in a way that allows for seamless, consistent, personalized service.

Keys to Successful Implementations

1. *The Keep It Simple, Stupid (K.I.S.S.) Principle*. There are a few home truths about successful CRM implementations. The K.I.S.S. principle is highly applicable. Over-complicating the process does one thing – it succeeds in extending the duration, potentially causing budgetary overruns. In the words of Dr. Chekitan Dev, associate professor of strategic marketing at Cornell University's School of Hotel

Administration, "Do not draw up a long-winded program. It is important to have quick hits that show short-term benefits – this will help to get people on board, since they want to see results. Maintain the built-in potential to upgrade...a simple process that grows organically will be the most successful, and yield the best results." If you must plan a gargantuan CRM program, "break it down into shorter-term, focused projects with clearly defined business benefits and success metrics"1 . This brings us to the second key to success.

2. *Actionable Measurements and Performance Metrics.* It is important to ensure that adequate emphasis is placed on establishing timely and actionable measurements. It is crucial to be able to identify the bottom line impact on an ongoing basis of the program that has been established.
3. *Stakeholder Ownership.* If you want to ensure a successful implementation, it is important to ensure that all stakeholders are on board. It is not merely sufficient if key players buy into the process. They must take ownership of, and be actively engaged in the process. For a successful project it is important to have internal champions.
4. *GIGO.* Better known as "Garbage In – Garbage Out," this is the test of stakeholder ownership. Realize that none of the exciting new capabilities are worth anything without good data. In our experience, legacy systems generally have errors in roughly half of their customer records. These could be as simple as an address that reads "road" instead of "street," or as complicated as multiple customer records for the same customer, each with slight differences. Yet you have countless opportunities to capture good data in the course of a guest experience. Part of your business process work has to be to ensure effective capture and

cleansing of customer data. Effective capture implies not sticking all of the good stuff in the comments field, where it likely resides today, completely unread in the hustle and bustle of the typical front desk.

5. *Consider the Value of the Customer.* Successful CRM is not about providing the best service on the block; rather, the key to effective relations with your customers is in providing appropriate service. We all know that customers are not equal. That's why loyalty programs were invented. Yet far too frequently we see clients that developed sophisticated segmentation capabilities and tiered loyalty programs who have no means of differentiating the service they provide to these segments of guests. One resort client was excited about his newfound ability to execute real-time marketing campaigns to fill short-term availabilities at the hugely popular property. Yet he had not considered the value associated with different customer segments and was disappointed when the realization from these last-minute guests was not up to the usual standards of the resort. Simply put, this client was ignoring all of its segmentation data and mass-marketing its limited capacity. Thus, it is important to provide appropriate service at every interaction based upon intelligent segmentation.
6. *Help Your Employees Help Your Guests.* All employees, at all properties, should have the training and up-to-date information that allows them to provide seamless, consistent, personalized service to the customer. According to Jens Thraenhart, director Internet strategy, Fairmont Hotels and Resorts, "A successful CRM and customer retention strategy in the hotel industry is dependent on the implementation at the property level. It is important to train front line employees to capture information from many offline touch points, in combination with online data capture. Training is vital to ensure consistency and cleanliness

of guest information." This information should be immediately available to front desk receptionists, call center agents, pit bosses, concierge and housekeeping staff, and so on, and should be served up at the right time.

7. *Strong internal partnerships around the CRM strategy.* We said earlier that CRM is a way of doing business that touches all areas of your organization. This means that you and your management peers need to form strong internal partnerships around CRM. If you and your organization are early on the road to CRM implementation, now is the time to bring your CRM needs to the table, and to be open to listening to the CRM needs of other areas. You may find that you have requirements that are, at least potentially, in conflict. Resist the temptation to go to war for what you need. If your organization has gone off the partnership road with CRM, then now is the time to come back together and rebuild partnership with the area that is currently championing CRM. Let them know that you appreciate what they have done. Let them know what data you have to offer and help them understand how you plan to use the data you request from them.

8. *Employees at all levels and all areas accurately collect information for the CRM system.* Employees are most likely to comply appropriately with your CRM system when they understand what information is to be captured and why it is important. They are also more likely to trust and use CRM data when they know how and why it was collected.

9. *CRM tools are customer- and employee-friendly.* CRM tools should be integrated into your systems as seamlessly as possible, making them a natural part of the customer service interaction. A major manufacturer of specialty pet foods redesigned the pop-up screens

for its toll-free consumer phone line. In the original design, the final pop-up screen prompted the representative to ask the caller's name and address. Yet, representatives had found that it was easier and felt more natural to ask, "What's your name?" and "Where are you calling from?" and "What's your pet's name?" at the start of the call.

10. *Report out only the data you use, and use the data you report.* Just because your CRM tool can run a report doesn't mean it should. Refer back to your CRM strategy, and then run the data you will actually use. And share that data with your team.

11. *Don't go high-tech when low-tech will do.* At Harley-Davidson outside of Milwaukee, WI, during the summer they often leave open the big metal doors to the manufacturing facility to let in any breeze and the cooler evening air. Unfortunately, open doors occasionally let in other things, including skunks. A team met to consider the problem and possible solutions. After discussing the pros and cons of screens, half-doors, or keeping the doors shut, they came upon the ideal solution. When a skunk wanders in, just leave it alone and wait till it wanders back out. Skunks may be Harley fans, but they never stay long. Organizations that successfully implement CRM look for the simplest solution when implementing their CRM strategy.

A low-tech solution that works for the people who actually use it is more effective than a high tech solution that is cumbersome, costly and apt to be discarded or inconsistently implemented.When aggregate customer information is strategically collected and segmented, you can target new customer prospects. When customer preference information is easily accessible, you can craft superior service experiences-be they face-to-face, via telephone, or over the Internet. And when information about changing or additional customer needs is captured, you can expand the depth of the customer relationship. CRM is the strongest weapon you have to create, maintain, and expand customer relationships and it's here to stay.

This is where the true test of CRM solutions takes place. There is nothing worse for your relationships than raising expectations and then failing to meet them.

— Does the call center know about the e-mail campaign that marketing just sent out?
— Does the front desk recognize that the repeat guest standing before them remembers the way to the elevator and doesn't need a 60-second refresher course complete with maps?
— Does the reservations agent realize that the potential guest on the telephone has used the onsite spa the past three times she has been at the property, and might just want to get services booked in advance?

Truly successful CRM implementations anticipate these kinds of issues and build the requisite business processes, employee training and integrated systems necessary to meet or even exceed growing expectations.

Technology certainly plays an important role in the implementation of a successful CRM project. However, it is not a silver bullet that will solve all problems or open all doors. It is important to remember that all technology decisions are only relevant in a business context. All the technology in the world is cool, but if your business processes aren't set up to effectively utilize these resources, your company will be added to the statistics of failed CRM implementations.

Data-ownership Dilemma

CRM's success is predicated on the ability to collect, analyse, and disseminate large amounts of timely and relevant information for customer-service operatives to act on to improve the experience at each point of customer contact. Thus, a CRM initiative cannot be successful without commitment among a critical mass of properties.

Hotel chains cannot provide a consistently high level of personal service unless customer data can be garnered from most, if not all, of the affiliated properties, organised and synthesised in one central location, and subsequently redistributed to each property on an as-needed basis. However, we propose that (technological constraints aside) this apparently simple theoretical proposition is difficult to realise in the lodging industry due to an inherent data-ownership conflict between the major industry stakeholders. In the following sections we present the main issues facing the brand, the management company, and the owner.

Brand

For brands, the development of an effective CRM initiative is deemed an important competitive move as it would facilitate the development of a deep understanding of customer needs and preferences, potentially resulting in a high level of personalisation, thus helping to improve service levels across the brand as a whole. As a result guests would have a strong incentive to remain loyal to the brand and patronise affiliated properties, thus increasing the value proposition for owners and operators through improvements in financial performance.

For the promised benefits of CRM to materialise, standardised information systems must be implemented throughout the franchise network to allow data to be obtained from all branded properties—a problem in the past, becoming less important as a result of recent technology improvements. Furthermore, the brand must be willing to share the customer knowledge generated by the consolidation of customer data chain-wide with the individuals that can take action based on it at each point of customer contact. Such data sharing presents the first dilemma. In some cases, the brand may be reticent to disseminate customer knowledge back to the property for fear that owners or operators might use it to poach high-value customers and divert them to competing brands within their own portfolios.

For example, imagine a management company that operates a hotel flying one flag (Brand A) in a particular market, and a competing flag (Brand B) in others. This company might be tempted to steer highvalue customers toward its Brand B hotels in markets where it does not operate Brand A hotels. Thus, Brand A is faced with a decision —either share the data it collects companywide to reap the benefits of large-scale CRM and risk the poaching of high-value customers by some of its partner management companies operating individual properties; or protect its customer knowledge from the interests of multi-flag owners and operators, thus forgoing the full benefits of CRM.

The Management Company. Management companies do not appear to have strong incentives to develop a CRM initiative for themselves. Such companies tend to operate a varied portfolio of properties, each flying different flags, on behalf of different owners. By definition a CRM initiative developed across flags is unlikely to generate brand loyalty and thus is of limited interest to most management companies.

The question arises, however, as to whether management companies should actively cooperate with the collection of operational guest data by brand-level CRM initiatives. As most companies operate a varied portfolio of flags, if the management company participates in a brand-based CRM initiative, it will stand to gain only in those properties that carry that particular brand. Conversely, participation will result in a competitive disadvantage in markets where it competes against the brand. As a result, management companies have little incentive to support brand-level CRM initiatives by contributing data about customers that stay at its properties. In fact, by doing so, they would in effect be undermining their own operations in markets where the brand operating the CRM initiative is a competitor rather than an ally.

Moreover, while the management company may not be interested in detailed customer data for branding purposes, it certainly finds value in customer data that allows it to create customer-value models and better target high-value prospects, particularly with respect to group business. Consequently, management companies have in effect an incentive to limit data disclosure and not cooperate with brand-level CRM initiatives.

Owner

While owners, like operators, typically have many flags in their portfolio of properties, they have a different focus in terms of profitability. Many primarily view hotel ownership as a real-estate investment, and have a marginal interest in the question, "Who owns the data?"Where their properties fly the flag of a successful CRM initiative, they may have an advantage over other competing properties; where their properties fly competing flags, they may be at a disadvantage. Thus, the same dilemma facing the management company seems to affect the owners—whether to participate in brandlevel CRM initiatives, or to refuse to cooperate with the collection and consolidation of customer data. The owners may also have interests that go beyond the use of the data strictly for operational purposes. Customer data may be used by the other entities (the brand and the management company) for marketing purposes and analyses that run counter to the owner's own interests (e.g., studying the feasibility of building new properties in the same geographical area).

CRM strategies appear most applicable at the brand level, but their success is dependent on the active cooperation of both the operator and the owner of each property. For CRM to succeed at the brand level, operators must supply the brand with in-depth customer data—a requirement with which operators in particular, and owners to a lesser extent, have little incentive to comply. Brands also face challenges in terms of maintaining control over the resulting customer knowledge and preventing its spread outside the brand network.

Because of this conflict, we believe that CRM in the lodging industry may never progress beyond its current, relatively limited, level of sophistication. While database-marketing techniques will continue to be used, we propose that few hotel companies will successfully implement large-scale, chain-wide, CRM initiatives. Only if significant change occurs in the structure or methods of operation of the sector are the full benefits of a CRM approach likely to be realised. In closing, we speculate as to what changes will have to occur for successful implementation of CRM initiatives. We see three possible scenarios: there will be a fundamental change in the way in which hotel brands are organised; a change in the nature of franchise agreements and management contracts; or there will be more cooperation among brands to take advantage of CRM's promised benefits.

The first scenario is that the need for adoption of a CRM approach will induce changes in the ownership and management structure of the lodging sector. If CRM truly provides compelling benefits, the large brands should begin to pressure the management companies and franchisees within their network to provide the data needed for successful CRM operations. Those brands that manage a relatively large number of their own hotels will be in a good position to take advantage of these initiatives quickly, should face little resistance as a result of the dataownership dilemma, and shoud be able to easily reap the benefits of CRM.

Wyndham International's ByRequest initiative demonstrates that highly integrated lodging brands are moving quickly to embrace CRM. If these pioneers are successful in their effort and are able to attract and retain high-value customers, competing brands will have to follow suit and develop similar CRM capabilities. Such companies would have to resolve the data-ownership dilemma either by "integrating down" or by restricting the number of flags that the companies operating their hotels can fly. Integrating down implies that brands would move aggressively to take over the operational management of their branded properties. Such integrated companies should be able to standardise the IT infrastructure needed to support CRM, mandate the collection and consolidation of customer data, and provide each property with dynamic access to the central knowledge repository. Since all operations would effectively be managed by the brand, there would be no conflicts of interest and no danger of high-value customers being poached, freeing the brand to take full advantage of the CRM initiative.

Obviously, taking over operational control of their unit properties would be a dramatic and high-risk strategy. Thus, brands, particularly in the short term, may instead concentrate on restructuring their management and franchise agreements to minimise the barriers to success discussed earlier. Redevelopment should focus on two main areas —data collection and data use. While many franchise agreements require properties to feed its customer-folio data back to the central level, few specifically mention any other data collected about the guest.

As CRM is dependent on building up a holistic picture of the guest's needs and behavior, this oversight may force brands to restructure contracts to force greater compliance with data needs. Such restructured contracts could spec-ify that all customer data generated at the property level be extracted and loaded to the brand's central data repository. Management contracts also need to be rewritten to offer protection to the brand as it disseminates customer knowledge back to the property level. Both of these measures mean that ties between brands and operators would be strengthened, which may ultimately result in further industry consolidation as owners and operators feel pressure to fly a limited number of flags. In an extreme scenario, each operator would effectively become aligned with one brand and fly only one flag.

The final potential scenario we envision is the emergence of an industry consortium that both develops and maintains the CRM infrastructure and standardises customer-data collection and distribution. As it has happened historically with hotel e-commerce systems such as THISCo (The Hotel Industry Switching Company), HDS (Hotel Distribution Systems) and Avendra (an e-procurement marketplace), competing brands could cooperate to develop the standards and the infrastructure necessary to capture, store, organise, and distribute customer information.

Such a scenario is attractive as joint development would mean that the infrastructure could be delivered and operated at a fraction of the cost of proprietary initiatives. Thereafter, rather than being used as a basis of competition, customer data would be shared and companies would compete on the analysis, interpretation, and use of such data. For example, competing brands could use the same data to market to their chosen customer bases. Competitive advantage would come from how well they could use the data to identify, target, and build a relationship with each individual.

We believe the latter scenario to be the least likely, even though it may optimise industry-wide performance. The likelihood of an industry consortium developing and managing customer information for the benefit of the industry as a whole is small, as the industry's belief in the proprietary value of customer data, the industry's structure, privacy issues, as well as a culture that precludes trust in this domain makes the cooperation necessary unlikely.We see a change in contractual agreements and in industry structure as far more probable. In any case, given the potential proposed for lodging-industry companies, careful consideration must be given to the data-ownership dilemma to avoid failure.

8

Operation and Management of Spas

Spas are becoming such a significant component of the service menu for resorts and fullservice hotels that their absence, especially in amenity-rich resort environments, is glaringly obvious.Within the leisure industries in 2003, revenues related to spas ranked number four behind golf fees and dues ($19.7 million), cruise line revenues ($14.7 million), and health club revenues ($14.1 million). At $11.2 million, spa revenues outpaced amusement park revenues ($10.3 million), box office receipts ($9.5 million), and vacation ownership sales ($5.5 million).

According to the International SPA Association research, between 2002 and 2003, 11 percent of the national population over the age of 16 made one or more spa visits. This statistic shows that one in ten Americans visited a spa during that period. Additionally, of these, 41 percent were visiting spas for the first time, indicating a larger population embracing spa usage. Age demographics show that 14 percent of clients are between the ages of 16 and 24, and over 50 percent are in the 25 to 44 age bracket.

An emerging national statistic is the number of male visits to spas. Twenty-three percent of spa visits and 29 percent of spa goers were men in 2003, trending toward special gender-oriented treatments and male-only spas being opened worldwide.

Spa selection criteria are determined by a number of factors. An established and known environment—for instance, as a part of an established resort, club, or destination spa—often influences the decision, as does atmosphere, quality of treatment, and friendliness of staff. Additionally, among spa goers, nine out of ten respondents report they would return for a similar experience.

Most spa customers believe they received good value for their spa dollar. On a 10-point scale, services were given an average of 8 for value, with massage generating 8.8 on the value-for-service scale.

Spa services demonstrated the highest and heaviest demand on weekends, followed by appointments after work on weekdays. Gender demographics also play a role in spa demand, as men are more likely to go for regular weekly visits after business hours or while traveling on business.Women, however, often visit spas during regular business hours.

The International Hotel Resort Spa Association (IHRSA) reports that branded resort spas such as Canyon Ranch are opening in the day spa market, adding new competitive pressure on the independents. Nontraditional players are also adding product supply. For example, corporations are creating in-house spa environments, hospitals are adding wellness as part of their repertoire, and medi-spas, with a primary focus on cosmetic surgery, are adding spa business as an additional profit center. Health clubs are also trying to capture a piece of the pie by adding spa practices.The rationale in this market is that time-crunched patrons can benefit from the one-stop-shopping approach to fitness and wellness, but the health club operator also uses the spa as an enticement to join the fitness center.

As the day and destination spa markets become saturated, it will become imperative for survival that each operator differentiate from the competition. The necessity for market segmentation to ensure clear communication with consumers will be a key to success in the maturing spa market.Another component of success will be a branding strategy that the consumer can immediately identify with respect to spa performance and the consumer's personal comfort level.

SPA DEMAND

Increasingly, spa goers are looking to create prolonged wellness that integrates and renews body,mind, and spirit.To that end, Eastern and Western lifestyle issues related to medicine, philosophy, and spirituality are becoming a mainstay of many spa/wellness experiences. To best deliver this, the wellness spa (located at day, destination, or resort environments) supports guest needs by creating an experience, not just a series of treatments. All the guest amenities, facilities, treatments, and programs must be seamlessly integrated into a personally tailored guest experience. These experiences should be targeted toward couples, parents with children, and teenagers.

In the early 1990s, spas were considered a natural outgrowth of fitness facilities and focused primarily on treatments related to body wellness. As market sophistication evolved, the body-mind connection attracted consumer focus. In the beginning of the twentyfirst century, spas and marketers are overtly addressing body, mind, and spirit connections in order to respond to emerging market sensibilities. Among the components one might find in a modern spa are services related to:

— Complementary and alternative medicine in mainstream lifestyles

- — Traditional Western medical and Eastern lifestyle/ wellness practices
- — A proactive approach to overall health and the quality of one's life

Body

- — Action spas are attracting a greater percentage of men who are looking for a way to unwind and keep active. Because of this trend, an aggressive array of activities — including cardio-circuit courses, squash, racketball and tennis, free and fixed weights, jogging, and bike paths, hikes, and water spots—is still a basic spa/wellness requirement.
- — As part of the wellness experience, medical affiliations are sometimes available to provide information and to check blood pressure, heart conditions, bone density, and so on.
- — Exceptional food can be tailored to virtually any dietary restriction or request.
- — When examining which body treatments to include, note that salt glows and exfoliant treatments are approximately four times more popular than any other body treatment. These items are a mainstay in successful spa services.
- — Guests must be able to upgrade their experience with add-ons such as eye-firming therapies and mineral-enhanced hydrotherapy soaks. Further, it is important to sell services in several time blocks so guests can select services that fit their schedule and financial budget.

Body, Mind

- — Educational programs at many levels include classes and clinics. These programs personally empower the guest, expand the wellness center's demand base, and encourage repeat visits. Health and wellness issues encompass cardiovascular health, holistic childrearing, the integration of Eastern and Western medical practices, indigenous spiritual practices, aging, intimacy, transition/death, vitality, strength training, cooking programs (macrobiotic, vegan, vegetarian, indigenous), women's issues, and so on. Traditionally, educational programs at spas have focused primarily on personal health issues.

— Mind-body techniques may include spiritual and cultural instruction. Examples include tai chi, visualisation, progressive muscle relaxation and biofeedback, labyrinth walking, meditating and chanting, sweat lodges, and storytelling.

— Extensive yoga programs should include Hatha yoga for body control, Ashtanga yoga for cardio workout, Iyengar yoga for balance and alignment, and Kundalini yoga for breath work.

Body, Mind, Spirit

— Comprehensive touch/alternative manual therapies including chiropractic treatment and deep tissue massage (rolfing, myofascial release, nueromuscular massage, acupressure/ shiatsu, watsu, Trager massage, etc.) are a necessary component of any wellness clinic. This modality is an extension of the basic massage offered at all spas and wellness/healing centers. Practitioners who provide manual therapies should be cross-trained in the areas of subtle energy work such as reiki, chakra balancing, and chi gung. Offering alternative touch/energy therapy as a component of traditional massage has the potential to accelerate market acceptance.

— Ayurvedic treatments are popular and provide an additional link between the East-meets-West philosophy showcased in many day spas. Elements of ayurvedic treatments can be incorporated into most touch therapies.

As far back as 1993, a well-known study by David Eisenberg revealed that one-third of all patients had visited a practitioner of alternative health care in the past year, at a cost of $13.7 billion. This indicated to the medical community that the significant out-of-pocket expenses implied not only lost revenues to traditional (allopathic) doctors but also a broad dissatisfaction with mainstream medicine. A great number of people were taking the issues of health and well-being into their own control, thus setting the stage for the popularity of proactive wellness programs.

In 1997, Eisenberg updated his study. He estimated the total number of visits to alternative medical providers at 600 million, representing an expenditure of over $27.1 billion.

The number of visits to alternative care physicians in 1997 was greater than the total number of visits to traditional primary care physicians in the same year. The increasing popularity of alternative wellness modalities, the aging of the population, and the strength of the economy are all factors that support the growth of this trend. As of this writing, it appears to continue to grow.

The use of at least 1 of 16 (alternative) therapies during the previous year increased from 33.8 percent in 1990 to 42.1 percent in 1997. The fastest-growing therapies were herbal medicine, message, megavitamins, selfhelp groups, folk remedies, energy healing, and homeopathy.The probability of users visiting an alternative medicine practitioner increased from 36.3 percent to 46.3 percent. In both 1990 and 1997, alternative therapies were used most frequently for chronic conditions, especially back problems, anxiety, depression, and headaches. In general, it can be concluded that alternative medicine expenditure increased substantially between 1990 and 1997, and this can be attributed primarily to an increase in the proportion of the population seeking alternative therapies rather than increased visits per patient.

SPA CLASSIFICATION

Spa development and its attendant popularity have deep historical roots and vast potential for the hospitality industry. The term *spa* was once reserved for European destination resorts where guests went to "take the waters" and restore a healthy and balanced life.

However, the term now is used to describe many types of facilities and amenities in the U.S. lodging industry. At one end of the spa spectrum are dedicated destination resort spas aimed primarily at those seeking a specialised combination regime of health, fitness, and pampering. Modalities and treatments include massages, unique treatments, custom dietary plans, lectures, and adventures that can include, but are not limited to, an array of activities ranging from nonsurgical facelifts to helicopter skiing.

Destination resorts, such as Miraval's Life-in-Balance and Canyon Ranch, with locations in the Berkshires in Massachusetts and the Arizona desert, draw demand because of their facilities and reputation. The primary reason for going to a destination resort spa is to enjoy the spa itself and its related activities. The destination itself is a demand generator.

Closely related to a destination resort spa is the amenity spa. Amenity spas provide services to resorts and full-service hotels. The primary difference between an amenity spa and a destination spa is the scope and depth of spa services. Amenity spas, while sometimes quite extensive, *support* the resort environment, whereas destination spas are the *focus* of the resort environment. In situations where a full-service, high-end hotel is located in an urban environment and has a significantly large spa component, the spa can operate as both an amenity spa (to the hotel) and a day spa (to the local community).

As the spa industry matures, certain development trends are emerging. In 2005, the spa industry was considered the fastest-growing segment of the travel, hospitality, and leisure market, showing 26 percent growth from 2002 to 2004. Spas are no longer considered a niche industry but rather an entity unto themselves.

The spa industry is made up of the following segments, each with its own characteristics and operational opportunities:

— Destination spas
— Resort hotel spas
— Day spas
— Medical spas
— Mineral springs
— Club spas

Destination Spas

A destination spa is one whose sole purpose is to provide programs and facilities that support lifestyle improvements and enhance guest health. The services offered are professionally administered and include fitness, education, and lectures on lifestyle, nutrition, and disease prevention. Because of their healthful orientation, destination spas often provide programs that support postoperative conditions, address various addictions, and provide tools to cope with serious, prolonged illness. The destination spa industry constitutes only 1.6 percent of the total spa industry, per the International Spa Association's Industry Study. However, the growth in the development and use of destination spas reflects the market's trend toward wellness and health as a major component in spa menus.

Resort Spas/Amenity Spas

Resort spas are located on the grounds of vacation resorts where treatments for mind, body, and spirit are offered to complement other resort activities such as golf, tennis, horseback riding, skiing, and water sports. Healthful spa cuisine is on the menu as an option, complementing traditional offerings. In the evenings, guests can enjoy resort pastimes like dancing and live entertainment. Children's programs are also offered. According to the ISPA Spa Industry Study, the resort spa represents 14 percent of spa locations in North America but accounts for almost 41 percent of the total industry revenue, 27 percent of all spa visits, and 26 percent of the industry's employees.

A luxury resort spa has the ambience of a secluded retreat on the grounds of a first-class resort. Set in beautiful surroundings, these resorts commonly have world-class golf courses and other excellent recreational facilities. Gourmet dining and exceptional spa therapies are not only expected but demanded.

Day Spas

Day spas are designed to provide a healing, beautifying, or pampering experience in a short period. Guests may book individual treatments that last as little as an hour or a package of treatments that take up to a whole day. Found throughout North America, day spas are freestanding or located in health clubs, hotels, and department stores. The day spa industry constitutes 72.2 percent of the total industry revenues, per the International Spa Association's 2004 Spa Industry Study. The large percentage of day spas and their growth pattern reflect spa goers' time crunch. Day spas can be owner-operated or chainaffiliated.

Preliminary data from ISPA's 2004 survey show that industry growth is still robust. As of midyear 2004, there was a total of 12,000 spas nationally, of which 8,700 were day spas. These numbers reflect 25 percent growth in the industry in general and 20 percent growth exclusively in this market. The total number of day spa visits in 2003 was 81.2 million. However, only 13 percent of the general population had used a spa in the prior three-year period, indicating that the industry still has large growth potential.

Medical Spas

Medical treatments in various spa environments represent a significant trend in the scope, depth, and inclusiveness of numerous spas. Medical spa treatments can range from elective, reconstructive surgery to noninvasive Eastern modalities incorporating elements of Eastern philosophy that draw on the body-mind-spirit connection to create positive, measurable changes in the client/patient. Slightly over half (51 percent) of the medical spas in North America have a partnership with a medical doctor, and 26 percent have a doctor on staff. The remaining configurations include being located in a doctor's office or having licensed staff members. Botox and microdermabrasion are the two most popular treatments, followed by chemical peels and laser hair removal. In North America, allopathic or Western medical procedures found in medical spas often incorporate Eastern-based treatments.

Day, destination, and resort/amenity spas are adding medical treatments to their spa menus. Part of this trend is directly attributed to market demand, and part is attributed to health insurance plans that reimburse for some procedures. According to the ISPA 2004 survey, medical spas are the fastest-growing spa segment with respect to number of locations.The average annual growth in medical spas by location since 1999 is approximately 45 percent. Cumulative growth from 1999 to 2004 is 205 percent and from 2002 to 2004, 109 percent.

Medical spas generated an estimated 1,900,000 visits in 2003, representing 1.39 percent of the total spa visits. However, this percentage of visits accounts for approximately 2.1 percent of the total industry revenues, reflecting the lucrative nature of this segment of the industry.

Mineral Springs Spas

Many mineral springs spas are considered to be the original spa prototype, where guests go to "take the waters." Mineral springs spas, by definition, are located at naturally occurring mineral springs, and by number of locations represent 2.8 percent of the total spa industry, or 1.3 percent of the total industry revenues, making this one of the more modest incomeproducing segments of the spa industry. The popularity of mineral springs spas is reflected in a cumulative growth from 1999 to 2004 of 143 percent. Growth from 2002 to 2004 represents only 15 percent, implying that the number of sites available directly affects the growth in this segment.

Club Spas

Club spas lack a lodging component, and their primary objective is to facilitate daily fitness activities. Many club spas' services complement the primary fitness component of the club by offering sports massage (deep tissue), chiropractic services, physiotherapy, and related treatments that address issues of pain management, flexibility, and mobility. By lo-cation, club spas represent 5.8 percent of the total spa industry in North America and account for approximately 3.7 percent of the industry's revenues. Growth in the club spa portion of the spa industry is the lowest of all spa segments. Between 2002 and 2004, cumulative club spa growth was only 3 percent.

SPA OPERATIONS

Historically, spa operations were treated by management similarly to other revenue departments, like catering and restaurants. These departments were simply perceived as an amenity needed to attract guests to the hotel. As long as the department broke even, or didn't lose too much money, their ability to increase occupancy was deemed sufficient justification for their existence. However, in the late 1990s, hotel spas followed the path of other operating departments and transformed from support facilities to profit centers.

This trend is strong and continues today. In 1999, PKF Consulting identified only 30 hotels in the United States, thousands that report data to the PKF, extensive spa facilities and analysed the financial performance of those properties and their spa departments. Dedicated destination spa resorts were not included in the analysis due to an insufficient sample.

While spas were a relatively small source of revenues for the sample properties, spa revenues grew at a relatively strong pace. In 1999, spa revenues for the subject sample represented just 3.3 percent of total sales. However, from 1998 to 1999, spa revenues grew 16.6 percent. This compares to revenue growth rates of 5.2

percent for rooms, 12.2 percent for food, and 3.2 percent for telecommunications, and a 0.3 percent decline in revenues for the beverage department.

During 1999, the spa departments in the sample of hotels averaged a departmental profit margin of 30.7 percent. However, spa department profits did grow a strong 51.3 percent from 1998 to 1999.

Spas mirror and enhance trends in the lodging industry. Drawing heavily from residential design and the use of technology, hotel designers and operators create a spa experience that:

— Complements the lodging experience
— Drives occupancy levels
— Enhances average daily rate
— Provides a distinctive marketing advantage

North American spas are rapidly becoming more segmented, pursuing market niches well outside the traditional ladies-who-lunch demographic. Adventure spas, fitness spas, children spas, family spas, and even pet spas are part of a new generation of spa facilities, spa programs—and, most importantly, spa aficionados. Spas now attract a much wider demographic that includes men, women, couples, children, teenagers, and families.

Since the early part of the twenty-first century, spas have been redirecting their menus to include stress relief and resultsoriented therapies. By focusing on the social benefits of hanging out in a safe, relaxing place, they not only address current market needs but also support the development of spa programs that can be incorporated into virtually any leisure-oriented environment or level of lodging. In particular, destination spas and full-service resorts provide platforms that have both the infrastructure and the economies of scale to support cutting-edge spa treatments, sometimes also referred to as spa modalities.

Spas are no longer solely about frivolous self-indulgence and luxurious pampering. They are being reevaluated and repackaged with a broader emphasis on self-care, stress relief, emotional balancing, and preventative (as opposed to reactive) wellness modalities. This trend is being embraced by aging baby boomers as an adjunct to traditional health care. Because of this trend in health care, hotels and resorts have acknowledged and embraced the need for full-service spas as part of their amenities and facilities. The inclusion of a well-integrated spa can provide additional (and lucrative) sales and marketing opportunities. Conversely, the exclusion of a spa facility may disqualify a property from consideration. Ironically, many hotel guests may dismiss a property out of hand for lacking a spa not because they require the services of a spa but rather because its absence may imply other areas of the hotel are also deficient in meeting current market expectations.

Numerous factors must be considered in developing or repositioning a spa, especially in chain environments where the lodging brand is already established. Because spas are capital- and labor-intensive, they must materially enhance the property's revenue stream to be considered viable. In addition to creating spa revenue, a spa facility also must extend length of stay, drive room rates, enhance shoulder and low-season demand, augment food and beverage revenues, and capture new market segments.

Successful spa operations start with a standardised level of procedures and a prioritised sensitivity to guest needs. As it is for all departments in a lodging environment, profitability is essential. Especially in a spa environment, a dynamic balance is essential to meet the fiscal requirements of the owners and the physical needs of the guest.

A savvy spa manager continually monitors the spa and hotel operations to ensure that everything possible is being done to enhance the synergy of the two entities. Constant monitoring also provides an early warning system to the spa operator if revenues are falling or if expenses are not in line with anticipated revenues or budgeted amounts. Spotting these trends early enables the manager to take efficient, proactive steps to ensure that positive trends are enhanced and negative ones controlled. Constant monitoring sets a standard of operations, which is an excellent way to train and motivate employees. It also puts employees on notice that the spa is a well-run business with extensive attention to detail, which should discourage any actions that might not be in the best interest of the spa's reputation and profitability.

Customer Service Training

A spa's reputation is easily made or destroyed by its level of customer service. Guests can forgive an occasional shortcoming if the level of service is exceptional. For this reason, it is essential that all spas have an integrated quality management program that provides ongoing training to assist its employees in addressing customers' expectations. Customer service training (CST) helps ensure that guests' expectations are exceeded. In a spa environment, expectations are usually very high, and a trusting bond can be quickly established if the spa employees are sensitive to guest needs.

The guest's arrival sequence, starting at the front desk, initiates the spa ritual that brings the spa guest to a place of trust, relaxation, and rejuvenation. CST is proactive and provides employees with the tools they need to meet or exceed guest expectations. Guest CST is a never-ending, all-inclusive process that bridges textbook training scenarios with operational realities. The traditionally high turnover of spa employees in the hospitality industry requires that CST be introduced as a part of the orientation process and reinforced regularly.

Nonproductive training time (time that does not directly produce revenue for the spa) is actually a minor expense when compared to the expenses related to employee turnover, poor service, dissatisfied customers, and, ultimately, loss of business and reputation. Budgets must include CST as a nonoptional employee expense. For long-term success, CST is vital when margins are tight, business is slow, and turnover is high.There is a strong correlation between high employee turnover and low CST. Employees should know that the training program is an investment in them.

CST gives the employee the means to understand what is expected of them as a representative of the establishment and identifies what guests expect from their visit. Seeing the process from the guest's point of view helps employees meet or exceed expectations. This minimises the need to provide discounts or compensation in cases of service delivery problems. Discounting or "comping" goods and services is a knee-jerk response to poor service and should be reserved for the last effort in service recovery; CST should stress this.

An inclusive training program is the engine behind stellar customer service and guest loyalty. CST should be seamless; while it predominately addresses the needs of the guest, the program also includes instruction on profitability and yield management, thus addressing the needs of the owner as well. In order to meet or exceed profitability goals, customer service must be delivered in a fiscally responsible manner. Employees must understand customer service in the operational context of the property in which they are employed. Minimising the expense of a CST program starts with the proper selection of employees. While there is no steadfast guarantee that a potential employee will work out over the long haul, first impressions, prior work experience, references, and, above all, attitude and enthusiasm are indications of whether or not it is appropriate to hire and invest the time and money in an applicant.

Management's expectations of guest service delivery should be clearly articulated and integrated into the corporate culture and reinforced daily at all levels and in all departments.

Employees, no matter what their responsibility, position, or tenure, must be treated with the same level of respect and dignity that management requires for their guests. Reinforcing the tenets of customer service within the corporate culture provides the employee with the tools to do the right thing—that is, to ask, "What do I need to do to make a spa guest happy? How do I exceed their expectations?" Sometimes the little details reap the greatest rewards.

Employee empowerment is a key component in CST. As an employee's experience and skill base develops (and as management becomes comfortable with an employee's performance), levels of empowerment should be increased proportionately. Empowerment is a vote of confidence in an employee and a way to quickly resolve problems as they arise.This situation is said by spa managers to increase job satisfaction, and the employee's ownership of his or her position.

CST also requires a strong foundation in the technical skills of how a department runs. Routine procedures, appropriate lines of oral and written communication, and what is expected of each employee in the normal course of his or her shift help minimise problems. When problems do occur, a strong foundation in technical skills makes it easier for the employee to create alternative solutions for the guest.

Training draws on employees' EQ (emotional quotient) as well as their IQ (intelligence quotient). CST requires that employees draw on their ability to empathise with the guest. This starts by training employees to suspend judgment of a situation, become attentive listeners, and know the right questions to ask. This allows them to understand what the actual problem is. Training employees in this type of customer service delivery assists them in focusing on the salient issues and creating ways to address them.

Because CST is ongoing, employees can benefit from their peers' experiences.Vehicles to exchange this type of information can be as informal as role-playing and round-table discussions, or as structured as an employee newsletter. Incentives, acknowledgments, and rewards for excellent customer service delivery are an integral part of the training program. Successful CST supports a skilled and unified staff, which translates into profitable operations. CST is an investment in property that owners can't afford not to make.

Value-oriented Services

Spa aficionados are savvy.They are looking to be indulged, pampered, and nurtured, not fleeced. Setting price points with market sensitivity can create tremendous customer loyalty. Because spas are no longer a one-time indulgence but rather a lifestyle choice, it is important to price services competitively and provide incentives for customers to return regularly.

Numerous variables are involved in the development and operation of a spa as part of a hotel or resort. Doing one's homework is essential to success.When a spa is developed or repositioned correctly, it can be a lucrative and rewarding experience.When it is not developed correctly, it can be a financial liability that haunts the spa director and jeopardises the hotel's market position.

If spas and their programming are not an integrated part of the hotel's future development, the property may lose a significant competitive opportunity. Spa-less hotels or poorly run properties have an inherent competitive market disadvantage. Not only do they find it more difficult to penetrate the market but they also often lose market share.

Resort Spas

The ratio of guest rooms to treatment rooms is based on many factors, including the anticipated return on investment to the owners, the topography of the site, the scope and theme of the spa, and the competition. In a destination resort, where the reason for the spa facilities is the reason for the trip, there should be an average of 1 treatment room for every 4 to 5 guest rooms. At the other end of the spectrum, such as a casino hotel, the spa is definitely an amenity, and 1 treatment room should be built for every 50 to 100 guest rooms.

The spas at lower-end hotel properties normally are limited in scope and are often between 3,000 and 6,000 square feet, whereas luxury spas at full-service, high-end resorts average between 10,000 and 35,000 square feet. These ranges vary based on each hotel's specific circumstances, including seasonality, accessibility, meeting space, fill patterns, and local demand. Each market and each lodging product must be individually evaluated to assess the appropriate ratio of treatment rooms to guest rooms.

Another matrix that measures the viability of a resort or hotel spa is the cost to build the facility. Once again, a number of factors support various outcomes in this process, including the amount of available land, the finishes of the spa, the finishes of the hotel (these should be compatible), and the need to develop a spa either vertically or horisontally. Vertical spas are most often built in environments where land is scarce or the allocated footprint for the spa is too small for one floor. Vertical construction always raises the price per square foot, as load distribution, drainage, and the weight of equipment and water must be factored into the construction design and budget. The cost to construct a resort or destination spa can range from as low as $200 per square foot to over $450 per square foot. High land-value areas and plumbing-rich design schemes will send cost dramatically above this range.

Day Spas

Day spas often lack the grand infrastructure associated with resort spas, and for this reason the ratio of spa revenue to treatment room space is much closer. In terms of number of square feet, day spa revenues account for 43 percent of the total spa space and provide approximately 52 percent of the total day spa revenues.The remaining 57 percent of the day spa environment is allocated to guest flow, check-in desk, retail, back-of-the-house support, and, on some occasions, food and beverage areas.

Medical Spas

Historically, medical spas have placed less emphasis on the aesthetics of the spa experience and more on the treatment provided.

Therefore, it is not surprising that 45 percent of the medical spa space provides 63 percent of all medical spa revenue. Retail sales are limited in medical spas, as outside of cosmetics and prescriptions there are limited branding opportunities.While resort spa goers are anxious to wear a sweatshirt or ball cap that announces to the world where they last vacationed, most medical spa clients do not share the same need or enthusiasm about their recent microderm abrasion or rhinoplasty. Medical spas may require the use of pharmacies to fill patient's prescriptions, which from a business model could be considered part of their treatment-related retail sales.

TREATMENT

To this point, we have evaluated the economics and use patterns of spa types.The focus of most spas dictates how the space is allocated and where the income is generated. Spas should aim to have at least 50 percent of their total space—their prime real estate—produce direct revenue. Secondary real estate is the support and public areas necessary for atmosphere and supporting functions that assist in delivering the spa services. Secondary spa real estate includes areas where people can prepare for or relax from their spa treatments.

These secondary areas are an important component in the spa development plan, as they allow guests to prolong their experience, which enhances the perceived value. If guests are hurried from their massage or facial out of the spa and back onto the street, the magic that is created can be abruptly snapped and the overall spa experience is compromised. Conversely, if a guest is allowed to soak and relax for hours after a body wrap is completed, emotionally speaking, the cost of the body wrap is amortised over the entire spa experience and not just for the time the client was enjoying the body wrap in the spa's prime real estate.

Combination rooms account for about 36 percent of North American spa spaces, but because of the various treatments offered in them, a revenue percentage generated from these spaces is hard to predict. Combination spaces allow the spa to address surges in demand for specific treatments and at the same time be flexible and respond to global market changes. Massage rooms account for approximately 27 percent of the total space in North American spas but 47 percent of the spa revenue. Given these factors, an operator would need a compelling reason to not include massage on the spa menu. Facial treatment areas reflect 19 percent of the total spa space and result in about 33 percent of the spa's overall revenue.Wet rooms, often the most underutilised portions of the spa, account for 7 per-cent of the space and revenue. Because many spa modalities involve water therapies, many spa developers and owners believe that wet rooms are essential, even if they seem underutilised. Because wet rooms are one of the most expensive components of a spa, it is essential that they be utilised to their fullest extent. Packaging wet room treatments with other spa services is one way to better utilise the space and create value for the spa.

Spa Industry Trends

Anti-aging treatments and products are driving much of spa menu and retail development. This calls for devoting a treatment room to outpatient medical procedures. Programming and spa menu items include sun damage treatments, chemical peels for skin renewal, and other rejuvenation techniques that build on repeat procedures. Commensurately, spas are developing retail product lines that can take the spa experience home and continue the wellness regime.

Gift card sales are driving new users to spas. In the friends and family sector as well as the corporate gift-giving world, day spa certificates are creating demand that is not directly user driven. Third-party purchasing brings to spas clients who may not normally have chosen the location or treatment, creating a large but undefinable market demand.

Regional specialties that relate to indigenous and climatic influences continue to create unique spa experiences based on site-specific supply. This has excellent leverage potential for spa operators working to differentiate their product matrices in densely operated areas.

Increased stress management. It is important to position services for stress relief, especially to the male business traveler. Spa programming that requires a limited amount of special equipment and minimal changes to a property's infrastructure can do this.

Impulse appointments. "Life is uncertain, but I want a massage (reflexology appointment, yoga class, etc.) now!" This trend may result in developing adjunct programs for oncall staff resources. The as-needed portion of the program limits a hotel's payroll burden and other related fixed costs. Of course, this implies existing core programs and facilities where these programs can be developed and supported.

Shift in perspective. Self-indulgence, pampering, and luxury are being reevaluated and repackaged with a new, broader emphasis on self-care, stress relief, and emotional balancing. This is reflected in spa programming, the menu of services, food and beverage outlets, and spa-related retail. The retail positioning and spa programming components represent huge untapped revenue opportunities.

Changes in demographic use profile. Historically, the greatest segment of spa goers was women between the ages of 35 and 55. More couples and families are expected to visit the spa together as an alternative social/ recreational activity. This trend has the potential to extend business-related stays, fill business hotels on the weekend, and create demand for destinations. It is important to understand this trend when evaluating ways to increase market penetration in a down market.

Medical affiliations. For some markets, an affiliation with a medical center or group in the area can be established to provide treatments such as acupuncture, nutritional assessment, laser therapies (hair removal and wrinkle reduction), Botox injections, collagen treatments, chemical peels, laser resurfacing, body contouring, microderm abrasion, and vascular procedures. When creating these types of relationships, it is essential that spa owners thoroughly investigate the legal disclosure and liability implications of being an affiliated medical service provider.

Green environments. A spa can be ecologically sensitive by incorporating environmentally friendly features into the operation. By proactively supporting programs and products that are earth friendly, the spa does something good for the environment, provides a service to the community, and creates a competitive advantage and a unique selling point that may provide significant returns, especially in a highly competitive market.

Trends in day, destination, and amenity spas influence each other. President of Spa Finder, a spa marketing company, after the rise of the medical spa and broadening spa participation by men and teens, spa use is expected to become more popular in 2005 and beyond. Spa Finder's trends to watch for are abstracted below:

— Those personal elements that make the spa experience special will find their way into the design of personal living spaces in private homes.

— Private, gated living communities will develop around central spa facilities, much like golf and fly-in communities.

— Some spas will compete on the far outer reaches of luxury, with ever-increasing rare and proprietary products and services.

— Spas will make house calls. Legitimate spas will offer out-call services where spa technicians travel with appropriate equipment and personnel to a client's home, office, or hotel room.

— Destination spas and resorts will develop market segments focused on personal goals—everything from spiritual awareness to sexual health to detoxification.

— The spa travel segment will grow, with more clientele booking through online portals.

— Medical spas will continue to be popular and will add alternative therapies and couple traditional medical treatment with spa luxury and innovation.

— Day spas will not grow their exotic menus much more but rather focus on the traditional; destination/resort spas will be the businesses that experiment with more exotic services and products.

— Specialised cuisine developed for spa guest consumption will find its way into mainstream grocery/specialty food offerings.

— Restaurants may also add lines of healthy spa cuisine to their menus.

— Eco spas—those designed and operated around green principles of management will become a growing segment of the industry.

9

Managing Hotel Security

Travellers not only do have virtually an unlimited choice of means of travel, but also have an exceptionally broad choice of accommodations when they reach their destination. A traveller might have some of the following choices when he reaches the hotel. The list choices go on from modest to luxurious, from full-service to virtually do-it-yourself. From casino resorts to private clubs, the traveller has never had such a selection from which to choose. Further, the traveller can avail himself of a property which functions as a multi-operation facility, at the same time offering long-term accommodations to some (an apartment), both room and food to others (a boarding house), and finally supplying the basic needs of an overnight guest (a traditional hotel.) For all practical purposes, there is little legal difference between any of these types of facilities when it comes to hotel protection management.

Hotel managers have been besieged with a multiplicity of terms which seem to surround the subject of guest protection. These terms, in and of themselves, seem ill-defined, perhaps non-defined, and certainly confusing. The terms such as security, risk control, safety, life-safety, loss prevention, asset protection, loss control, crime prevention etc., are bandied around constantly. They may be separate and distinct to the professional who deals with protection on a full time basis, to the average lodging manager.

By choosing a secure hotel, you're choosing a well made, fire-resistant property. However, many hotels abroad are not as fire-resistant as those here: it may be difficult to contact a fire department; there may not be reliable smoke detectors or sprinkler systems; there may be too few exits and escape routes may not be posted; escape routes may not be posted in hallways; and, fire-fighting equipment and water supplies may be limited. Experts tell us that if a fire starts, try to call the fire department or the police for help—do not rely on a security guard. If you speak the language, tell the fire department or police your room number. If you cannot reach the fire department, call the front desk—tell them your room number. Grab your key and crawl to the door on your hands and knees. Don't stand—smoke gases rise while the fresher air will be near the floor. Before you open the door, feel it with the palm of your hand. If the door or knob is hot, the fire may be right outside. Open the door slowly. If your exit path is clear, crawl into the hallway. Be sure to close the door behind you to keep smoke out in case you need to return to your room. Take your key as most hotel doors lock automatically. Stay close to the wall to avoid being trampled.

Firefighters remind us to not use elevators during a fire. They may malfunction, or if they have heat-activated call buttons, they may take you directly to the fire floor. They recommend that as you make your way to the fire exit, stay on the same side as the exit door. Count the doors to the exit. Follow the plan that you organised. When you reach the exit, walk down the stairs to the first floor. If you encounter heavy smoke in the stairwell, don't try to run through it. You may not make it. Instead, turn around and walk up to the roof fire exit. Prop the door open to ventilate the stairwell and to keep from being locked out. Find the windward side of the roof, sit down, and wait for the fire fighters to find you. If all exits are blocked, or if there is heavy smoke in the hallway, you'll be better off staying in your room, according to the Fire Department.

If there is smoke in your room, open a window and turn on the bathroom vent. Don't break the window unless it can't be opened. You might want to close the window later to keep smoke out, and broken glass could injure you or people below. Fill the bathtub with water to use for fire fighting. Bail water onto your door or any hot walls with an ice bucket or wastebasket. Stuff wet towels into cracks under and around doors where smoke can enter. Tie a wet towel over your mouth and nose to help filter out smoke. If there is fire outside your window, take down the drapes and move everything combustible away from the window.

Emergency evacuation is a part of hotel security procedures. It is especially relevant in high-risk countries. Here are the general guidelines. First, you must verify the source and validity of a notification of danger. Move directly, without delay or hesitation, on the predetermined escape route. Consider airport security conditions and proceed accordingly. If the airport is expected to be unsafe use alternative means of transport. Hotel rooms are not safe places for discussions of confidential business matters or classified information. Hotels in certain countries invariably put business visitors in designated rooms, presumably for ease of eavesdropping. Use the hotel to practise your communication skills when travelling abroad. Hotel security also involves effectively utilising hotel personnel as resources for information. Inevitably this includes asking for directions. There is an effective or right way, and an ineffective or wrong way to get directions. The most useful tool for getting or giving directions is a map. Be sure to have one with you when you ask for help. It is much clearer to mark out a route than to describe it.

Elements of Hotel Security

The basic security elements for hotel industry are: deadbolt locks, viewing devices, chain locks, doors and frames, and communication devices. In some instances, when the risks of crime are known to exist, additional security has been recognised as fundamental under the circumstances. In these cases, courts have often held that the following elements are required as a matter of law: track bars for sliding glass doors, closed circuit television, and security guard personnel.Very often hotel chains have corporate security departments consisting of only a few people. This generally happens not because the company ignores its security needs, but because the security employees are assigned as staff to various corporate facilities. So while dozens or even hundreds of people may have a full-time or part-time security function, the corporate staff is limited. Each facility staff member should have a specifically assigned role to play in the security programme.

From housekeeping and maintenance to front desk and executive management staff, everyone should be trained and encouraged to participate in security programmes. Special areas that require total participation of the staff include: general disorders and bomb threats, fire emergencies, overall surveillance, first aid response, maintenance checks, parking lot patrols, response to calls for assistance, record keeping, eyewitness testimony, and internal security. Whether security personnel are employees of the facility or are provided under a contract with a security service, or even if they are part-time off-duty law enforcement officers, among the things to be considered are the following:

- All personnel should have a copy of, and be familiar with, the security manual.
- All personnel should undergo a competent training programme emphasising those subjects that deal with the institution's security needs.
- All personnel should be readily identifiable as security officers if they are to have public contract.
- All personnel should be issued and trained in the use of appropriate equipment.
- All personnel should be regularly supervised and evaluated with a record maintained of their performance.
- All personnel should undergo a background evaluation, which can reveal suitability for employment in a hotel.
- Contract security personnel should be employed under a contract that sets specific duties and responsibilities for which they can be held accountable.
- All personnel should possess a licence necessary for their employment and for the possession and use of weapons and equipment.
- All personnel should receive regular and updated training and testing on their skills and knowledge to their employment.

Thoughtful analysis should be given to the manner in which law enforcement officers are employed. Different regulations of the country govern the employment of police personnel in private security assignments. In addition, civil liberty issues and conflict of interest possibilities may also be considered in the decision to utilise off-duty police. Decisions on these issues should be made with the advice of the counsel.The hotel should employ any technology it acquires to its full capacity. The reason for this is, that by purchasing it, the hotel is both acknowledging the need for the system, and advising the guests that they are under the protection of the equipment in place. In the event of loss or injury, that might have been prevented if the installed equipment had been working to its full capacity, the hotel-owner has more claim to defend against.

Close circuit television can be an effective security tool when installed and used properly. It should be placed in areas with the greatest likelihood of effective use. Generally remote areas, such as parking lots need coverage, because other eyes and ears are not available for security purposes. Electronic door locks are useful to gain better control over room access problems. Maintaining adequate key control has long been a vexing problem. Mini-safes have become useful because theft from guest-rooms are responsible for the greatest percentage of reported hotel-related crimes Maintaining adequate insurance against claims of negligent security is essential both to defend against claims and to pay damages if awarded.

Not utilising an investment in security equipment can be as bad or worse than not making the investment at all. The development of a clearly defined procedural manual is the backbone of the security programme. The procedures manual not only directs the security effort, but also serves as evidence that security considerations have been carefully and logically thought out. Good lighting is an important crime deterrent and prevention tool.

In an environment of increasing all-round crime, increased crime in hotel-related matters is not a matter of surprise. Hotels in particular are looked at as targets for local criminals, who see a fertile source of victims carrying cash and valuables. It is common to find criminal elements from adjacent neighbourhoods or those who are even willing to travel relatively long distances for the promise of a good haul from unsuspecting victims. Among the leading causes of hotel-related crime are:

— employee dishonesty;
— failure to recognise and respond;
— inadequate maintenance;
— absence of effective security procedures;
— lack of training;
— ignorance and carelessness;
— purchase of inferior hardware and security apparatus; and
— inadequate supervision.

Certain categories of guests require special security consideration because of behaviour-patterns, special needs, cultural differences or other characteristics that cause security problems to develop. These individuals and groups require special attention to ensure that their stays do not result in preventable losses or injuries to themselves or others. Foreign visitors are often victimised by criminals because they are tricked or misled into placing trust in dangerous individuals or bad advice.

Convention guests or large groups are frequently targeted by burglars, prostitutes and con artists because of the ease of penetrating the group and learning about patterns of movement and conduct. Convention groups should receive special reminders about security hazards, should be encouraged to practise stringent requirements concerning the use of deadbolts, chains and peepholes, and encouraged to cooperate with overall hotel rules and security personnel. Women travelling on business now represent 40 per cent of business travellers. These women often travelling alone, and have in recent years become the victims of especially brutal crimes including assault, rape and murder. Care should be given with room assignments, and every effort should be made to place women on notice of foreseeable risks. Airline flight crews, and particularly female members of these crews, have been identified by criminals as targets because the regular patterns of their stay is so easy to identify. Room thefts and personal assaults are higher than average for these crews. Student groups, especially those attending proms or other school functions, often lack adequate supervision to ensure that they conform to rules and procedures. Trade shows, especially catering to industries involved in valuables such as jewellery, furs and electronics, attract thieves from all over the world.

Group tours, because of their scheduled departures and the practice of leaving luggage and purchase in lobbies, storage rooms and unattended guest-rooms, suffer a high incidence of loss. Celebrity guests, especially entertainment groups or sports teams, regularly suffer attempts by fans, curious, and persons with criminal intent, to accost them in public spaces, on sidewalks around the hotel, and even in their rooms. Always make reservations ahead of time and secure them with your credit card. Otherwise, if area facilities are overcrowded, you may find yourself stranded in unfamiliar surroundings or in an unsafe room. If your room is not ready, ask to store your luggage in a locked room.

Many hotels have a "dry room" where you can put your luggage and freshen up. If the hotel has more than one building, request a room in or near the main building. Request a room that faces inward towards other rooms or towards the lobby. Request a room that does not have easy access to the window, such as from the roof or street. Request a room on the second floor, but not higher than the seventh floor, near a fire exit, away from stairwells, elevators, ice machines, basements or garbage/refuse rooms. A room near (but not next to) the elevator helps avoid long walks down stairways. If you have valuables or important documents, e.g., passport or airline ticket, store them in the safety deposit box at the front office and get a receipt. Use a room safe to store only items of moderate value. Large sums of jewellery or money should be placed in the safe at the front desk. If there is no room safe, put valuables in a money belt that you may wear, or bring along a "portable safe". These come in many forms: hollow books, shows with hollow heels, suitcases with hollow compartments, etc. Always use the deadbolt lock when in your room. Always use the chain lock which should be securely fastened to the wall and a solid core door. Windows should open and close easily from the inside. Use the extra lock or stick on windows, sliding or patio doors so that they do not lift out of their tracks.

If someone comes to the door, use the peep hole and ask the visitor to identify himself/herself. Call the front desk to confirm the identity of the visitors, even if they reply they are with room service, janitorial, etc. If you are expecting someone, pre-arrange an exact time of arrival, as well as some form of introduction or identification: a secret knock, business card under the door, or a phone call from the lobby. Completely close the curtains, especially in the evening or if you will be away from the room for sometime. Public announcements are a means to disseminate information about terrorist threats and other relatively short-term and/or transnational conditions posing significant risks to the security of American travellers. They are made any time there is a perceived threat and usually have Americans as a particular target group. In the past, public announcements have been issued to deal with short-term coups, bomb threats to airlines, violence by terrorists and anniversary dates of specific terrorist events.

Reasonable Security Programme

Although the risks may be well understood, management lacks the necessary financial resources to implement what the prudent security professional would consider to be an adequate, reasonable security programme. There are none the less certain basic security steps that can be taken with only a modest expenditure of funds. These are:

— manage by walking around;
— screen job applicants, at least those who will be in positions of trust;
— make security a responsibility of all employees;
— work with the local law enforcement;
— communicate with neighbouring businesses; and
— patrol the premises.

Most hotels and motels are concerned with security and have measures in place to prevent crimes against patrons. At the same time, however, hotels and motels continue to be targeted by criminal elements. Security in the lodging environment presents a wide range of challenges if only because the lodging business is in operation every hour of the day, every day of the year.

Inexpensive safeguards can usually be implemented at a budget motel, but the more significant and costly safeguards tend to be put on the back burner. Unfortunately, it is the absence of the significant safeguards that leads to litigation. On the one hand, budget motel management may recognise the need to upgrade security and appreciate the attendant liability risk, but on the other hand, may lack the financial resources to do anything about it. Even with new construction or retrofitting for expansion or other non-security purposes, management may be unable to find enough capital to fund needed security improvements. With the exception of safe deposit boxes at the front desk, which limit a motel's exposure to property loss, no codes or laws require a motel to provide physical security. Courts across the nation have mandated that motels must merely take "reasonable" precautions to protect their guests from physical harm.The public has become more educated concerning personal safety. In an overbuilt lodging market with heavy competition and fewer people travelling, hotel and motel owners are responding to their customers' concerns about personal safety.

Six very fundamental security steps that involve time but little cost can be implemented at the budget motel:

— Managing by walking around (MBWA) involves getting into the trenches and seeing what's going on in the business, and getting close to customers and employees. The really small "Mom and Pop" motels practiced MBWA before Tom Peters put a label on the concept. The larger, multi-unit motel chains are often lacking in this valuable practice. MBWA is a caring attitude that is imparted to employees and guests alike. Many security professionals emphasise having a written policy and programme, and although written materials can be helpful, they cannot engender the caring attitude and genuine concern that must be projected for security to succeed.

— A background investigation that includes contacting prior employers and making criminal records checks should be conducted before employees are hired. This is the second step. This is important because applicants may falsify prior employment information in order to conceal personal defects that make them unsuitable for assignment to high-trust jobs. The value of background checking is apparent at the budget motel where only one or two employees are present in the evening hours. At stake are the care and custody of the motel and its assets, and the protection of the patrons and their valuables. These are awesome responsibilities that cannot be placed into the hands of people about whom little is known.

— Employees need to be involved in security. One way to promote involvement is to make employees aware of security risks, how the risks affect the motel, the staff and the patrons, and what the staff can do to offset risks. The American Hotel & Motel Association offers a series of training video workshops on the basics of lodging security. Workshops cover everything from awareness to handling disturbances. Another consideration is to motivate employees to carry out their security responsibilities, especially with respect to emergency response procedures. Programmes that provide rewards, such as a deserved thank-you from a supervisor, a certificate of appreciation, recognition by co-workers, a day off or a merit bonus, can go a long way to building a security programme. It is not unusual in the lodging industry for an employer to pay for performance as opposed to paying for time spent on the job. The quality and quantity of work, especially work that is central and essential to the business, is recognised as having a higher value than hours spent at the workplace.

— Having a liaison with local law enforcement is crucial to the small property operator. Without adequate police protection, the budget motel is at extreme risk. The property management can contact the local crime prevention unit to identify the criminal threats confronting the motel and to learn what the police and the management can do to improve security at the property. At a minimum, the local management needs to know the nature of the police services that are available, the manner in which those services are performed, and the officers who deliver the services.

— The motel manager needs to communicate with neighbours. The idea is to share information about crime in the neighbourhood and to look out for each other's interests with respect to spotting and reporting suspicious activity. Neighbours can also share details of their successes and failures in setting up countermeasures to local crime. These are the kinds of activities that defend against allegations that the motel management was negligent by not recognising crime risks that can impact its patrons and by not having a security programme at least equal to that of nearby competitors. The motel manager should be active in the local business organisations, especially with organisations that serve the lodging industry. The contacts and information obtained through networking can be invaluable.

— Patrolling of the premises should be done during the hours of darkness and whenever crime presents a threat to property or people. Patrolling can be handled on a proprietary basis by designating in-house employees to perform the patrol or patrolling services can be handled on a contract basis with a security guard company.

Whatever the approach, four considerations are important.

— First, screen the persons to be selected for patrolling. Ensure they are drug-free, psychologically stable, trustworthy, and possess the physical ability to meet the rigours of constant movement in an outdoor environment.

— Second, provide the selected persons with the knowledge and skill to do their jobs effectively. Teach them how to look for the indicators of crime and hazardous conditions, and how to respond when the indicators are present; make sure they understand the limits of their lawful authority; and motivate them to convey an interested and caring attitude in their dealings with people.

— Third, give them the proper tools to carry out their jobs. Distinctive uniforms, inclement weather gear, flashlights, and a means of communication are essential.
— Fourth, give them plenty of supervision and lots of positive guidance.

Unlike other security specialists, the lodging security manager operates in an environment where the protected group is nearly always changing. With the exception of the employees working on the property, the guest population changes nearly everyday. A wide spectrum of society is represented in the guest population; also represented are the problems the guests bring with them. As with any facility security programme, the security manager will develop a loss prevention plan and programme based on the results of a survey. Ideally, although seldom the case, the survey will occur prior to the facility being constructed.

The survey of a hotel is similar to that of a survey for any other facility, except possibly that more attention must be paid to the surrounding area. The foreseeability of crimes is a concept that has great significance at lodging facilities, requiring careful analysis and formulation of effective countermeasures. Lodging operators have been placed on notice by the courts that the owner/operator "may be liable for failure to warn guests and to prevent criminal assault where prior criminal activity in the area should have made the attack on the hotel guest foreseeable to the owner/ operator". Lodging industry professionals are clearly faced with a duty to act to protect guests. The security survey is an element in meeting the duty.

Zone Approach to Hotel Security

In zone approach, the facility, the land it sits on, and the surrounding neighbourhood are compartmented in four zones. Zone 1 is the neighbourhood immediately surrounding the property. Obviously, if the hotel staff is afraid to walk the sidewalk in front of the property after sunset, there is a real problem. While the hotel staff may be aware of crime in the immediate area and may in fact have developed personal strategies for dealing with it, the guests will have no awareness, no warning, and no personal defence mechanisms at hand. A good way for the security manager to begin to appreciate the crime problem is to walk the area during various times of the day and week, and determine first-hand the types of activities occurring on the fringes of the property. A next step for the security manager is to establish working relationships with officers in local, county, and state law enforcement agencies. These may be the supervisors of patrol operations in the neighbourhood, vice squad officers, and robbery and burglary detectives. The security manager can learn from them the types and frequencies of crimes, the criminal methods of operation, and the nature of the criminal threats, e.g., whether the criminals act individually, in small teams, or as large gangs.

The security manager will follow a logical progression from analysis of threat to analysis of vulnerability to formulation of countermeasures. This is also another way of describing how the security manager will construct an overall protective programme. As a small example: in a walk-through of the neighbourhood the security manager observes gang activity (threat); joggers make up a good percentage of the clientele (vulnerability); the security manager asks for increased police patrol presence along the jogging route.

Zone 2 begins at the property boundary and extends to the wall of the first building. In nearly all cases, this area will include parking areas. The swimming pool, tennis courts, and other outdoor recreational facilities might also be in this area. The zone 1 analysis will provide clues to the types of security problems that can be anticipated in zone 2. Other factors requiring consideration are: the perimeter, parking areas, exterior lighting, recreational areas, and the exterior walls of the lodging facility. The security manager should examine the boundaries of the property to determine needs for psychological deterrents and physical barriers. It may be possible to inexpensively create boundaries by linking a natural barrier, such as a stream, with a hedge row, or by installing a short fence that extends from a fence or structure on neighbouring property. Lodging facilities are often constructed amid shrubbery and trees. Although aesthetically pleasing, these offer concealment to criminals who would prey on unsuspecting guests walking on the grounds or moving to and from their vehicles in the parking areas. Parking schemes for guests vary widely in the lodging industry. There is close-in parking, in which the motel guest's vehicle is parked within a few feet of the guest's room, garage parking, valet parking, on-street parking, parking lots in walking distance, and parking lots with shuttles to the facility. Within the limitations imposed by the type and configuration of parking areas, the security manager must set up safeguards that primarily protect the guests and secondarily protect their vehicles.

Good lighting is both a deterrent to crime and an aid in detecting and apprehending criminals. Lighting is a basic security tool that can also be pleasing to the eye; for example, when it is artfully integrated with foliage and water. Security lighting in a parking area is essential. Unfortunately, a parking area is sometimes not lit properly because management wants to avoid projecting an image that the lodging facility is in a high crime area. In open general parking areas it is recommended that between 0.9 footcandles and 0.6 footcandles be maintained on the pavement. Lighting may go as low as 0.2 footcandles when there is a low level of night-time activity. In covered parking facilities, the recommended illumination levels increase to 5 footcandles for general parking and pedestrian areas; 10 footcandles for ramps and corners; and 50 footcandles at entrance areas.

The security manager must consider the routes and means of transportation utilised by guests going to and from outlying recreational areas; the times of utilisation; the types of guests; and the valuables they may be carrying with them. These considerations will aid the security manager in assessing the security risks involved. The nature of the recreational activity is also a consideration. A swimming pool, for example, may be used at all hours of the day or night when it is fenced or inside a locked building/area where entry is controlled, and where some degree of staff attention is given to the safety and security of guests while using the pool. However, if the pool is near an unfenced/unprotected perimeter, the relative security of the using guests may drop to a level that would require either closing the pool during high-risk hours or increasing the protection. Hiking, walking, jogging, and biking on unattended trails present similar risks.

The innermost line of defence in zone 2 is the exterior of the lodging facility. Passage through the walls can be made by guests and trades people at any number of entrances. The control of access through the entrances is typically by lodging staff whose training and experience permit them to discriminate between authorised persons and unwelcome visitors. During late evening hours when traffic into the lodging facility is minimal, many or all of the remote entrances can be secured, requiring persons to enter through one or a few entrances that are under the direct observation of staff. Unwelcome visitors who are able to pass through an entrance unchallenged or by subterfuge would be confronted with the safeguards of zone 3. The term unwelcome visitor is substituted for the term intruder because zones 2 and 3 are essentially public areas. It is not the movement of people through public entrances that is of greatest concern to the security manager—it is the movement of criminals through exterior doors and windows that lead directly into guest rooms or into areas containing the lodging operator's assets.

Zone 3 consists of public space that may include restaurants, lounges, shops, rest rooms, and reading areas. Guest room corridors and fire exit stairwells are technically public but from a practical standpoint the security manager will insist that the lodging staff be alert to suspicious persons in these areas. The main thrust of security with respect to zone 3 is not to keep people out but to exercise subtle controls over human activity inside the zone. Security awareness should be second nature for all employees. It means being aware of the methods that criminals use, being able to spot suspicious persons and activities, and knowing what to do when the indicators are present. An awareness technique that incorporates both courtesy and attentiveness is for staff to greet persons who are on the premises and to offer assistance when it appears they are not sure of their bearings. To the guest, the employee making the greeting is seen as a helpful person; to a criminal looking for the opportunity to commit a crime, the employee is seen as a potential adversary and witness.

Robberies at motels, motor lodges, and hotels occur more frequently than property owners care to admit. The foreseeability issue is strongly connected to robberies because of the potential for injury or death to guests and employees. Data gathered in the zone 1 analysis will indicate the probable nature of the robbery threat. Employees should not be permitted to congregate in the lobby for two reasons. First, an unprofessional image is presented to arriving guests by the appearance of too many employees. Second, the security manager will be concerned that a dishonest employee will have the opportunity to observe guests entering with expensive valuables and act upon this information or pass the information to a confederate. On the latter point, thieves who specialise in victimising lodgers will wait near the registration desk looking for a prospective victim (the "mark") as he or she checks in and hoping to overhear the registration clerk mention the assigned room number. Registration clerks should be trained to simply point to the room number on the registration card when checking guests in.

Zone 4 comprises the guest-rooms within the facility. The guest-room is the traveller's home away from home; a sanctuary from the rest of the world. The major separating point between the sanctuary and outsiders is the guest-room door. The door should be a solid wood or steel door. In most areas, local building codes and/or fire codes will specify doors with a specific fire rating. Hollow core doors should never be used at the entry point to a guest-room. The door should be equipped with at least one viewing port or peep hole. With the recent enactment of the Americans with Disabilities Act (ADA) serious consideration should be given to providing two peep holes in every door: one at a standard height and one at wheelchair level to accommodate guests in wheelchairs. These view ports or peep-holes should provide the guest with a 180-degree view of the corridor outside of the room.

The door lock is another important element. Whenever possible electronic locking systems should be employed that permit a "key/lock change" with every guest's arrival and departure. Electronic locks also make it possible to determine which key card was used to open a door at a particular time. This audit trail feature can aid investigations that involve unauthorised entries to guest rooms. It is not uncommon, however, to find smaller properties continuing to use the standard lock-in-knob arrangement, which is well known for problems associated with key control.

Even the best hardware can be defeated when a key has been stolen or duplicated. The worst thing that can happen is for a master key to be compromised. Professional thieves are always on the lookout for lodging employees who will sell or rent master keys. It is absolutely essential that mechanical locks be changed immediately whenever a key is missing. This includes keys that the guest forgets to turn in. The guest-room should not be sold to another guest until the locks have been changed. Each employee must turn in at the end of the work shift any lodging facility keys. It should be policy that only a responsible manager, such as the general manager, chief engineer, or manager of security, will be permitted to take keys off of the property.

The door should be equipped with a deadbolt with at least a one-inch throw and self-closing hinges that cause the door to swing into a closed-and-locked position. The self-closing feature must be reliable because guests will expect the doors to always and perfectly close behind them; if the feature fails, resulting in a loss or injury to the guest, the management can expect a claim for damages. The sliding glass or patio door often used in resort properties must be capable of resisting forced entry, including the technique of lifting a door panel out of its sliding track. The rule of thumb is to augment the locking capability of a sliding glass door with the use of a secondary device, such as a charley bar.Consideration must also be given to where a guest will store valuables. Nearly all states have some version of an innkeeper's law requiring the lodging operator to provide safe deposit boxes for guests. Consideration should also be given to providing a guest with an in-room safe. The survey should determine why and how often employees enter guest rooms. Entry is usually related to the need to make heating, ventilation, and air conditioning (HVAC), mechanical, and plumbing checks, but includes also the need to determine damage to or theft from rooms.

More important, these checks make it possible to discover if a guest inside a room is ill or injured. The standard practice is to conduct a check of each room in every 24-hour period. Unlike office building security, where the office population is generally stable, the lodging security approach is tailored to address the unique problems of an unstable, ever-changing guest population. In coming to grips with these unique problems, the lodging security professional must take into account the diversity and the changing nature of the clientele. The relatively young lodging guests, those in their 30's and 40's, have different values and expectations than guests who are younger or older. The security manager must be able to balance the need for security, the guest's desire for privacy, and the organisation's need to reduce liability and losses.

Structure of Security Department

A typical department structure consists of the security manager, assistant manager, shift supervisors, and security officers. The structure ideally coincides with the size of the property, which usually is categorised by the number of rooms. In most hotels the department head usually will be called the director or manager. Commonly, the title "Director of Security" is used to denote multiple property responsibility or multi-job function responsibility. He or she reports to a member of senior management—either an operations manager or directly to the managing director. A "Security Manager", on the other hand, is usually responsible for a single property, or else has the primary job function of security and reports to varied levels of management depending on the company. It is very important for the department head to have an assistant who can substitute when the manager is not present and manage the department operationally on a daily basis. A security department will encounter difficulties operating effectively with just a single person in charge. There will always be some situation to which the department head cannot attend, due to the usual limitations of a regular work schedule. A hotel cannot afford to depend on the availability of a single individual. The role of the assistant security manager should be just that—to assist the director/manager by shared job tasks such as scheduling, payroll, training, hiring and firing, and coordinating department meetings. The assistant in most hotels must be capable of working flexible hours and days.

The management structure of a security department should include shift supervisors: individuals designated as being responsible for the officers working a given shift. The supervisor is the vital link between employees and security management. The supervisor represents management's needs and views to the officers and at the same time has the responsibility of representing the needs and views of the officers to management. Without a knowledgeable supervisor available, the staff are left to make decisions in haphazard ways. A lack of structure could lead to an increase in poor decisions. Even if there are no actual supervisory personnel, some system of supervision must be in place.

Little instruction material is available concerning the individual lodging security employee's role, contribution, or importance in the overall security function. It must be remembered that regardless of how knowledgeable security management may be, the line employee's performance is the ultimate measurement of success. The security officer's daily patrolling and presence have a deterrent and prevention effect that must be acknowledged. This is true both for employees and would-be criminals intending to commit a crime.

The size of a security staff required will generally be proportional not only to the number of rooms, but also to size of the facility and the number of employees on the hotel payroll. It also will depend on a number of factors that must all be considered simultaneously. In a pre-existing hotel, it is somewhat easier to determine staffing needs by reviewing the history of problems and guest-related issues addressed by security. If there are records available for review, a workload analysis can be conducted to indicate the types of calls for service and their distribution according to times and days of the week. One rule of thumb that deserves mention concerns the number of staff required to cover a single post around the clock, for three eight-hour shifts. The number is not 3, but 4½ or 5 persons, to allow for days off, vacation, sick time, training and other administrative tasks. Other important factors to be considered include the design of the property and the location of the property relative to both the neighbourhood and the type of setting.

An urban hotel in a high crime district should anticipate overflow problems from the neighbourhood, such as streetwalkers, vagrants, and trespassers. A hotel in a suburban location that is accessed only by motor vehicles and is surrounded by a residential community is less likely to experience the problems of the urban property. Crime rates, economic growth or decline, climate conditions, and the availability of public safety resources such as police, fire, and ambulance services must all be taken into account when planning staff size and distribution.

The level in an organisation to which security reports will greatly affect the ability of the department to achieve desired results. Lodging security departments have been known to report to a wide variety of managers, including the managing director, general manager, operations manager, human resources manager, building superintendent, and—perhaps most commonly—the rooms division manager. Ideally, however, the security department should report to the highest level as possible; the operations manager is practical, for example. If the property is operated in such a way that the general manager is accessible to the security manager, then this is the person to whom security should report.

A general manager's schedule is often so busy that it precludes regular accessibility except to a few senior managers. The security manager needs to be able to communicate routinely with the senior manager who oversees the security department.

There are other problems caused by having security report to middle- or lower-level managers or to a manager who represents only one area of the company's operation.

— Each layer of management that security must penetrate to reach the general manager must be acutely and accurately aware of the problems. The more layers of people a manager has to communicate through, the greater the chances of misrepresentation.

— Not everyone in an organisation is an advocate for the security and prevention needs of the hotel. It is clearly possible for a middle-level manager who oversees the security department to lack the enthusiasm needed to both advocate for and utilise security successfully.

— In order to maintain a global perspective, it is critical for the security manager to be aware individually of all aspects of the hotel's operation, including sales, accounting, human resources, and so forth.

Some security professionals lack a broad company-wide perspective on the role of security. Their narrow view does not take into consideration how the entire operation is affected by their department. Security solutions must be consistent with the overall operation of the hotel. Closing the general storeroom at night, for example, may reduce losses in inventory, but such a "loss prevention" decision will also have an adverse effect on other departments such as banquet and food and beverages personnel who need items immediately.

Selection of Security Personnel

It is essential for all security personnel to be hired directly by the security department managers and not by the human resources department. In most cases hotels will hire personnel based on their immediate need, forcing themselves to hire the next available applicant. It has been a common practice for hotels to hire retired police officers and would-be police officers who for some reason have not been accepted onto the force and so work in security. There are clear pros and cons to this approach related to hiring managers, supervisors, or officers.Many security managers are hired because they have a work history that includes experience such as law enforcement for a municipality or a federal agency. Traditional management thinking has been that this type of candidate has had extensive experience handling crime-related problems, is usually trained, and has many contacts within the police force or city/state government. For these three reasons, such a choice would seem reasonable and appropriate.

Senior management must consider, however, the actual needs of their hotel. Not all properties are inundated with crime and seldom is the job of security solely focused on crime. Furthermore, it is far more cost-effective to deter crime through broad-based prevention programmes than to expend resources trying to apprehend and prosecute criminals. Another drawback frequently encountered by hiring the retired local, state, or government employee is his or her view that the lodging security job is only a second source of income and, hence, not that important. These comments are not meant to say that no former police officers or government agents can succeed as security managers, because many have, but simply to point out the problems associated with their basic orientations, lack of management skills, and, perhaps, lack of incentive. A preferable candidate for such a position is one who is able to understand and work within a business organisation.

Hotels are more likely to have an emphasis on prevention, management principles, and labour issues, rather than on arrest and prosecution. Thus, a person with well-rounded management skills is far more likely to succeed than one who has a limited sense of the role of security. Security managers are the most important people in the security department because they set the tone of the organisation by their example. However, careful selection of other security personnel should be the second-most important task for security managers filling a department. Lodging security is still a developing profession and, in some people's minds, is subordinate to police work.

Many younger security officers see their positions as interim steps to becoming police officers. This is fine; working in hotel security allows them to develop experience and maturity. Although police officers currently may enjoy a better public image, they are not necessarily better paid, have better training, or have better opportunities for advancement compared to those in the lodging security industry. Still, many people do see lodging security as a path toward public law enforcement. The problem human resources managers, or anyone else involved in the selection process, need to be sensitive to is hiring the frustrated would-be police officer who has been unsuccessful in getting a public sector job. It is one thing, for example, to hire a law enforcement or criminal justice student who wishes to gain experience. It is quite another thing to hire the individual who cannot be a police officer and must settle for the security job.

Promoting from within is a common practice for all types of organisations. The sense that you are getting someone as a supervisor or a manager who has established a track record and who knows the company is more comforting than hiring the unknown candidate. Prior performance, consistency, quality of work product, and reputation are all factors that should be considered. Past performance usually is a good indicator of future performance, there are some drawbacks to adhering to a strict policy of promoting from within. First, those promoted are likely to reflect the views and values of those above them, and thus this practice will maintain the same types of people throughout the organisation. It may be all right to perpetuate a type of person when it is good for the company, but when the type is not as effective as needed, it could be harmful.

Positive and constructive discipline is training that corrects, moulds, or strengthens an employee in the interest of achieving departmental and hotel goals. Punishment, which is feared and disliked by everyone, is secondary. Any punishment connected with discipline always be a means to an end, and that end should be organisational, not personal. In other words, the effective disciplinary process condemns the act, not the employee. It is also important that discipline should be swift. Whatever the nature of the problem, be it simple tardiness or careless oversight, the long-range effect of coming to grips with problems immediately is better than putting off what probably will have to be faced later. All employees require constructive discipline. Most employees want to do a good job. If care is taken in giving assignments, there will be fewer failures and fewer disciplinary problems resulting from failures. However, there are six fundamental rules in the disciplinary process that have universal applicability.

A hotel's reputation as a safe, well-run, clean, and comfortable establishment is essential for its success. The same argument can be made for the reputation of the security department and, certainly, the hotel's reputation will depend in good measure upon the success of the security programme. That programme's success is tied directly to the reputation and image of the department in the opinion of the hotel's employees, its guests, and the general public. Capable and effective from the employees' perspective, the members of the security department and the manager, in particular, must project a positive image. Image is affected by a variety of factors, including outward appearance—grooming, demeanour and attire, personality, consistency in treatment of employees in situations requiring security intervention, and emphasis on the positive aspect of services provided to fellow employees. It is a popular trend, for example, to eliminate the traditional security uniform and replace it with business attire.

The security manager sets the tone for the organisation and should maintain positive interaction with all levels of employees, never using authority as a means of exerting influence or pressure on the employees. From the guest's point of view, image and reputation will be determined primarily by the nature of the guest's contact, if any, with security while staying at the hotel. Most guests do not have any direct contact with security, and those who do will generally have it under adverse conditions, such as a theft of property or some other negative situation. Any victim, regardless of the seriousness of the loss or inconvenience, will behave in a fairly predictable manner, frequently blaming the security officer for not doing his or her job. It is essential that security personnel recognise that the guest's response is a normal reaction to stress. Furthermore, most victims know that it is unlikely that the harm they suffered cannot be undone and, therefore, really only look to the officer for some compassion and information. Most victims simply want someone to listen to their plight, which suggests that the security officers must have developed good listening skills. To the outside world, the public at large, the reputation of a hotel's security department will depend on all the factors cited above, and the relationship the department and its members—especially the manager—have established in the community. That community includes other hotels, the local police, the courts, the general public, visiting travellers, and criminals themselves, who have been known to have their own information system. Prostitutes, for example, know which hotels are easy to work in and which ones are not.

ROLE OF SECURITY PERSONNEL

The most basic function for the security personnel in any hotel is to perform regular patrols of the property, both inside and outside. There are three different types of security patrolling that have been utilised in hotels for decades, yet continue to serve the needs of guests, employees, and the property in general: random routine patrol, lobby patrol, and basic rounds. In random routine patrol, the security officer walks, or in some cases drives, around the property on a random basis to check for irregularities, suspicious circumstances, and intruders. There are two objectives achieved by this type of patrol.

First, any irregularity or suspicious circumstance hopefully will be discovered before a major problem develops. For example, there may be a leaking roof, broken pipes, dark hallways or stairways, and other unsafe conditions that may cause injury to a guest or employee.

The second objective is crime prevention. By patrolling in a randomised fashion, potential assailants or other wrongdoers can be detected or deterred from committing their acts. It is essential that this form of patrol not become too methodical or predictable. The officer should never patrol a site in a fixed schedule or pattern; however, it is critical to have key checkpoints throughout the patrol.

The second form of security patrol commonly employed in a hotel is lobby duty or surveillance. Any area of the hotel open to the general public requires a different type of patrol. The officer who is assigned to a public area, such as the lobby, must stay in one general location for extended periods of time to fulfil his or her duty. There are three benefits or purposes filled by this type of security presence: observance of undesirable persons or behaviour; assisting guests or others; and, deterring crime as a visible presence.

The third and most traditional form of security patrol is the fire watch. It differs from randomised patrol, although both may be accomplished simultaneously. On a fire watch, the officer patrols every floor and section of the building, including locked areas, in hopes of discovering any potential fire hazard, smoke, or actual fire. It is a common practice to utilise some type of watch clock, checklists, or an electronic wand to record what items or areas were checked and at what time. Caution should be taken by security managers to control the keys and discs that are imprinted from this equipment to prevent tampering and destruction. Accurate records should be maintained with the daily log books and incident reports, mostly for insurance purposes but for legal purposes also.

A contemporary version of the watch clock is an electronic device that reads barcodes similar to those used in grocery stores. The officer carries the device, which is about the size of a hand-held calculator, and passes it by a code placed on a tag at the location to be checked. At the end of the shift, the officer can insert the device into a recorder, which will read all rounds made, critical areas missed, and so on, and generate a hardcopy printout. Any of these measures is helpful to enhance the level of watchfulness necessary during late night hours. An important aspect of patrolling for all security personnel is the awareness of arson signs. Arsonists are known to use hotels as avenues for committing theft by setting fire to one location and, while everyone evacuates, stealing the guests' or hotel's property. Other arsonists like to watch people evacuate from buildings and will usually blend in with the crowd watching the scene. The typical arsonist has little concern for a facility's occupants or the firefighting personnel. Arsonists, particularly a professional "torch", will use flammable liquid in quantity. Look for liquid containers that may hold accelerants that can turn a small fire into a major fire in a short time.

One accelerant of which most people are unaware is the basic corrugated cardboard; it will burn intensely. Other items to be noted and acted upon include: dynamite charges connected with primer cord; hydrants or sprinkler valves that have been shut down or have deliberately damaged threads to prevent hose hook-ups; and unusual odours such as gasoline, kerosene, or fuel oil. Documentation is essential to the proper operation of a security department in any environment. Reports usually generated by a hotel security department include incident reports, activity or shift reports, and safety rules violations. Well-written, typed, and accurate record keeping is very important and helpful to the future planning of the hotel in general and of security specifically. A security manager should be able to review the previous year or more of reports and identify patterns of activity that will help direct available resources in the security programme.

Security reports are important as records for insurance or prosecution purposes; they should be thought of as important management tools, not locked away in a storage room or discarded. It is easier to maintain and research incident reports if they are kept chronologically. Caution should be used when storing these records; a fire file safe is recommended. Be sure to check the state statute of limitations for civil action suits and keep all records for the required time, as well as keeping records for specific pending cases until the cases are completely settled; check with your legal department.

Hotels offer a wide variety of services to guests, and like most other businesses they also maintain a lost-and-found department. The number of found items a hotel can accumulate varies with the size of the hotel and the volume of business within the hotel. Property that is turned in to security can potentially belong to a guest, patron, employee, or someone passing by the hotel. For ethical reasons as well as ensuring that all found property is secure, all lost-and- found items should be turned in to the security department daily. The property should be logged in and only given to its rightful owner on request. Lost-and-found sheets are critical, as well as a lost-and-found log book tracking the property chronologically.

Security Policies and Procedures

The company-wide manual covers policies and procedures that are general for the entire company. The manual may include vital, yet basic practices and procedures for each department within a hotel. This type of manual usually is used only as a guideline, while each individual facility develops its own manuals and handbook based on its geographic location. Most lodging facilities will also have a detailed manual for each department with emphasis on its operational departments. A separate manual specifically for the security department is an indispensable tool to give all security personnel the same information regarding the purpose, functions, and procedures carried out by the department. Security department manuals typically contain a series of policies and procedures, directives, and references to information which may be critical to security personnel. Manuals should be designed for quick reference whenever a need arises and they also should be readily accessible. Little is accomplished when a well-written and well-designed security manual is locked up in the security manager's office after regular business hours. Ideally, every officer is given his or her own copy of the manual, and all manuals are updated as needed, generally on an annual basis.

The contents of a manual should fall into three basic categories:

— general information;
— department policies; and
— emergency procedures.

The "general information" section often includes a description of the department's mission, organisational chart, dress code, and job descriptions for security personnel. "Department policies" are written statements that indicate the objective of each policy and any relevant procedures the officer is expected to follow. Finally, the "emergency procedures" section includes detailed information on steps to be taken by security and other hotel personnel during an emergency.

Policies and procedures need to be developed for every aspect of the security operation. By using a generic outline format, you can fill in the substantive information as you develop your manual. This ensures that there is a set way to deal with specific tasks and situations. Not all the employees of a hotel will have access to or even be aware of the existence of the security department's operation manual. Every hotel should, however, have a general company-wide policy and procedure manual that includes a variety of essential documents. The fundamental policies and procedures of each department need to be covered in the company-wide manual. This is especially true in the area of security. Many people think security policies only involve how to patrol the premises or the methods employed when conducting an investigation. However, there are many areas that fall under the realm of security, and all hotel employees need to be aware of the appropriate steps to be taken in a multitude of situations that are likely to arise. By including in the company-wide manual the essential steps to take in certain circumstances, it can be assured that proper policies will be followed, and that employees throughout the hotel will act in a similar and consistent manner.

Report writing is designed to inform readers as simply and clearly as possible of the facts assembled. Including all pertinent facts and using a clear and effective language to express thoughts are critical to report writing. The hotel security department is an integral part of a business. Therefore, the security manager should think and act like a business manager. This includes generating various types of reports that disclose and describe the issues, problems, and concerns encountered by the security department. Many security managers spend too much time trying to support the efforts of law enforcement and lose sight of the fact that their departments are a vital component of the hotel. By producing reports, the security department will:

- — Have an accurate record of the number and types of incidents it deals with.
- — Learn how to most efficiently allocate manpower.
- — Determine areas of weakness and potential security violations.
- — Ascertain which policies and procedures need modification.
- — Identify new areas of concern for which there may not be a set policy.

The security manager must ensure that all essential parts of any incident report are written down by all security personnel and that they are the facts. Names, descriptions of individuals, vehicles, buildings, surroundings, correct dates, and times are critical when attempting to reconstruct on paper what actually took place. Often a report is not written immediately after an event occurs. People who can provide answers may no longer be available for questioning. Every security person should always carry a pen and a small pocket notebook to document key facts as they arise. Names, titles, and descriptions can often be noted quickly—even during an emergency. This information can prove to be critical months later. Use the six questions, who, what, where, when, why, and how, to complete any report. All reports, log books (including front desk or manager's log book), and checklists have the potential to become legal documents. Therefore, it is critical that information be recorded completely and accurately. In criminal prosecution cases against the hotel, the defence counsel has absolute access to all such reports. In civil actions, insurance claims require the production of all relevant reports to defend a claim.

Any type of report generated by the hotel pertinent to a claim will be considered a relevant report. Also, when a lawsuit commences, the discovery process will require the hotel to produce all documents, including reports, memos, notes, and so on. Corporate attorneys' work products and investigations done at the local attorneys' requests are not necessarily available. The accuracy of the reports is paramount when considering the potential legal problems wrong information could pose, as well as the unprofessional image it might give the department, and ultimately the entire hotel.

First, false information may lead to defamation and libel suits. Such additional charges only complicate the original suit, and increase the amount of time and money spent on the matter. Further, the torts of libel and defamation are avoidable with the accurate and factual recording of information.

Second, the professional image of the security department, and in turn of the hotel, is affected by the quality of the reports produced. Sloppy and erroneous reports reflect sloppy and apathetic employees.

Professionalism means that reports are prepared prudently. It also means that reports are not merely filed away after they are generated. Professionalism dictates that reports be analysed for content, distributed to appropriate personnel, and examined for benefits and concerns they may offer to the department. Internally, it is the senior management that reads most reports. Externally, however, attorneys and insurance company representatives read the security department's reports. Depending on your state's requirements and your legal advisor's recommendations, a general time period should be established for retaining various types of records.

Special Concerns

A hotel's reputation is, without doubt, its single most important asset. No matter how professional the hotel's services may be or how good a value may be offered, no one respectable will stay at a hotel if a bad type of activity is allowed to take place openly. It is probably safe to say that prostitution has been around as long as the concept of inns for travellers. Some of the comments frequently heard about prostitution is that it is a victimless crime and that society should not care what consenting adults do in privacy. However, prostitution is a problem that, if not controlled, can ruin a hotel's reputation. The word controlled was used intentionally, for prostitution cannot and will not ever be eliminated. The security objective should be to reduce such activity to an absolute minimum.

There are a number of simple control methods a hotel can employ. First, guest registration procedures must be established and followed closely. All guests must be required to show valid photo identification such as a driver's licence and preferably a credit card when checking in, even if they are paying cash in advance for their stay.

The reason for the tight registration process is that most streetwalkers will not carry identification. The more sophisticated "call girl" or "escort" type of prostitute will have identification, but she or he also represents less of a threat to the innkeeper. The second method of control can be utilised in properties that have computerised front desk procedures and can print out a complete list of all guests by room as well as list the number of occupants registered in that particular room. Once given that list, particularly at night when guests are returning to their rooms with visitors they may have just met in the local bar, the security officer can screen all incoming guests at the front door. This method has two benefits. First, the innkeeper is entitled as a matter of law to additional revenue if a second person is staying in the room. Second, if in fact the "visitor" is a streetwalker, not only will he or she not have identification as noted above, but the guest may not want to risk having a second person listed on the registration folio. The final two methods of prevention include employee cooperation.

The housekeeping department will know if a certain guest-room has heavy traffic going to and from it and can alert security. Secondly, hotel managers must maintain a no-tolerance attitude toward prostitution while supporting security in its efforts to deal with the problem. Common meeting places for prostitutes are lobby pay telephones, bars, and easily recognised hotel fixtures such as chairs, plants, and the like. There are two general types of problems associated with bars, restaurants, stores, and the front desk in a hotel. They are check and credit card fraud, and theft of merchandise including food and beverage items. Incidents involving "walk-outs" are common when non-paying customers enjoy a meal and/or drinks in a hotel and then proceed to leave without offering to pay for the items consumed. Unfortunately, this type of crime is only a misdemeanour in most states and innkeepers are very limited in what they can do after the event.

Frequently, if the patron is caught leaving, they can be confronted and—if they refuse to pay—be held long enough for security or the public police to arrive. The thief then can be identified for future reference or prosecution. The amount of the loss usually is not worth the time required to prosecute, so it is recommended that the name and description of the individual be recorded and distributed to all outlets in the hotel. You may try alternate means of payment. If the person tries to obtain food or drink again, they can be refused until they pay for the previous bill. Credit cards very often are used as a means of payment by patrons because of their convenience and the generation of tax records for business purposes. This convenience, however, has caused some problems for the hotel operator, particularly in food and beverage outlets and stores.

The security department must face problems ranging from guests using stolen cards and cards over their allowable limit to dishonest employees inflating gratuities or even writing in gratuities. The best means of avoiding these and other scams is to develop detailed policies and procedures for authorisation of use, and to train employees to follow the procedures. Charging store merchandise to a guest-room, for example, must somehow be verified first. Management must then follow up to ensure compliance with the rules, and violators should be dealt with appropriately. If security is called to investigate alleged wrongdoing by employees and the allegations are proven, swift and severe disciplinary action should be taken after all levels of disciplinary action are considered. Disciplinary action can range from counselling to termination.

The sale and use of illegal drugs are major issues in any industry, but appear more complicated in the lodging industry. The innkeeper must be concerned not only with employees, but also with guests and patrons who become involved with using and selling drugs. The use of drugs by employees on or off the job presents some serious consequences for both performance and safety. With the cost of workers' compensation insurance rising so high and representing one of the largest line expenses for liability, employers must address the increased use of drugs by employees.

Only recently have employers begun to consider the possibility that some employee accidents are directly related to drug use on or off the job. Even employees who do not use drugs but who are aware of others who do are affected. Morale problems are likely to arise among employees who want to do their job well, but see others not performing because of drug use. Furthermore, a work environment that allows employees to sell drugs to co-workers will create the impression that management does not care or is incompetent. Although still controversial at this stage, employers may wish to consider the possibility of drug testing on employees who either have declining performance levels or who have exhibited unusual behaviour or evidence of drug use. Legal counsel should be consulted before this action is taken.

A number of legislative reforms on intoxication on the job have been enacted recently, including denying benefits in cases in which accidents are alcohol- or drug-related. Talk to legal counsel about your state's legislation. Effective ways to deal with substance abuse problems are complicated. The long-term solution is education and awareness, not policing employees. The hotel should have an Employee Assistance Programme

(EAP), which may reduce the incidents and cost of alcoholism and other abuse at work. Yet we must be realistic and acknowledge that both alcoholism and drugs do exist in the lodging industry. Most hoteliers wait until drug dealing is rampant before they act on tips about drug usage. This does more harm than rapid action because, by the time management reacts to the problem, more employees are involved and affected, which may result in having to remove more staff from the hotel. Security managers also can consider using undercover investigators posing as employees to determine who the dealer and buyers are, as evidence for termination. Drug use or sale by guests is not an unusual problem, but is one that hotel operators should be prepared to resolve. It is very unlikely that a hotel manager will be able to prevent a guest from using drugs in the privacy of his or her room.

Depending on the size and location of a hotel, certain types of public figures are likely to stay as guests on occasion. In larger, convention-class hotels, political figures are often in attendance for social events. Public figures, whether they are politicians or people such as rock stars or sports teams, often will draw crowds. These crowds may be admirers, or they may be demonstrators protesting the appearance of the individual. In either instance, security is faced with the difficult task of controlling the crowd while protecting the public figure. One should not assume that the local police will always take care of or even be aware of these problems. Instead, the security manager should be prepared to work with the authorities in planning for the person's arrival, stay, and departure.

Occasionally, hotel security will not receive any advance notice of the person's arrival. However, if your hotel security procedures include how to handle this type of scenario, coordinating this process should not take very long. Generally, though, there will be varying amounts of lead time available before the event. If this time is adequate, detailed planning will avert risk with minimal difficulty. The following are issues to address during this stage:

— *Communications systems.* Be sure all equipment is operating and rent additional radios if needed.

— *Transportation.* Plan transportation of the celebrity to and from the hotel and airport; in conjunction with their dignitary protection staff or secret service, work out alternate routes and possible escape routes from within the hotel.

— *Emergency equipment.* Have medical equipment and an ambulance, if needed, standing by.

— *Access control.* Limit bystanders' and other hotel employees' access to the areas where this person will be located. Provide for crowd control by roping off areas or using barriers.

— *Intelligence.* If this public figure recently has been at other hotels or events, contact the security and/or police in that area for any information that might be helpful in planning for the celebrity's arrival.

The hotel may make reasonable regulations governing the conduct of its guests, provided such regulations are applied to all persons, without discrimination. These regulations can be designed to prevent immorality, drunkenness, or any form of wilful misconduct, e.g., loud obnoxious behaviour, drug activity, etc., that may offend other guests, may bring the hotel into disrepute, or may be inconsistent with the generally recognised properties of life. The hotel has the right to evict any guest who wilfully violates these rules. Obviously, the eviction must be done in a reasonable manner. If guests refuse to leave the hotel after their attention has been called to the violation and they have been requested to leave and given a reasonable opportunity to do so, the hotel may forcibly evict them. The hotel may use only such force as is reasonably necessary to accomplish this goal. Management personnel and security officers should be carefully instructed on this point and the hotel should obtain the assistance of the local police. When a hotel guest becomes ill with a contagious disease, the hotel management, after notifying the guest that she or he must leave, has the right to remove the guest in a careful manner and at an appropriate time to a hospital or other place of safety, provided this does not imperil the guest's life.

Bibliography

Beale, Joseph Henry. *The law of innkeepers and hotels: including other public houses, theatres, sleeping cars.* Boston: William J. Nagel, 1906.

Boni, G. de. *Hotel organization, management and accountancy.* London: Pitman, 1939.

Boni, G. de and Frederick Francis Sharles. *Hotel organization, management and accountancy.* London; New York: Sir I. Pitman, 1931.

Boni, G. de and Frederick Francis Sharles. *Hotel organization, management and accountancy. Hotel organization and management.* London New York: Sir I. Pitman, 1926.

Boomer, Lucius Messenger. *Hotel management; principles and practice.* New York: Harper, 1931.

Dahl, Crete M. *Housekeeping management & organization for hotels & institutions.* Stamford, Conn.: The Dahls, 1945.

Dahl, J. O. *Restaurant management, principles and practice.* New York: Harper & Brothers, 1927.

Dicksee, Lawrence Robert. *Hotel accounts.* London: Gee & Co., 1905.

Eckert, Fred William and Howard L. Dayton. *The hotel lease; a study of the business elements and principles involved in making leases that are equitable to both lessee and lessor.* Chicago: Hotel Monthly Press, 1947.

Fisk, Warren Wells. *Evidence of needs of hotel managers in regard to training and education.* 1947.

Gill, Winifred Ethel. *Business affairs for institutional management.* London: Evan.

Hamilton, Francis Frazee. *Hotel front desk management, a treatise on the best methods and procedures in use in small hotels.* Miami, Fla.: Francis Frazee Hamilton, 1947.

Hamilton, W. I. *Promoting new hotels: when does it pay?* New York: Harper, 1930.

Heldenbrand, Howard Van Woert. *Front office psychology.* Chicago: The Hotel monthly press, 1930.

Hitz, Ralph and National Hotel Management Co. *Standard practice manuals for hotel operation.* New York: Harper, 1936.

Holmes, F. H. *Hotel training course.* Chicago: F.H. Holmes, 1937.

Horwath, Ernest B. and Louis Toth. *Hotel accounting, including departmental control, food costing, and auditing.* New York: The Ronald press company, 1928.

Hotel Management Clipping Bureau of Good Ideas. *Hotel Management Clipping Bureau of Good Ideas.* New York: Ahrens Pub. Co., 1931.

March, C. A. *Building operation and maintenance.* New York: McGraw-Hill, 1950.

Martyn, Charles. *The financial side of hotel keeping.* New York: The Caterer Pub. Co., 1903.

O'Brien, Daniel J. and Charles Bennington Couchman. *Hotel administration, accounts and control.* New York: McGraw-Hill book company inc., 1927.

Ramage, Edward D. *A study of minor operated departments: based on the operating statements of one hundred eighty hotels.* Ithaca, N.Y.: [E. Ramage?], 1931.

Rogers, R. Vashon. *The law of hotel life; or, The wrongs and rights of host and guest.* San Francisco.

Tellman, John. *The practical hotel steward.* Chicago: The Hotel monthly, 1913.